Praise for Trauma Family

"Much has been written about PTSD; less on the secondary trauma inflicted upon the family members of those who struggle with it. Bill McBean's TRAUMA FAMILY – a remarkably compassionate and clear-eyed account of his life as the son of a troubled World War II combat veteran – helps to remedy that. McBean's wry, unflinching memoir of his own alcoholism and other issues, skillfully interwoven with useful research and information, makes compelling reading even for someone not directly affected by PTSD; for those in such situations, it will undoubtedly prove a godsend."

– Gwen Florio, author of *Silent Hearts* and *Montana Noir*

"Written with the flair of a born storyteller, Trauma Family is a searing search for the roots of one family's dysfunction and darkness. McBean's memorable memoir makes a convincing case that the aftershock of war echoes from generation to generation. This is a harrowing portrait of a troubled family told for all the best reasons–to understand who we are and why we do the things we do."

– Mark Stevens, author of *Antler Dust* and *The Melancholy Howl*

"Bill McBean has shattered one of America's enduring myths — that The Greatest Generation came home after WWII, got jobs, raised families, and rebuilt America, all without complaining. Based on his father's letters home from the front, the secret but violent post-war dysfunc-

tion in the McBean family, and extensive research into PTSD, McBean realizes that the life he and his siblings suffered under his father's alcoholism and erratic stoicism was widespread in GIs. What's more, it was passed to the children. McBean's painful discovery that he ended up like the man he hated is a sobering, must-read revelation for veterans and their families of all wars."

– Jim Carrier, author of *The Ship and the Storm and Letters From Yellowstone*

An epic battle for mental health awaits too many spouses and children of returning soldiers. Hardboiled journalist William McBean reports from the frontline of growing up with his shell-shocked father to offer this unflinching yet ultimately compassionate account of secondary family trauma, the uphill skirmish from self-destruction to healing, the science behind trans-generational trauma and the tactics families can deploy to shield children from the life-destroying friendly fire of PTSD.

– Heather Lynn Mann, author of *Ocean of Insight, A Sailor's Voyage from Despair to Hope*

TRAUMA FAMILY

A Memoir of PTSD's Collateral Damage

Bill McBean

Climacteric LLC, Edina MN

Published by Climacteric LLC
Edina, MN

Cover Design by Asya Blue
Cover photo of Peter McBean © Bill McBean

ISBN: 978-1-63684-818-1 (E-book)
ISBN:978-1-63684-819-8 (Print edition)

For all my children

CONTENTS

CHAPTER 1: HIGHLIGHT REEL

On a glittering Vermont morning, my father showed us how much he enjoyed bloodshed.

During those August days in the late 1950s, our family vacationed in an old wooden farmhouse just north of Brattleboro. Mornings started pretty much the same — cocks all around the foggy Connecticut River Valley began their clamor, Grandma made us pancakes, and then my sister Mary Jo and I dashed outside to practice croquet.

On this morning, the grass was heavy with dew, and our sneakers got soaked. The humidity made the exposed skin of our thighs stick together. The sun bore down on our sodden surroundings, assaulting our nostrils with the stink of fungus. Mary Jo and I tired of it, and as we trudged back to the house, we heard a ruckus.

"Over there!"

"Quick, quick!"

"Oh, my God!"

"Hah, hah, *hah*!"

This last phrase came from deep within the throat of my father, a noise so passionate and uncouth, I wondered how he could have uttered it in front of my grandmother, who stood with her yellow-on-gray floral backside to the door, protectively blocking our path inside.

"No, now children, please, please stay out, stay out, please..."

But it was too late, for we could look around her through the screen door. He stood in the kitchen, the inky stubble of his unshaven, ruddy face upturned at the barbeque fork he held in his hand. He'd skewered a rat through its midsection with the tool we used to toast marshmallows. He held the wiggling rodent high, staring at it, his eyes swelling.

Because I knew I'd witnessed something forbidden, I couldn't take my eyes off the writhing rat. The animal's blood poured off Dad's fingers and down his wrist. My eight-year-old mind flipped like a circuit breaker. My father had been transformed from the bedrock of my life into a seething killer, and I just didn't get how that could happen.

This scene led the highlight reel of my childhood. It spotlighted how Dad passed his trauma on to his brood. It would be decades before anyone understood that the trauma of war could be passed on to the family of the warrior. Naturally, no two of us became traumatized at the same time or in exactly the same way. Yet all five of the McBean children eventually suffered from at least one symptom of Secondary Trauma Stress: panic attacks, anxiety disorder, alcoholism, depression, and attention deficit disorder.

Today, millions of American soldiers just like my dad have returned home from Middle East battlefields, many with PTSD. They are having children, some of whom won't have the sheltering resources of the McBean clan. They will face homelessness, prison, addiction, and untimely death.

◆ ◆ ◆

No one ever mentioned the rat incident in my presence. Typically, no one ever tried to explain my father's behavior. Dad revered J.P. Morgan and attributed to him the old chestnut, "Never explain, never apologize."

After all, why should he ask forgiveness for the emotional scars he suffered while saving our country from Hitler?

Thus, it fell to his children to explain the strange things that happened in our house.

For much of the time when we were young, an unearthly sound somewhere between a scream of terror and a bellow of aggression awakened us in the night. Sometimes it would last five minutes, and although we knew Dad was the culprit, the house was very dark and it was hard to convince ourselves there was no danger.

At first, the sharp eruption of a man in imminent fear of death reverberated through the walls. Then there would be desperate snarling, the kind made by an animal caught in a leg trap. Sharp commands that didn't take the form of words but nonetheless sounded like warnings were broadcast from their bedroom, followed by the soft incantations of my mother as she tried to get him back to bed.

Then silence would once again settle over our house, and we children would wonder if Mom had prevailed or if the troll that seemed to live just behind my father's eyes had triumphed. Yet when the early sunlight again set the tree limbs in relief, they'd both appear, dressed and ready, as if nothing had happened.

If the nightmares had served as the sole manifestation of his PTSD, perhaps our relationship wouldn't have gotten so badly off-track. The use of whiskey to suppress his symptoms, however, brought out his anger, and much of his wrath fell upon me, his oldest child and only boy.

When Dad and I reached the crescendo of our power struggle in 1961, my mother, hoping to calm her household, offered to let me read the letters he wrote from the European battlefield. She brought the old brown envelope containing the correspondence to my bedroom and pleaded with me to read them, but I turned my nose up in the way only an angry teenager could.

Thirteen years later, in 1974, Dad died at fifty-five. His medication, Black & White Scotch Whiskey, along with tobacco, killed him. My mom died in 1993, basically from the same medicine, and the letters passed into my hands.

I thought I should read the correspondence, but I just didn't want to. It would mean thinking about him, and he had fallen into the dead letter file. He needed to stay there. Sometimes I wondered what I was missing. Maybe the letters were as good as Mom said — but I'd shake off the thought. Thinking about our broken bond still brought up painful bile.

Decades went by. I worked as a newspaper reporter for twenty-three years but decided to quit journalism in favor of commercial real estate. Time to make some money, I thought, but the mere pursuit of cash became entirely too boring, so I got involved with housing the disabled. I became mired in government rules and rule-makers as I struggled to build an altruistic kingdom; I hired and fired employees; I floundered to save myself from drowning in an ocean white-capped with paperwork.

During these years, I had various personal vexations, including a big problem with alcohol. Yet I kept my life more or less on track. I stopped drinking at forty, I hoped for good. I became much more honest. Anxiety never left, though. It was my constant companion, telling me something about my past needed to be addressed.

Then, more than fifty years after Mom offered to let me see Dad's letters, I heard a story about World War II veterans on National Public Radio. The piece described five former servicemen, all of whom were very successful in their postwar careers and all of whom committed suicide in their mid-fifties.

For the first time I thought about how PTSD might apply to men who fought in the "Good War." I pondered my father's demise, and although it wasn't a conventional suicide, it did occur by his own hand—the hand that brought whiskey to his lips thousands of times as I grew up.

I thought hard about where I might have put the letters. I hadn't seen them in fifteen years, and my Denver home had many deep closets and a dank cellar. For a moment I panicked, but after taking several deep breaths, it came to me. The old brown envelope sat no more than fifteen feet from me, in the back of the closet off my study.

I began reading with a firm goal in mind. I wanted to see if I could pinpoint the actual time and place where Dad's re-occurring nightmare began.

Although he never discussed the nightmare, Mom and I talked about it just before my departure for college. As I packed, I came across the brown envelope as I rummaged around in a closet looking for something else. I wanted to know what all those letters said and thought quizzing my mom would be easier than reading them.

I sat at the kitchen table as she bustled about, getting dinner ready. A yellow apron covered a purple crushed velvet dress. One of the ministers from Christ Church, for whom she had great fondness, was to dine with us. My parents came back to the church late in life and behaved like newly minted converts.

"Mom, does Dad still have that dream?"

She gave me a guarded look, as if to say, "Since when did you care?"

She didn't answer immediately, but after taking the hot

casserole from the oven, she removed her thermal mitts and gave me her full attention.

"It happens occasionally, but not nearly as often as it once did."

"Do you know what he was so scared about?"

"Yes, Bill, I do know."

Because cocktail hour had finally arrived, she took her glass of sherry from its hiding place in a kitchen cabinet and sat down across the table from me. She gave me the weathered look a parent saves for an intransigent child.

I suspected she wanted to remind me of how I had behaved as a teenager but decided it wasn't worth it. Instead, she began talking about Dad dreaming that he got lost in Northern France's hedgerow country and wandered into a German trap.

Before she could provide details, the doorbell rang. Mom ushered in the priest and sat him in our living room's most comfortable chair. The tinkling of ice cubes followed, and the storyline went unfinished.

Now, decades after our talk, I wanted to try to answer those questions myself. Obviously the dream had no literal truth to it. Dad hadn't been captured by the Germans. But what *had* happened? Did the letters actually address the genesis of the nightmare? Could I learn what caused the tectonic plates of my dad's mind to shift so violently, or did his yelling and screaming arise from a hodgepodge of shelling and machine gun fire that caused a frightened mind to erupt?

I cleared my desk and emptied the brown envelope of its contents. In addition to letters, out tumbled pictures, official Army paperwork, and maps. Decades had corrupted the correspondence. Although Dad wrote many of the letters on sturdy Red Cross stationery, some of them were on low-quality scrap paper that had turned yellow and crumbled at the margins. Rusting paperclips held some together.

Over the next couple of weeks, I photocopied the letters and placed the originals back in the brown envelope. As I reproduced the letters, I haphazardly read a few, hoping I would get lucky and find an answer to my question.

I didn't procrastinate often, yet in this case I knew I might learn something about my parents and probably about myself. Thus, instead of diving straight into the letters, I got to work on research to help me understand what the times were like when Dad finally returned to New York in 1945.

Nearly everyone coming home from World War II faced enormous pressure. Dad's father sent him an application for Columbia Law School when he was still fighting in Europe. Two weeks after his return, he found himself sitting in a classroom.

Nine months after that, he had a child to contend with (bellicose, ungrateful me). One of New York City's swankiest law firms hired him, and he became a fast-talking cash cow who commuted more than three hours a day and revisited his battlefield horrors only between lights out and the alarm.

In the decades prior to the Vietnam War, if you had a battlefield-related mental problem, you handled it with alcohol, the only medicine commonly available. If your contemporaries saw the war's aftermath had mastered you, your choices were stark: hit the road or get locked up. Many men found it vastly preferable to ride the rails; even if there wasn't any dignity in it, there was at least freedom.

Others were so crippled by their crazies they were shipped off to gulags run by the Department of Veterans

Affairs. By 1947, the Vet had about one million "psychoneurotics" incarcerated. They occupied about half of all available VA beds.[1] Yet America abounded with guys like my dad. They liked whiskey, and they put it to good use. Its sedating effect kept them in the box — but it never allowed them to tell their stories. Or more accurately, it never let them express their feelings.

Today, more than seventy-five years after World War II ended, researchers have established that having Post-Traumatic Stress Disorder (PTSD) and alcohol problems at the same time can make both problems worse.[2] While today's treatment can make both ailments better, it was largely unavailable in 1945. My father could have sought out an infant organization called Alcoholics Anonymous, but he didn't want to quit. Twenty years later, a heart problem forced him to put the plug in the jug, but even then he wouldn't confess to suffering from anxiety and depression.

After deciding I wanted to write a book about PTSD and my experience with it, I interviewed veterans I found in the parking lot of a VA facility in Lakewood, Colorado. Most said they never talked about the battlefield. Some said no one wanted to hear it, and others said even if someone did, most people couldn't understand how being afraid day after day turned you into an animal, how it changed your perspective on everything. People tried to understand, but they just didn't. How could they possibly comprehend it if they weren't there?

Dad believed that no one appreciated how many rats there were in the world and how badly they needed to be killed. He thought that few truly comprehended how bad the Nazis — indeed all Germans of that era — were, and how much they needed to be eliminated. He thought almost no one recognized how much he had to change himself to get that job done.

So when Dad saw the rat scampering across our farmhouse floor that morning ten years after the last wartime bullet had been fired, he leaped into action. He killed the rodent and held it high for his family to see. It was an ancient ritual performed for an audience that had become far too civilized for such rites. His mother told him to bury the thing in the vegetable garden.

The rat episode represented the earliest example of my father's aberrant behavior I could remember. Many, many more episodes followed, but until I sat down to write about those early years of my life, I'd compartmentalized Dad's conduct and my reaction to it.

As I began to read his letters, my defenses departed as abruptly as air escaping a vacuum-packed can. I realized I was about to embark on a project that would help me understand why my life had been such a persistent game of hopscotch on land mines, such an unconscious exercise in self-destruction.

CHAPTER 2: LOVE LETTERS

Prior to my confrontation with the brown envelope, I always approached research projects from a standpoint of strict neutrality. Reading my father's words tossed objectivity out the window. Suddenly a little kid again, I wondered if his hand could leap out of the brown envelope and slap me in the face.

It took weeks to get the letters in chronological order. Some days, I'd only be able to date-sequence a few letters before running into something that would summon up a rancorous event from my childhood. It didn't take much. A word. A phrase. When I read those triggers, I'd be back in the Bronxville, NY of the 1950s and 1960s, a world I thought had been boxed up and put away forever. It spawned something deeper than mere depression, more poignant than fear; feelings like worthlessness, hopelessness, defeat — and rage.

At first, when attacked by those memories, I'd walk away from my desk and seek escape. Often, I turned on the television and watched the news. After the events of here and now washed away the events of yesteryear, I'd put the letters away.

Finally, I arranged the missives — over a hundred of them extending from May 1944 to September 1945 — in chronological order and began searching for Dad's *bête noire*.

I imagined the nightmare must have started shortly after he got back. I could visualize him studying for law classes late into the night, having the hideous dream and then dragging himself to long lectures on torts or contract law. A less than ideal existence, to be sure, but compared with most soldiers, my dad's reentry was as smooth as the top of the mahogany desk at which he studied.

Many men came back to nothing. Wives deserted, employment went AWOL, and friends shied away. By 1946, after the hero worship ebbed, America began to realize many vets were causing big problems. Some chose barroom brawls over settling into prescribed family life. Many were labeled "shell-shocked," and America quickly tired of their antics. The press abounded with stories of postwar misbehavior. One historian called it "the shock of peace."[3]

Once, in my late teens, I asked Mom if Dad ever thought of getting help for his enduring postwar trauma. She was clearly appalled by my naiveté.

"If it had ever gotten out that your dad was shell-shocked, it would have ruined his legal practice. People would have lost faith in his judgment. It would have been the end of him!"

Finally, I began reading the letters. I expected accounts of freezing nights in water-filled foxholes. I had heard plenty about that growing up.

The first missives, however, were love letters with a war backdrop. Although none of my mom's letters survived, Dad's words of love were lush and unrestrained.

May 22, 1944:

Darling, I don't think that I have ever properly told you how much our short married life together has meant to me. It's been a lot of big things, Mary, and a lot of little ones. All your work to find a home for us, getting up at foul hours to get me breakfast, your loyalty and sweetness, ad infinitum. You mean everything to me, darling. When I see how the sex habits of the community have deteriorated, I really book on you. You carry all my hopes for now and for the future, and I have no fear you will let me down and you have no idea of what that means to me in my present situation. It was a lucky day when I met you, dearest.

◆ ◆ ◆

My parents weren't an obvious match. A dedicated Midwesterner and a relative "hick," Dad moved to Bronxville from Omaha when he was about fourteen. Mom, born Mary Louise Sills in New York City in 1920, grew up in Bronxville and spent her final high school years at the St. Catherine's School in Richmond, Virginia. She didn't know my father in Bronxville. He vaguely remembered her before she left Bronxville for boarding school as "the fat girl who played violin."

They never formally met until they bumped into each other while registering late at Swarthmore College, both delayed getting to school by the hurricane of 1938.

Although Mom often depicted their meeting at the registrar's office as "love at first sight," her social calendar during her freshman year was full. She went out with four other lads, one quite steadily, so she obviously kept her options open.

Yet Peter McBean had a quality the competition apparently didn't have: an outstanding ability to convey sincerity and confidence, to take you by the hand and assure you things would come to a completely satisfactory and happy conclusion.

When they attended Swarthmore, Mom spotted this sincere streak and fell for it. She must have looked into those hazel eyes with their orange flares and thought the instability of her adolescent years had ended.

Although they didn't get married until 1942, their matrimonial fate was probably sealed in the spring of 1939 when my grandfather Alan made it clear that he thought Mom an unworthy distraction and the sole cause of Dad's mediocre freshman year grades. Alan McBean insisted his son transfer to Dartmouth, a school he had originally steered him away from because of its "roughneck" reputation.

Dad's letters from Hanover, NH, confirmed Alan's doubts about Dartmouth. Although Dad graduated *cum laude*, it seemed like he got drunk at least twice a week and badly wanted my mother to hop on a train and come join him. Mom came to New Hampshire much more often than Dad came to Philadelphia because her mother (who by then had divorced her dad) lived in nearby Woodstock, Vermont.

Dad and the woman who would one day be my grandmother, Jo Sills, became close, and Dad often visited her even when Mom couldn't come up from Philadelphia. By then, Jo had earned herself a reputation for exotic adventure. In the mid-thirties she traveled to Cuba and Puerto Rico for "vacations" without her husband and later let it be known she had found an assortment of fascinating men, reportedly among them an heir to the Bacardi fortune. By 1939, Mom grasped her mother's predilection for the forbidden and must have wondered if Dad qualified. She got up to Hanover whenever she could.

In January of 1942, they almost eloped, but pulled back because they didn't want to deprive her mother of attending the wedding. Jo said she had no objection to the marriage as long as she could be there, but she pointed out her daughter would be alone in New York City for years and might fall in love with someone else while Dad fought in Europe.

Clearly, Dad was worried about that, too. On February 9, 1942 he wrote:

I experienced a terrible wave of fear. That idea doesn't often occur to me, probably chiefly because I can never imagine myself falling in love with someone else. Please don't fall in love with anyone else, Mary. It took me quite a while to fall in love, but I am head over heels now and am afraid that I would take it awfully hard if you were to give me the air. Know your power and have care of those at its mercy.

They finally made it official over the Columbus Day weekend of 1942, just before Dad left for Officer Training School at Fort Benning, Georgia. Mom wanted her father to give her away, but by whimsical coincidence, he'd just married his second wife and was honeymooning in Maine. The State Police volunteered to hunt him down, and Ken Sills, with his new spouse, Dixie, came trailing in moments before the event began.

In September of 1945, the same month Dad returned from the war and started law school, they conceived me. Two years later, Mom became pregnant again, and thus a beauty from the country's finest Quaker college became a drudge in a quiet, parochial village more removed from New York City than the literal sixteen miles to Times Square. Her life consisted of coping with me, waiting for Mary Jo — and then three other children — to be born, keeping the house straight, and longing for her husband to return from the strenuous days of a beginning associate at a Wall Street law firm.

We hadn't yet moved into the 3,400-square-foot Bronxville house. Dad purchased a tract home in Eastchester, a couple of miles from the Summit Avenue abode. Roughly 1,400 square feet, the white tract house had two baths and three bedrooms. My grandfather Alan gave Dad the Summit Avenue house in 1951 so I could attend the Bronxville schools, but he first wanted Dad to understand how lucky he was.

I knew the Mary Louise of the rounded tummy and varicose veins, so her application to the 406 Club, my father's lodging in Hanover, surprised me. It introduced me to the playful, innocent woman who lived in my mother's skin before she and Dad shellacked themselves with alcohol and the war's aftermath.

The application, taken when she was twenty-two, listed her weight as "a floating" 122 pounds. She said her skin color was "pink," her hair color "varies between washings," her eyes were "cat green," and the color of her teeth was "mottled." Her complexion was "fine, when leading a good eye." The application inquired about her previous condition of servitude. She said, "Slave to McBean."

◆ ◆ ◆

Dad wrote his amorous war letter days after his arrival in England, where he spent roughly two months training for the invasion of France. His artillery unit bivouacked in a manor house requisitioned by the military in southwest England near Cornwall.

We have a beautiful set-up here. Woke up this morning to sun with the birds singing and big sprays of lilac, laurel and rhododendron pushing in the windows...

Soon, however, it began raining, the plumbing stopped up, and after dark, rats "as big as fox terriers" invaded the mansion. Tensions rose as the men contemplated the coming invasion. Days filled with physical conditioning, artillery drills on blustery moors, and hour after hour driving military trucks among swarms of English bicyclists who apparently thought they had the right of way.

Men of Cannon Company with 105 mm howitzer. Dad is standing, right.

During the evening hours, Lieutenant McBean wandered through local pubs. About half of the two dozen letters he produced in England concerned his opportunities to consume ale, gin, and particularly Scotch.

He expressed a disdain for the off-duty behavior of his men, especially the sexual actions of his fellow soldiers with English women. Apparently, the men didn't even need to leave the manor house to find females more than willing to satisfy their needs.

...There are a goodly selection of sluts who come creeping up in the bushes near the back door every night. Most horrible looking creatures I ever saw. I can't imagine what makes some gals sink as low as that.

He asserted other officers, "Practically to a man," had "shacked up" with English women. The men in his company resented his obvious dislike for this kind of behavior. They called him "Creepin' Jesus."

When he went out to the pubs, he was often approached

by local females.

June 18, 1944:

Went to town last night and had a poor time. The theaters were full as were the pubs. I finally found myself picked up by a gal and we spent the evening wandering about. I'm afraid she was disappointed in me. She kept luring me into semi-private hedgerows, but I suspected her past and would have none of it. I finally tactfully got rid of her and ended up in the Red Cross drinking coffee and eating innumerable donuts. Mary, you've ruined me as a Lothario. Nipped me in the bud. I can't get interested in these girls to save my life. If only they would stop trying to 'make' a man every second and talk a bit. These English gals can't carry on a conversation worth a damn.

I hope my accounts of going out with other women don't bother you. I thought you would like to know everything that I've been doing. The last girl I made love to was the one at 71 Washington Square South (Jo's apartment) and the next one I make love to will be the same one. You gave me permission to philander, but the desire is lacking. I can't see sharing something that belongs to us with some slut.

Although he must have been apprehensive about the immediate future, he wrote extensively about what he thought might happen after the war.

I am eating up all the news of the operations in France. The faster they go, the sooner Mr. and Mrs. Peter C. McBean will settle down to a life together composed of many parts such as eating steaks, drinking rum in Vermont, listening to the phonograph, putting up our Christmas tree, giving a few discreetly wild parties and of course regular sessions of 'cuddling' as you choose to call it. The word hardly seems adequate somehow. I have also given some thought to the little boy with red hair and freckles which you intend to conceive one of these days. I think I might be persuaded to give him his start in life someday fairly soon.

I found the letters from England unsettling. His display of tenderness didn't match up with my experience watching my parents as I grew up. A peck on the cheek, a fond smile — that was about it.

Although my parents had a traditional marriage in that he worked and she tended to home life, they had a solid connection and seldom disagreed — at least in front of their children. Despite their bevy of offspring, I felt sure theirs was a love based not on sexuality but on mutual intellectual respect and a bond cemented during our nation's fight for survival — and the battle's aftermath.

Mom served as Dad's psychologist. They were "in session" every evening from the time he walked in the door until lights out about three hours later. They closed the kitchen door. The children, having been fed, were told to do their homework, play outside or amuse themselves in any way that didn't run a cropper of their many rules, paramount of which were no bickering of any kind, no TV and no bothering them. Dad needed time to process; Mom needed time to listen.

They depended on each other, and it worked to a remarkable degree. Yet when I read the first war letters, I found myself wondering what had happened to his human warmth. It pervaded every word he wrote Mom from England. Occasionally, as I grew up, I felt it, but infrequently enough that I remembered each act of kindness. His prewar acquaintances, including my maternal grandmother, his college friends and others, told me frequently how lucky I was to have him as a father. As I listened to these adulations, I thought he must be a master of disguise, a shape-shifter of the first order, for so many people to have missed his demonic nature.

Even as I struggled to understand life as a child, I never dreamed the questions about my youth would deepen as I grew older. I never imagined I'd need to understand my father, and most of all, I never suspected examining these questions in my old age would threaten my emotional stability.

CHAPTER 3: HOW MANY MEN DID YOU KILL?

Reading the letters posed almost as many problems as they solved. Dad's tone proved the biggest impediment to my research. At once jocular and sarcastic, his superior manner could leave my mother no doubt he'd come out of the abattoir alive.

Yet this war-time voice sounded to me like the same man who mocked my childhood problems — bed-wetting, learning difficulties, mouth agape, defiant, stubborn, angry, good at absolutely nothing.

The look on his black-whiskered face, his slightly sneering lip, the thunder-cloud pouches under his eyes wrinkled with disdain, would come to me as I tried to solve the nightmare mystery, and I'd be rendered helpless to think, sure that any effort to reason would fall miserably below his standards.

I forced myself to snap out of my funk and focused on the task at hand. I tried to sort out what role Dad played in the European campaign.

He was a big man in a very small outfit.

For much of the time he was in Europe, he served as the first lieutenant executive officer of the Cannon Company, 134th Infantry Regiment, 35th Division. His responsibilities included meshing the activities of about a hundred men, six 105mm howitzers (maximum range, 8,300 yards)[4], and ten to fifteen vehicles. He coordinated the firing of the guns and did much of the advance scouting. He answered to the company commander, a captain and career army man.

My father, somewhere in France, 1944

As I went through the contents of the brown envelope, I found a map. Inscribed *Carte Michelin, Les Grandes Routes*, he traced, in purple pencil, the path of the Cannon Company from its beginning July 8, 1944 on Omaha Beach to the time it left France that December to join the Battle of the Bulge in Belgium.

The purple line led first to the transportation hub of St. Lo, about twenty miles south of the beachhead. In the month preceding the Battle of St. Lo, the Allies struggled to maintain their foothold in German-held territory. The Nazis would throw the Allies back into the harsh, gray English Channel unless they could gain a secure staging area.

The British had failed to establish a secure foothold on the continent in 1940 and were forced into a frantic retreat at Dunkirk. No one wanted that to happen again.

Arriving on the outskirts of St. Lo, the Cannon Company dug in. Using collapsible entrenching tools — short-handled shovels that could also be converted into picks — they hacked their way through roots, rocks, and mud to make their dugouts.

The Norman pastures that served as the St. Lo battlefield had previously been used for the nurture of livestock, and thus the soldiers frantically excavating their way to safety became covered with several shades of manure that almost, but not quite, matched their olive drab.

Even the completed dugouts could hardly be referred to as sanctuaries. Night after night, soldiers suffered the shattering concussive shock of German artillery and mortar shells landing nearby.

During the most frenzied hours of St. Lo, the men of the Cannon Company worked twenty-two hours a day, firing the howitzers so continuously that water had to be poured down the barrels to keep them from melting.

The gods supplied plenty of water. It rained constantly, and as it hit the muddy pastures, it percolated through the soil and into Dad's foxhole. On one occasion, as shells shook the ground, an earthworm slithered out of the dugout wall and down his collar — causing a struggle that ended up severing the telephone lines.

Dad did most of his communicating with regimental headquarters by field telephone, a less than reliable conduit of speech since something constantly cut the lines. Radios had very limited range, and soldiers hesitated to use them because they feared (rightly, as it turned out) the Germans would intercept their transmissions.

If a telephone line went down at night, Dad had to wait until daylight for repair, meaning hours of isolation in a cold hole that gathered more water as time passed. He occupied himself by writing letters, his digs lit with a candle and a German helmet he used as a reflector. His writing table was a square, canvas GI pillow in his lap.

Dad had company in his foxhole. On July 31, 1944, there was a full, bright "Bomber's Moon" and the German air force...

...caused us some restless moments. I turned over a few times in my moldy hole in the earth and soon slumbered unbothered by anything but a profusion of fleas which crawled all over me. This morning I look like a pincushion. Great red splotches all over my skinny carcass.

The blood-sucking bugs stayed with him for a month until finally succumbing to a combination of insecticide and gasoline.

Dad didn't lose his life at St. Lo, as many men did, but he did lose his innocence. Bronxville, Dartmouth, basic training, and prolonged stateside maneuvers hadn't emotionally prepared him for the theater of war.

July 19, 1944:

The little country villages of Normandy are a pitiful sight. Most have been leveled to the ground by artillery fire. They are dead places with only the occasional dog prowling around. The silence is complete. The bodies in the streets do not speak. The outstanding characteristic of them all is the same. The awful stench that hangs over them... Some of the sights that greet your eyes are almost too horrible to believe. I often get the impression the whole thing is a fantastic dream.

No men inhabited in the villages, he said, because they were all dead or in German concentration camps. The retreating German army took the women.

Although the Cannon Company operated two to six thousand yards behind enemy lines, death visited regularly. Every time the Cannon Company fired a round, they exposed their position by the puff of smoke from the howitzer muzzle, and German artillery would react accordingly.

For Dad, the personal danger involved creeping close to, or sometimes beyond, the front lines, searching for proper gun emplacement sites.

When the front lines moved forward, the artillery positions also had to change, and before the cannons could be moved, someone had to scout out the new position. Loading and firing artillery took technical skill, but finding a new firing position took someone who had excellent military judgment, someone who had been to artillery training school — and that often meant Dad.

In Normandy, the location of the front line was often ephemeral. No digital displays or heat-sensing satellites existed then. Hedges up to fifteen feet high bordered a maze of sunken roads. The hedges divided the countryside into a checkerboard of small pastures.

One War Department publication said aerial photos showed about 3,900 hedged enclosures in an area of less than eight square miles.[5]

The sunken roads provided the Germans with ideal ramparts, and the hedgerows gave them perfect cover. One enclosed field looked very much like another. The invisible Germans hid in the hedges until they started shooting.

The scouting, therefore, had to be done on the crawl, and men often measured forward progress in feet per hour.

As I read about Dad's scouting duties, it became obvious to me that this must have been the sort of situation that provided the raw material for the recurring nightmare, but the letters from St. Lo never even hinted he became lost behind enemy lines. It made me wonder if Dad's nightmare came out of the fear of getting lost rather than any actual event. Or perhaps he didn't write about his mistakes because he knew military censors read his letters.

I began to realize that although reading the letters might help me to understand Dad, questions would multiply like single-cell animals.

As I continued to read, I stumbled across an odd statement:

I have gotten one Nazi for you personally and have accounted for untold numbers through our guns. But that is not personal.

I could imagine Mom saying to Dad, during the hours just before he boarded the *Queen Mary* in New York, "Kill one of those nasty old Germans for me, darling." What I hadn't been able to put together was how an artillery officer would have an opportunity for "personal" killing.

As I read the letters, it occurred to me that he undoubtedly had to kill people as he searched for gun emplacements. He probably needed to kill not only German soldiers but also anyone he tripped across who might give him away to the enemy.

This thought brought back a conversation I had with Dad as a thirteen-year-old. I sometimes watched him shave, my bony rump seated on the edge of the bathtub so I could get a side view of the male morning ritual I'd soon be practicing. He had a face full of soap applied with a brush. He used his left hand to pull his skin tight so the other hand could employ the razor to maximum effect.

Out of nowhere, I asked him how many men he had killed during the war.

His eyes, which had been fixed on the mirror image of his face, found mine.

"With our howitzers? Thousands, tens of thousands probably."

"No. I mean you. How many men did *you* kill?"

I felt free to ask him the question, because we talked about the war all the time — primarily about how much good the discipline had done him and how I could benefit from a similar experience.

But we also talked about many other aspects of military life: trucks getting stuck in mud wallows; an artillery shell that landed in the center of their encampment but didn't go off; the intricacy of German booby traps.

He told stories of women, hiding in the basements of their homes, who had to throttle crying children. He talked about the justification for shooting men who disobeyed a direct order in the heat of battle. I often got the impression he had forgotten the age of his audience.

I asked him how many men he killed because I wanted to see if he would prevaricate. I rather hoped the question would embarrass him.

Yet he didn't hesitate.

"About twenty," he said and then shifted his eyes back to his shaving.

I found his reply so stunning, I didn't ask the obvious follow-up questions. Who were they? Did you shoot them or kill them in ways that made less noise? Were they all soldiers, or were some of them civilians? Women? Children?

As I recalled the conversation, my insides fluttered. I couldn't imagine what it would feel like to be matter-of-fact about killing twenty people. Still, it fit in with Dad's hard-core attitude. He probably *could* kill people without compunction.

Yet if he had no regrets, what about the nightmares? Did they represent the memory of an actual situation? Was he unconsciously projecting toward the day he might be held accountable by God? Or would I never understand, no matter how many questions I asked?

Not asking wasn't an option. If I stopped, I'd never make sense of what happened between my father and me. Worse, I'd never know myself, for by this time I had in my sights the primary purpose of my inquiry.

Yet my quest wasn't without a price. Recent PTSD research indicates that reliving trauma can make it worse.

"Talking about the trauma, even just *trying* to put what happened into words, can actually worsen a victim's trauma by reactivating it in the brain and embedding it deeper," said British therapist Mark Tyrrell. He believes "talking it out" may work for 75 percent of people who are traumatized, but for the rest, it just makes matters worse.[6] Although a great deal of disagreement exists about how to treat PTSD and secondary trauma (like mine), I think researching and writing this book retraumatized me.

Shortly after deciding to write this memoir — which I hoped would stand the Greatest Generation archetype on its head — I wrote out the anecdotes that appear in this book.

After I'd been working for a month, my then-wife said to me, "Bill, have you started drinking again?"

Her question startled and offended me. I hadn't had a drink in over twenty years.

"God, no," I said. "Why would you ask such a question?"

"Because you haven't said a word to me for three weeks."

I had been preoccupied. I knew that, yet I didn't know I had become so withdrawn. I apologized and made an effort to be more rational about my father's chimera. His bones had, after all, been residing under a blustery Vermont hillside for over forty years. Perhaps I could summon up the mental bravery to write about him without lapsing into a fugue state.

Although I had every intention of being "rational" about my subject matter, I had no intention of stopping. I badly wanted to write a book about my life experience, and giving up just because it made me feel bad wasn't an option. As a result, I became increasingly depressed.

As my mental condition deteriorated, I became snappish and argumentative with my wife. Although I don't believe my secondary trauma was the only reason we got divorced, our marriage of forty-two years ended in 2016.

CHAPTER 4: TRANSGENERATIONAL SHOCK

German shells penetrated the gray-green sludge near my father's foxhole during the battle of St. Lo, turning it into a whirling mass of dirt, pulverized insects, shredded rodents, and manure particulate. When the high explosives erupted, fire and shell fragments obliterated anything above ground. Below the earth's surface, shock waves juddered everything in their path: the viscera of worms, the shells of beetles, the legs of centipedes, the brains of voles, the hearts of low-land nesting birds, the fresh-born offspring of hares — all the earth's underground creatures, including Dad. The sonic assault smacked the side of his dugout, splattered him with mud, penetrated his ears, entered his brain, and stayed there. Time after time, minute after minute, hour after hour, night after night, month after month.

If not in a foxhole, he hunkered down in the basement of some destroyed house or the corroded boiler room of an abandoned factory, but the sonic thug always found its quarry.

The laws of thermodynamics tell us energy cannot be created or destroyed. I'm convinced the blasts from the German shells were transformed into sonic concussions that entered my dad's brain, only to leak out slowly during the 1950s in the form of verbal assaults against his children. Sometimes the attacks came in the form of nettling sarcasm, occasionally embarrassing mockery, and often in bellowed military commands like "AT EASE!" shouted so loudly anyone walking their dog down on the street fifty feet below could easily have heard it.

Although the letters made it easy to see where Dad's negative parenting techniques came from, they weren't that helpful to a person trying to determine the details of his military mission.

He could only say so much in his letters; certain things were off-limits. For instance, he couldn't provide vital information respecting tactics — how a cannon company worked, how it spotted and hit targets, and how it defended itself from German infantry. The correspondence said little about the range of the 105mm howitzer, its use in close quarter battle, or coordination with the rudimentary fire control center.

The letters also said nothing about the company's day-to-day location, its mission (other than to kill Germans), or where it was headed. Regulations strictly prohibited any mention of casualties, so even on days when Dad's unit had suffered revolting butchery, he'd most likely lead his letter with what the chuck wagon served for dinner that night.

Thus, using the letters — or even available historical texts — wasn't going to provide me with the kind of truth I sought, for even though my investigation had just begun, it hadn't escaped me that I had turned out to be a lot like my father, despite all my efforts to the contrary. In addition to alcoholism, there was my penchant for newspapers, sarcasm, fedoras, railroads, reverse snobbery. In truth, anyone who knew us both could add to the list.

As I began to think about how to put our kinship in some sort of perspective the outside world could understand, I fished around for scientific concepts — or at least psychological ideas — that might help explain what had happened between 1944, the year the shells started dropping on my dad, and now, when they continued to reverberate around me as I wrote in the perfectly peaceable city of Denver, Colorado.

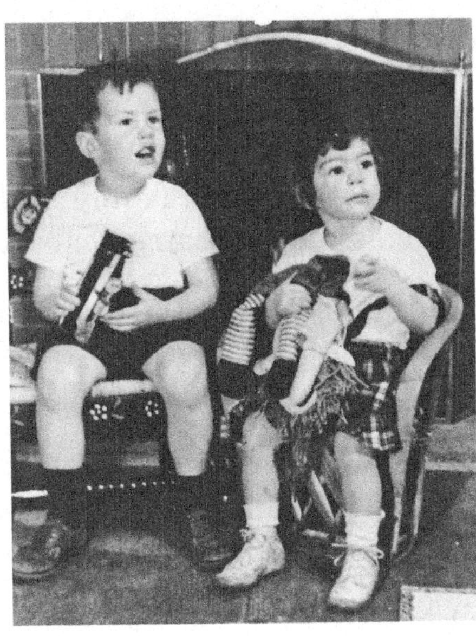

My sister Mary Jo and I, Christmas Eve, circa 1950

An old friend suggested I call his sibling, noted Chicago psychoanalyst Dr. Prudence Gourguechon. She introduced me to the "transgenerational transmission of trauma," a phenomenon first noticed among the children of Holocaust survivors. The survivors' children were damaged by observing their parents' secretive, suspicious, and even paranoid behavior.

"So if you're a child of parents like that, you're learning as a child how the world works and what to expect," she said in the interview. "Are things going to be okay? Is it right to expect that things will work out? That's a very important part of growing up. If I get married, is it likely to work out? If I get on an airplane, is likely not to crash? If I talk to a stranger, is it likely to be benign? These are lessons we learn growing up, and to be a sort of functional, optimistic, resilient person, you've got to have a certain positive outlook. If your parents convey deep anxiety, suspicion, and isolation as a logical way to approach the world, some of that...gets through to (their children) and affects (their) entire development of (their) sense of (themselves) in the world."

Research done by the Veterans Administration backs up Gourguechon's view. Secondary PTSD, the VA maintains, results in "compromised parenting, family violence, divorce, sexual problems, aggression, and caregiver burden."[7]

It's a new field, and since the US chose to engage itself in three major wars over the last forty years, there will be ample opportunity for further investigation.

After World War II, psychologists missed a big chance to study the effects of PTSD on families because they were so overwhelmed with caring for pschoneurotic soldiers.

In the months following the war's end, as the government packed a million psychoneurotics into VA hospitals, millions more, like Dad, toughed it out. That means there are an immense number of Baby Boomers that could be victims of transgenerational transmission of trauma.

A recent national study concluded "People in the Baby Boom generation (born between 1946 and 1964) have been shown to have a higher risk for depression, anxiety disorders, and substance use disorders than people born before World War II. As Baby Boomers age, the number of older people with mental illness will grow."[8]

It's probably not a coincidence that divorces among couples fifty and older now represent one in four divorces nationally.[9]

The VA says 18.6 percent of deployed Army troops and 20.6 percent of deployed Marines serving in Iraq and Afghanistan Wars were afflicted by PTSD.[10] This statistic obviously doesn't include thousands who refused to admit they had a problem. Children will be produced from this great legion, and some of them will observe a parent who is either silent and withdrawn — seemingly uncaring — or harsh and brutal, seemingly without cause. In all likelihood, some of those children will grow up angry and filled with anxiety. They won't have the slightest idea why they're on edge, but they'll know they need to take that edge off, and many will use alcohol, drugs, or both.

Having done this research into the field of PTSD, I was almost able to cut myself some slack. Maybe the problems I'd encountered in my adult life weren't really my fault. I had secondary PTSD, given to me by my father directly and Adolf Hitler indirectly, so why beat myself up?

This explanation satisfied me for a couple of days, but then it began wearing thin. I was, after all, trying to be a journalist as well as a memoirist, and good journalists are wary of easy answers. Sure, Dad's PTSD didn't help my emotional development, but even a cursory examination of my personal history revealed I had several serious problems Dad somehow managed to avert.

When I finished my list of anecdotes — to use as a skeleton for my book — I was subsumed by desolation, by mistakes I made that could so easily have been avoided, by the wrath that had become a part of me. Still I found moments, as I tiptoed through my youth, that were both enchanting and discouraging, moments that provided gist for both love and hate.

No one told me how to balance all these factors to tell a personal story that was even-handed, interesting and devoid of self-pity. Yet I spent decades as a newspaper reporter writing about the lives of others. I could be dispassionate about them. Clearly, I needed to try to turn that skill on myself.

CHAPTER 5: TWO MOONS

I never moved down the path to maturity quickly enough for my parents, and neither did Mary Jo. We were slow in school and in achieving most other watersheds of maturity. Trying to deal with this problem, Dad and Mom didn't have the tools of modern psychology. There was no Internet to Google "persistent bed-wetting." The only written advice commonly available was Dr. Spock. If he couldn't solve the problem, my parents fell back on ancient shibboleths like "spare the rod, spoil the child."

Occasionally we succeeded in covering up our childish mistakes. More often, we got caught, but in the process we formed a union which for a while transcended the fear that whips many children.

Sometimes, our bond seemed to take on a magical quality. So it was one owlish night in Vermont shortly before we left for a family trip to the Maritime Provinces. At the time, I was eight and Mary Jo was six.

Our parents tucked us into bed in a room referred to as "the Chapel" because, legend had it, the original owners of the 1787 structure used it for prayer services. It had a high, vaulted ceiling crossed by coarse wooden beams. Broad maple boards planked the floor. A large brick fireplace gave the room a smell of charred wood. The scent of flowers drifted in with the breeze, fluttering the lace-curtained windows.

Sometime between midnight and dawn, I dreamed of urinating in a toilet, but when I awoke, I found myself peeing in bed. Something my parents thought of as a character defect squished under me. I groaned in frustration.

Quickly, I launched into my cover-up procedures. As I removed the sheets and hung them over a lampshade to dry, I woke up Mary Jo.

"Oh, Billy," she said, her face contorted by anxiety and her two little fists clenched in the folds of her flannel nightgown, "Mom's gonna be mad!"

"Not if she doesn't find out."

"But even if they dry, they're gonna look yellow," Mary Jo said, sounding increasingly desperate. "And they're gonna stink!"

"What if I rinsed them in the bathtub?"

"Then they'll never get dry in time!"

She was right. The sopping humidity of the chilly Vermont night would prevent that.

"Maybe we should run away," Mary Jo suggested.

"Really?"

"Well, what else?"

"I dunno."

Mary Jo collapsed on the floor. I could hear her weeping in the dark. Witnessing my parents' punishment upset her greatly.

I nudged her with my foot.

"Don't worry. They'll probably just take away my dessert or make me pull weeds or something."

"You don't think you'll get the belt?"

"Nah! That's just for playing with matches. You know, the big stuff."

Actually, I didn't understand what caused the belt to come smacking down. Covering up a bed-wetting might be interpreted as playing fast and loose with the truth — one of the most heinous offenses imaginable.

I went back to the big table lamp over which my bottom sheet hung. It had a white cloth shade and an old sea-green jug as its base. I decided to take the risk of turning the light on for a moment to see if the urine was noticeably yellow, and then it occurred to me the piss could leach into the lampshade. I rashly pulled off the sheet, sending the lamp crashing to the floor.

"Ooooooh!" cried Mary Jo, sure the noise would awaken our parents.

We were very quiet for several minutes, and when it became clear they had slept through the incident, I lifted the lamp back up to the table and closely examined the shade. Sure enough, a big crescent of urine discolored it. My heart wobbled. The belt was becoming more likely. I turned the lamp so the urine stain faced the wall.

Mary Jo was sitting on the floor, leaning against her bed, weeping quietly. I sat down next to her and put my arm on her shoulder. I thought about saying something comforting. Then I noticed I was seeing the details of her crumpled little self too clearly. Our room, generally very black indeed, was filled with a dim, eerie light. I ran to the window, and that's when I saw it.

Our room had a door leading outside. Very quietly, we crept out onto the lawn, wet with the chill of dew.

"You see it, right? Two moons?"

In her most reticent manner, Mary Jo said, "Yes. I mean, I

guess so..."

After blinking several times, I convinced myself of their authenticity—both full moons and fairly close to each other, hovering over New Hampshire's distant hills. A nearby poplar glistened with lunar grace, but there was no wind, so the leaves didn't spoil the mood with pedestrian chatter. The absence of clouds allowed the moons to dominate the black sky.

"Why?" Mary Jo said quietly. "Why did it happen?"

"I dunno."

"But there's only supposed to be one, right?"

"Right."

For a couple of minutes, we gaped. The moonlight twinkled off the wet grass. A nearby stone wall, made of gray, flinty granite, glowed like a phosphorescent river.

Nearby, an owl hooted. It seemed like a promise, an affirmation of this miracle's authenticity.

Knowing this memory would be challenged, I sought to enlist my sister as a witness.

"Mary Jo, let's make a promise we'll never forget this."

"Well, okay..."

"I mean, when everybody else says it didn't happen or that it's impossible, we'll stick together, okay?"

"Okay, Billy."

Her assurance made me feel better about being believed, because though two years younger than me, my parents regarded Mary Jo as serious and not given to fable. I, on the other hand, had been accused of having an overactive imagination, so I needed my sister's endorsement.

The chill of grass made our feet cold, so we went back inside, seeking the warmth of our beds. Mary Jo soon slept, but I wanted to stay awake so I could remake my bed when the sheets were less wet. I lay down on the floor beside my bed. Before I knew it, my shouting mother awakened me.

"Young man, you promised me this wouldn't happen again!" she yelled, stomping her foot in frustration. "I'm so disappointed in you, I could cry!"

The klaxon of the adult world had sounded, and our truth was blown into a corner like so much dust.

A few minutes later, I walked into the dining room and found my father consuming pancakes and drinking black coffee. He brought his eyes up to mine, lifted his lip in a sneer, and shook his head with disgust.

"I hear you left another fine mess for your mother to clean up," he said.

I turned my eyes to the floor.

"You're still kind of a baby, aren't you?"

One of his robust black eyebrows rose.

"I think maybe you need a diaper."

"I'm not a baby!" I shouted at him.

"Well, you act like a baby!"

"But I'm not. I'm not!"

Refuting his assertion was impossible, however, so I crumpled to the floor and screamed — just like a baby.

It doesn't seem a bit strange that my father had nothing but scorn for my extended bout with enuresis. A black-and-white sort of person, he thought my problem a symptom of psychic weakness. He may have thought my mother mollycoddled me.

Mom knew little about raising children — only the skills passed down to her from her mother. What she did know came from the 1946 edition of *The Common Sense Book of Baby and Child Care* by Dr. Benjamin Spock. The book, which served as a Bible for millions of postwar mothers, asserts shaming a child for his bed-wetting problems will make it worse and create a rebellious adolescent[11] — which is exactly what happened in my case.

Since the problem went on for at least five years past the time it should have abated, why did my mother not heed its advice? I think she may have been overwhelmed by dealing with Dad's PTSD and her own alcoholism and wasn't emotionally capable of heeding Spock's advice.

The animosity toward my parents over bed-wetting began our extended internecine conflict. I thought they punished me for something I couldn't control, and that made me furious. It made me view all other interactions through that lens. It took more than sixty years and extensive research into PTSD for me to understand how Dad must have felt.

As the years rolled out, my propensity for mocking my old man became ever stronger. I enlisted my sisters in the battle against this crazy person who also served as our leader. Eye-rolling, crossed eyes, wall-eyed looks, derogatory noises all became part of my arsenal. When she wasn't frightened to death, Mary Jo often thought my wise-ass antics were pretty funny. Since he represented the enemy, we didn't care how Dad felt about our behavior.

Recently, I came across an article that suggested fathers suffering from PTSD viewed scorn from their children as a form of "friendly fire."

"Being spit on by strangers is one thing, but being symbolically spit upon with sarcastic looks and words by one's own children is quite another. Such behavior on the part of adolescents can deepen the veterans' depression and sense of isolation — as well as ignite his rage. The stage is set for an ugly family fight where no one wins."[12]

To say our childhood was one long struggle would be to tell only a fraction of the story. Joy often bubbled to the surface, especially when we traveled with our parents.

Almost every summer, in addition to going to Vermont, we took a trip of some kind. On a couple of occasions we set our sights on Canada's Maritime Provinces.

A few minutes prior to the beginning of one such trip, I pumped my tree swing — a tire hanging from an old oak in front of the farmhouse — as Dad packed our black 1946 Chevrolet sedan.

My efforts arced the tire far above the orange crust of dawn. The nip of the new day raised goosebumps all over my skinny body, but I didn't notice, for the coming adventure subsumed me. We planned to board the MV *Bluenose*, a ship that would carry us on the unruly Atlantic from Maine to Nova Scotia. During the twelve-hour journey, it would be all blue and no land in sight! As the old oak groaned under my weight, I thought of the rise and fall of the ship and of the frothy display of foam breaking over her valiant bow.

It certainly would be better than the past few days.

Ever since we arrived in Vermont, our acquaintance with the silent woods had become all too intimate. There were fields of Queen Ann's Lace and Indian paintbrush, bastions of granite among the gloomy trees, a brook full of darting fish — and absolutely nothing to do.

But in just a few minutes, all of that tedium would be over. The land of festive bagpipers and picturesque tourist cabins awaited us.

Hoorah!

At that age, I imagined the future as a cream pastry filled with glee. Although the misery of the seven-hour car trip from our New York home had occurred just nine days before, my brimming imagination would not tolerate the notion that such wretchedness would be revisited.

As the sun broke the crest of Mt. Monadnock, Dad ordered me off my swing and into the back seat with Mary Jo. The black Chevy rattled down the gravel driveway, leaving our smaller siblings, Anne, Susan, and Joan, behind with the grandparents.

Our parents kept the windows rolled up and turned on the heat. Then they both lit up cigarettes.

The minute I smelled the smoke, my cornflakes became restive. Back in the gas chamber! We had been here before, and there could be only one outcome. I looked over at Mary Jo. Her impish face seemed gray, and she already had it pointed toward the saucepan in her lap. She had a history of carsickness, but *I* had graduated from all of that. Yet my stomach told me otherwise, and I envied Mary Jo's pan. I felt it was quite possible I would embarrass myself unless I could persuade the warden to pump in some fresh air.

"Mom, would you roll down the window?"

"It's pretty chilly out there, Billy," she replied.

"But Mary Jo is gonna get sick."

"I'm sure she is. That's why she has the pan."

"But I don't feel so good either."

"So *well*, darling."

"Okay, so *well*. Would you roll it down just a crack?"

"Oh, all right!"

The gush of fresh air did indeed help. I immediately felt better, and Mary Jo lifted her head and looked out the window as we passed the white Congregational Church in Dummerston Center. But then Dad took a hard left and swooped down the hill leading toward Route 5. Mary Jo's eyes got very wide, and she redirected her gaze back to the silvery bottom of the pan.

As Mom promised, the cracked window did make the back seat chilly. We both had on t-shirts and shorts. I drew my legs up to my chest, grabbed them with my arms, and tilted toward Mary Jo, and she, wary that any outside vector would interrupt her fragile equilibrium, edged away from me.

"Billy," she whispered, "don't!"

My mom looked back, and seeing us shiver, closed the window. A blue plume of smoke jetted from her freckled nose.

Almost immediately, my stomach headed toward bedlam, and Mary Jo began to coil her little body into hurl position. I was desperate. I tried to roll down my window but was greeted by the rattle of broken gears. The window went down an inch and then stuck in place.

My mother looked sharply at me and then at the broken window.

"Oh, for heaven's sake, Bill! How many times have I asked you not to do that?"

"Well, when are you going to get it fixed?"

"Bill, AT EASE!" Dad bellowed.

His eyes fixed mine in the rear-view mirror. I shut my mouth and focused my anger on the vast array of mosquito bites that adorned my shins.

"Peter, you'd better pull over and jiggle that window back in place," Mom said. "I'd be happy to let them freeze, but then they'd catch cold and we'd have to deal with *that*."

So it went for the rest of the day. Mary Jo did a great job and didn't get sick until just outside Hillsboro, New Hampshire. That pushed me over the edge, but Mary Jo was generous with the pan, and the fact that she got sick first gave me a little cover. To my parents' credit, they didn't tell me I was a big baby. Instead, they complimented us on sharing the pan and not besmirching the car's gray corduroy seat covers. They knew the smoke made us sick, and they happily noted we had learned to manage the problem.

After puke faded as the day's primary theme, Dad did his best to entertain us with historical vignettes. He began with some family history. After the American Revolution, the McBeans mustered out of the 42nd Highlanders military regiment and moved to Fredericton, New Brunswick, a town through which we'd travel on the return leg of our trip. He asserted that at one time the city had more McBeans in the phone book than Smiths!

I was impressed by his anecdote, but the tale posed an obvious question.

"Dad," I asked, "how did we get back to America?"

"Some of us didn't take to farming, Bill. We hired on to logging crews that made their way west through Canada and somehow ended up in Montana."

Wow, I thought. Centuries in the backwoods. That got me thinking about the story of Pocahontas, the Native American princess who helped early settlers of Virginia. I imagined the early McBeans must have spent some pretty lonely years trudging through the timber.

"Do you think any of 'em married an Indian princess?" I asked.

Dad's eyebrows shot straight up. "Of course not!"

With the exception of the docking procedures in Halifax, the *Bluenose* failed to live up to my dramatic expectations. Our tourist cabin, which faced the Bay of Fundy, also disappointed me. I thought it might resemble the cottages of European elves, but it turned out to be an asbestos-shingled shack with a knotty pine interior and kerosene stove. It struck me, a lad accustomed to nothing but the finest, as distinctly...impoverished!

Knowing that my father would inevitably contrast our accommodations with his foxhole in France, I spared him my critique.

An hour of sanctuary from his children sat at the top of Dad's agenda. He wanted us out of the cabin, but removed from the natural hazards that surrounded us. He forbade us from taking a path down the steep bluff leading to the ocean. The pools of sea water trapped by rocks near the ocean's edge held a large population of rapacious crabs that often ganged up on unsuspecting children in much the same way wild dogs victimized deer.

We believed him, but from our vantage point a hundred feet above the water, Mary Jo and I could only see a wide swath of mud, punctuated by rock formations that looked like teeth from a skeleton. The tidal basin, a large ochre bowl steaming under the afternoon sun, was festooned with skanky seaweed and moldering fish. It provoked nauseating memories of my mother's tuna casserole.

Hundreds of yards to the north, we saw the ocean's quivering blue line, but it didn't seem to pose much of a threat.

About a half-hour into our exile, things began to change. The ocean, like an army of angry Visigoths, rolled onto the mud flats in a three-foot-high crest. We later learned this happened twice a day and constituted a major tourist attraction. Nonetheless, it seemed to us a threatening and somewhat supernatural event.

Shortly after that, the balmy day began to shatter around us. The hazy white horizon blackened and quickly staunched the signal from an outlying lighthouse. The sky became a steadily advancing mass of charcoal-dark cloud. Farther away from shore, the few small sailboats that delighted in the strong gusts preceding the storm squirted for cover. The buoy's lulling canon freshened into clanging concern. Although loath to interrupt our parents' sacred ceremony, we saw bolts of lightning within the advancing black wall.

"What if the black cloud grabs us into the ocean?" Mary Jo asked.

A fair question, I thought. I tried to pull my little sister to safety but abruptly discovered I couldn't talk, and then that I couldn't breathe. I fell to the ground and clawed the earth with the frenetic energy of a wounded animal. I used all my strength to pull in air, catching little snatches of breath but not enough to sustain consciousness. As the first rain began to lash my face, my writhing slowed as I began to give up.

I woke in the small, tiny bathroom of the tourist cabin. The place was full of steam, and Dad had me in his lap. His warmth wrapped me tightly.

"Come on, Bill, give me a deep breath. Now another. There's a good lad. I think you're getting the hang of this. Come on, one more."

Later, he told me I survived an asthma attack. He said if the steam therapy hadn't worked, his bag of tricks would have been almost empty. The nearest doctor was ten miles away and the closest hospital about twenty-five miles.

I asked him what he would have done if the hot water vapor hadn't gotten me breathing normally. My earnest need for an answer provoked Dad's urge to clown.

In his goofy, pseudo-serious voice, he said, "Well, Bill, I do have one medical solution that cures all ills. When I was in the army, it calmed the nerves, cured the common cold, and provided courage where there was none to be found."

He pointed to the green bottle of Black & White Scotch sitting on the kitchen table. "I think if I had poured a few ounces of that down your gullet, you would have been breathing again in very short order."

The Nova Scotia incident proved to be the beginning of my career as an asthmatic. One evening, later that summer, my parents put me to bed about 8:00 p.m., but the light still played on the tall grass outside my bedroom window. As I gnawed on my resentment at being put to bed so early, my ability to breath suddenly vanished. I could still take in shallow breaths, but I struggled even to do that. I wanted to cry out to my parents for help, but of course that proved impossible. I thought about getting out of bed to find them, but I feared even moving slightly might rob me of my last bit of oxygen. I began to feel the panic that would become a hallmark of my existence and follows me even to this day.

Mom came to check on me and found me awake and gasping. She and my father once again gave me the steam cure, soothed my anxiety, and got me back to bed. When we returned to Bronxville, sinusitis plagued me. They sent me to a doctor who inserted cotton-swabbed wires covered with a bright blue tincture up my nose. Eventually, my tonsils and adenoids were removed, which solved the sinusitis problem but didn't do a thing for my anxiety disorder. Although I felt low-level anxiety most of the time, actual panic attacks were forestalled until I began to have hangovers during my college years, those good old days that eventually proved to be my undoing and rebirth.

CHAPTER 6: DUMP SURPRISE

Shortly after our return from Nova Scotia, a low-pressure system centered over New England brought a deluge. It rained for days. It came down so hard, the leaves on the trees looked limp and helpless. Mold crept out of the woodshed and into the house. The dirt roads turned into brown soup.

Our family of nine became housebound and fractious, splintering into two distinct interest groups: my parents and grandparents, plus my younger siblings, fell into one cohort, while Mary Jo and I fell into another.

Because our younger siblings, all under four, needed constant attention, my parents expected Mary Jo and me to entertain ourselves.

Shortly after breakfast on normal summer days, our elders expelled us to the great outdoors. Given a thermos of fruit juice and a few cookies, we wandered among the abundant sugar maples and beds of soft moss.

On rainy days, Mary Jo and I became an underclass of two. While my parents and grandparents sat at the large dining room table, drinking coffee, smoking cigarettes, and laughing, my dad told us to play harmoniously with each other until lunch—only four hours away. Dark penetrated the living room's every crevice as stuffy and burly blue-tailed flies bumbled against windows made opaque by rain. An ancient collusion of dust, wool, and old wood stifled movement of air. The smell of mold made us sleepy.

Two uncomfortable antique chairs and a rigid pearl-gray divan furnished our prison. A repeating pattern of faded red-and-gold gilded picture frames made up the wallpaper. One after another, no pictures, just frames.

A crumbling fireplace of flinty granite and mortar stood as the room's centerpiece. An antique clock sat there, loudly proclaiming the passage of each and every second.

A record player and a Mitch Miller album temporarily salved our mumpish boredom. We listened to it three times, but when the music stopped, there was only the sound of rain and the relentless percussion of the clock. Occasionally, from behind the closed door, came an outpouring of laughter. Then the rain, and the clock.

Desperate, I lifted the latch on the dining room door.

"I'm bored," I said.

This struck everyone as hilarious. My father slapped his knee, my mother gave me her precious smile, and my gray, asthmatic grandfather began a lengthy, productive cough.

When the mirth faded, my father addressed my complaint.

"Bill, rainy days are boring for everyone. Use your imagination. I'm sure, given sufficient effort, that you will find a way to entertain yourself."

"But there's nothing to do!"

"That's correct. There is nothing to do. That's why I recommended the use of your imagination. Now get out and shut the door behind you."

"But..."

"Out!"

I closed the door, hard. The injustice of it all! When I turned back to Mary Jo, she had a silly look on her chimpy face.

"Let's play Coster, Chickie, and Mad Doctorie!"

I groaned. That again. That stupid game of hand puppets that cast me as the manly Coster and Mary Jo as his wife Chickie. A third character, Mad Doctorie (also played by me) represented our common enemy. We had played this game for nine days straight. I hated it because Mary Jo always wanted to follow the same script. Chickie would be kidnapped by Mad Doctorie and Coster would rescue her. I hated that part. Why couldn't Mad Doctorie ever win?

I could not, however, listen to any more Mitch Miller, so the game began again. This time, Mad Doctorie twisted Chickie's fingers during the kidnapping. Coster, instead of tracking down Mad Doctorie and freeing his bride, decided to malinger at the soda fountain with his buddies.

Eventually, Mary Jo's face knotted up, and she began pulling at her brown corduroy smock before she pitched herself to the floor and emanated a keening wail.

Instantly, my father opened the dining room door. He walked towards us in large, sweeping steps, threatening with his old army boots, which he wore every day in Vermont. He came to an abrupt stop and put his hands on his hips. It wouldn't have surprised me if he picked us up by our necks and knocked our heads together.

Then something changed. A smile crept over his face like the first lick of a new fire.

"Obviously, this glum weather has gotten to you. So let's do something useful. Let's go to the dump."

When we looked dubious, he said, "Aw, come on! It's better than sitting around here, isn't it? And guess what? I've got a surprise for you when we get there!"

I couldn't imagine what sort of surprise might be staged at the dump. I looked at Mary Jo. She seemed to have faith that the surprise would be swell. I suspected my father's motives but felt grateful for any change of pace.

We ran upstairs and got our slickers and then went to the trash storage in the woodshed. Dad handed each of us a large paper bag filled with garbage.

In our yellow hooded raincoats, we tottered down the woodshed steps out into the rain. Skirting as many puddles as we could, we made our way toward the Chevy. Normally, the dowdiest of conveyances, it glistened in the downpour.

Mary Jo and I got in the back seat and placed our bags in between us. I wondered if he'd take us to Ho Jo's for ice cream. He hadn't ever done that before, but why not start now?

When the doors closed, our malodorous cargo made its presence known, and we both held our noses and giggled. Dad lit up a Chesterfield, pulled out the choke and pressed the starter button. The Chevy groaned two or three times but then cooperated, and we were off down the driveway, throwing water out of our way and acting like this awful rainy day never even happened.

The dump sat about a mile and a half distant, and the soupy dirt road went steeply downhill through a tunnel of sodden greenery. Dad seemed in a particularly good mood. He drove way too fast and sang the "Wabash Cannonball." By the time we reached the dump, we were a jolly bunch indeed.

"Okay, kids, throw your bags over the edge. Take care you don't throw yourselves over in the process."

We chortled with excitement. We had never been allowed to take this step toward adulthood. We clambered out of the car, grabbed our bags, and cautiously approached the precipice.

Then we heard the sound of the Chevy's gears engaging and the roar of the engine. Tires spun, splattering us with mud. We turned around and watched as the Chevy headed back up the hill.

"Why'd he leave us?" Mary Jo asked, tears beginning to mix with the raindrops pelting against her upturned face.

I felt like a tumor took root in my stomach as I watched the car disappear through the trees.

"To get rid of us."

"But what're we gonna do?"

"Walk back, I guess."

When we got back to the house forty-five minutes later, the assembled cast of parents and grandparents greeted us with great good cheer. Did we have a nice walk? Wasn't getting some fresh air better than sitting around in the living room bickering?

I have no doubt my mom and grandmother expressed some concern about the prank, and I feel equally sure Dad said, "Nonsense. Good for 'em. Little rain never hurt anyone."

Dad didn't believe in babying children. He wanted to toughen us up and thought he should pass on the lessons of World War II. "Life is war, and they need to be ready." No young mind should be unprepared for tragedy. Reading his letters, decades after the "Dump Surprise," I stumbled on one possible explanation for his unorthodox ideas.

CHAPTER 7: RAZOR BLADES

I noticed Dad often applied perverse levity to his wartime predicaments. When he wrote home during the war, his facetious nature sometimes masked misfortune.

On August 10, 1944, about two weeks after the Battle of St. Lo, he wrote a veiled missive about being routed by German soldiers who ended up in possession of his shaving gear.

Had a little personal fracas with the Krauts yesterday from which I emerged unscathed, but lost all my personal property and am at present an orphan dependent on my companions for all the necessities of life. I even lost my prized razor and all the beautiful blades which I have been receiving (from home). The supply sergeant claims, however, that he can make all the losses good. I hate to think of all the blades you and Dad policed up going for the beautification of a Panzer Grenadier, but that is the so-called fortune of war.

When I read this letter, typed on a small Victory Mail or "V-Mail" form, I thought it pretty odd. I felt sure he minimized the danger to spare Mom's feelings, but I couldn't understand how such an attack could have happened. His company worked far behind the front lines, so how had the Germans gotten the jump on him?

The anecdote puzzled me greatly. I tried to invent a context that would be innocuous, but his account of the incident defied all reason.

Since Dad's letters never supplied a precise location or a context for much of what he wrote, I consulted the 134th

Infantry Regiment's *Combat History of World War II.* It said on August 6, the 134th, as well as the rest of the 35th Division, peeled out of Patton's Brittany-bound force and prepared to defend against an anticipated German counterattack at Mortain, about twenty miles south of St. Lo.

Downed German aircraft.

As elements of two German armored Panzer divisions moved toward the strategically important town of Avranches, they attacked the Allied Forces at Mortain in a pincer movement from the north and south. Although the Allies had expected the attack, British code-breakers didn't decipher the information until the night of August 6, and particulars didn't filter down to combat units until the Germans were upon them.[13]

The Germans believed if they couldn't cut Patton's supply lines, all of France would be lost. From a military standpoint, the counterattack was a major blunder. As General Eisenhower later said, "The enemy showed that fatal tendency to stand and fight when all the logic of war demanded a strategic withdrawal."[14] Within a week, most of the Germans involved in the effort were either dead or captured, albeit with significant Allied losses.

Dad never mentioned that the Mortain battle resulted in the death of ten men under his command.[15] By military regulation, imparting such information in his letters was forbidden, and it was never discussed in my presence.

After the Allies repulsed the German assault, however, his letters relayed a little more information about what happened to him personally.

On August 31, 1944, he authored the following lighthearted note, in which he attempted to reassure the family about his close call:

In regard to the issue of the lost razor blades...I'd hate to have anyone feel that he was indirectly a part of the 'Wehrmacht Four' section. Mortar shells were dropping all around (my) Jeep and several platoons of German infantry were on location. In addition, a German Nebelwerfer (rocket launcher) was blasting in our direction. My forces consisted of one radio operator and one wireman. A split-second command decision on my part dictated a withdrawal. I withdrew and they got the razor blades.

I spent some time trying to imagine what the counterattack must have been like for him. Hedgerows dominated Mortain, and where the sloping landscape wasn't divided into pastureland, thick beech forests prevailed. From a hillside, one could see the town's venerable gray cathedral spire and its crumbling stucco-and-brick homes.

I presume Dad stood with his communications men in an enclosed pasture. But his location must have been on high ground, because he obviously had to call the shots for his artillery team. This constituted "safe" duty, the reason he signed up for the Cannon Company.

Dad's command jeep.

The official 134th Infantry account of the battle makes it clear the Germans outmaneuvered the entire regiment. Confusion ruled the day. As a reporter for *Omaha World Herald* put it, "Everybody had everybody else surrounded. It was a sandwich... One of our lieutenants tapped a man on the shoulder to ask if he was from K Company — and the German turned around and fired at him with his 'burp' gun."

Nonetheless, the Mortain counterattack was a German blunder, and it led to a great Allied victory — the mauling of the enemy's army from August 12–21, 1944 in the so-called Falaise Pocket. The "pocket" represented the inroad into Allied territory the Nazis used to attack Patton's Paris-bound Army. The Germans sought to protect the "pocket," which they hoped would be their avenue of escape. But the Allies collapsed it, with disastrous results for the Third Reich. The Germans suffered sixty thousand casualties and lost five hundred tanks. Four days later, Paris was liberated.[16]

Once American troops defeated the counterattack, Dad undoubtedly went looking for his men. I see him wandering over pastures and through hedgerows, turning over dead bodies with his boot. He must have had the bitterest sort of regret, that sorrow they call survivor's guilt.

Dad's suffering didn't manifest silently. His guilt twisted into anger and carried forward into our family. He made fun of the common-place deaths our household experienced as I grew up — the canary eaten by our Border Collie, the hamster that turned up dead one morning, the cat that went for a walk and never came back. He'd often quote King Lear: "As flies to wanton boys are we to the gods; they kill us for their sport."

He felt as removed from his brood as Shakespeare's monarch from his. He believed our family lived in Bronxville due to his hard work, and with any luck we'd get to stay there — beyond that, he didn't want to be bothered. He didn't care about the mundane aspects of bringing up five children because he couldn't — the struggle to become a partner in the law firm enveloped him completely. He probably expended all his emotional resources not acting psychoneurotic at work.

I think Mortain may have had something to do with a word of wisdom he passed on to me at least once a week as I grew up: "Anticipate, William, anticipate." He maintained almost every folly known to man could be avoided with a little forethought.

One day, as a teenage driver, a guy rear-ended me. I felt confident I couldn't be held responsible. Yet Dad said I could have foretold the actions of the man who slammed into me.

"How?" I gasped.

"Well, did you allow enough distance between your car and the car in front of you? Could you see his rear tires?"

"What does that have to do with it?"

"If you had left enough room, and had your eye glued to the rear-view mirror, you could have seen him coming and pulled out of the way before he got there. The car in front of you would have gotten hit."

Vintage Dad.

◆ ◆ ◆

Mortain must have sliced open his psyche, but he had almost a year of trauma left before getting shipped home. As he rode through France, Belgium, and Germany in his mud-splattered Jeep, the conflict left layer after layer of trauma in his long-term memory.

The management technique Dad used to keep his psychoneurosis under control—alcohol—caused no end of problems. It may have helped him avoid a few nightmares, but the side effects rippled way beyond the damage it did to his heart and liver.

It inundated our family.

Dr. Gourguechon isn't the only academic convinced that these problems cascade onto the returning soldier's family.

"...the volatile and unpredictable behavior of the alcoholic parent (is) sufficient to create an environment of fear and apprehension in other members of the household," said the University of Colorado's Dr. Robert Scaer. "(A) child learns through a thousand tiny wounds to view the world with suspicion and fear, and he will carry a heritage of diminished resiliency to subsequent life traumas. Alcoholism is now known to carry a genetic propensity. If that child turns to alcohol to keep a lid on underlying anxiety, as many do, the child's alcoholism may then be attributed to genetic factors. It is likely, however, that the persistent state of threat involved in being reared in an alcoholic household contributed significantly to the activation of that genetic trait."[17]

Obviously, my parents couldn't have known in the 50s and 60s about passing trauma on to their children. Yet every popular publication of the day carried information about alcoholism. Dad and Mom surely read about it and apparently didn't think it applied to them. At that time, society countenanced heavy drinking, and my parents weren't about to give it up.

◆ ◆ ◆

While we vacationed in Vermont, the transgenerational transmission of trauma and its cure, King Alcohol, were background noise. The superbly perfumed month of August soothed us with the scent of butter melting in a large bowl of mashed potatoes, the sweet herb smell of Indian paintbrush, and the pungent odor of moss. Dad relaxed enough that he could think about making life fun for his children. He took us on tractor rides across the flower-filled fields; he and the uncles got down on their hands and knees so we could ride them over the broad front lawn, and Dad told bedtime stories about the Native Americans terrorizing the Vermont countryside during the French and Indian War. They appeared from the dense foliage without any warning, kidnapping women and children and caving in the heads of fathers and sons. These tales frightened us nearly to the point of sleeplessness, but every night we begged for more.

But it lasted just a month. A couple of hundred miles south, reality waited: the luxurious Village of Bronxville, NY. Most people in the world would have done anything to live there. Mary Jo and I would have done anything to get out.

CHAPTER 8: DOLLAR BILL

The drive back to Bronxville, since we generally headed for home over the Labor Day weekend, took nine or ten hours. Often, traffic jams would have us at a standstill. No one had air conditioning, so if the car stopped, the heat escalated from feverish to torrid.

When we finally reached the site of an accident causing a jam, a macabre sight occasionally awaited us: crash victims covered by tarps on the side of the road. Dad's eyes took in the sights and no doubt smelled the rotting battlefield corpses.

Finally, as evening arrived, we'd reach our exit on the Hutchinson River Parkway, and a few minutes later we'd pull into the driveway of our home at 72 Summit Avenue.

Our house perched on a hillside, and the garage sat under the house. Granite retaining walls defined our driveway as it snaked into the garage. Dad slowed the Chevy to a crawl as he pulled in.

When the car finally stopped and the torture ceased, Dad instructed us to play outside until Mom readied dinner. We didn't have much play left in us. Instead, Mary Jo and I sat on the crumbling granite steps by our driveway, squished a few ants, and used sticks to pick away mortar from masonry. While we indulged in this sullen, peevish destruction, we contemplated the affliction of school.

Both mediocre students, neither of us thought things would improve in the coming nine months. There would be more distressed teachers, more negative report cards. In response, my parents would employ the only character modification with which they were acquainted: the carrot and the stick. If you didn't have time for excellence in academics, you didn't deserve an allowance. Since we both tested out as intelligent children, we obviously weren't spending enough time on our homework. Therefore, we'd be grounded until our grades improved.

I think we wanted to be academic achievers, but previous years taught us the Bronxville School's curriculum lay beyond our ken. Had we been born in the twenty-first century, we would've been classified as attention-deficit-disordered. However, we lived in the fifties, and since the Stanford Achievement Tests showed us to be of above-average intellect, our parents figured we were just lazy.

Because we loathed our lives, neither of us had the slightest appreciation for our surroundings, nor did we understand the colossal advantage we had over other children living in most other parts of the New York metropolitan area.

We grew up in a terrarium of wealth. Subjected to none of the commonplace disadvantages, we had the best housing and the finest clothing. We needed only to put one foot in front of another to stay at the very top of American society.

Our parents feared we would waste our head-start. From their point of view, our family had arrived just two generations ago. Prior to our paternal grandfather's success, our predecessors struggled just keeping the family fed.

In fact, we lived in Bronxville only because of the largess of grandfather Alan. He installed our family in the twenty-room house on the hillside and then left it to my father to figure out how to stay there.

Our family's unhappiness caused us to largely ignore the beauty of the place.

Five great trees — three tulips and two ash — canopied our tan stucco Tudor home, their limbs infested by screaming blue jays and cardinals calling "purdie, purdie, purdie."

During the six months the trees bore leaves, the sun barely penetrated. The ambient light filtered inside the house faintly green and very dim. This pallor blended with Mother's interior decorating scheme of jade-green carpets and pagoda wallpaper.

The green dome also held in the summer's humidity, so much so that our bath towels, hung over the shower stall to dry, developed mildew almost immediately. The smell of mold permeated the air.

In the fall, the trees produced an overwhelming ocean that Dad and I would rake together every Saturday morning during October and November. Lack of clean air laws meant everyone burned their leaves in the streets, producing the primeval smell of men reducing chlorophyll to carbon.

The overture to winter almost always began with a shrieking nor'easter that dumped several inches of rain sometime during October or November. Then came twenty to thirty inches of snow. I shoveled the steep stairwell up to our front door from the street, and the path leading from Hobart Street to our back door, from age nine until I ventured off into the real world seven years later.

When the heavens coated our streets with ice, the tires of cars trying to climb Hobart Hill would wail, spinning and spinning in a futility that gave those of us inside safe, warm, and smug satisfaction.

Winter also produced icicles that sometimes reached two feet in length. These Dad would slip into the beds of snoozing children who ignored earlier requests to rise and get ready for school.

Then came May, the very best time of year. Our yard turned into a glorious hallelujah chorus of pink and white flowers blooming on the azaleas and rhododendrons. The trees turned gold before they became green, and for a month we became part of a congregation worshipping the onset of spring.

◆ ◆ ◆

In the few days between returning from Vermont and my first day of classes, I needed school supplies.

"Today, young man, we're going to get you organized," Mom would say with great relish.

Prior to going to Woolworths, she sat me down and asked me to write a list of what I needed. Pencil poised above yellow pad, I'd try to recall what materials school entailed. It had, after all, been three months.

Mom, busy cleaning up the kitchen but still sharp-eyed, spotted me dithering.

"You need notebook paper, right?"

"Oh, yeah."

I'd scrawl in a nearly illegible hand, "paper." Then my pencil would revert to the ready position and I'd wait for my mother's voice.

"Well, what else do you think you'll need?"

My mind swam. I'd been up at least an hour, but I felt immersed in sleep. I could probably tell her almost every brand of candy available at the drug store, but school stuff, well…

"Bill, *think!*"

"I'm *trying!*"

The stand-off would invariably end with Mom buying me what she thought I needed: a blue-gray cloth-covered notebook, paper, an assignment notebook, subject dividers, pencils, pens, a pencil sharpener, and a couple of erasers. We'd work together to get the whole thing assembled. Neatly organized, I'd briefly feel enthused. Orderliness would be the watchword this year: all assignments written down and each day's work done each day. Without fail!

For the first couple of days, I'd devote myself to my new scheme, but soon I began to slip. I'd forget to write down an assignment, and not wanting a lecture from Mom, I'd blow off the homework and get behind. Notebook pages were ripped from their moorings, graded papers folded up and stuffed in schoolbooks.

Then came the inevitable day the notebook would mysteriously go missing. I tried to remember the last time I saw it, but my brain swirled. When I attempted to skitter out the door the next morning, Mom would grab me by the collar.

"Bill, where's your notebook?"

"I think I left it at school."

"You *think*?"

"Yeah, it's in my locker."

Mom would give me a look of green-eyed skepticism. "You make sure you bring it home tonight, young man!"

Mom, circa 1950, during a rest stop on our way to Vermont. In her hand is a cup of Gallo dry sherry. My dad had one too – in those days, they didn't think of it as "drinking."

When I showed up that afternoon without the notebook, Mom's eyes narrowed and began to jitter back and forth. Her hands contracted into fists at her sides, and she thrust her head forward.

"William Seaton McBean, you've had that notebook four days! How could you possibly lose it so quickly?"

"I dunno."

"Now I suppose I'll have to go back down to Woolworths and buy you a new notebook. Like I've got nothing better to do! But I'll tell you one thing, young man. This Saturday you're going to polish every piece of silver in this house."

A kid as flummoxed as I would have tested the patience of most parents. Yet six hours of immersion in silver paste solvents probably didn't help the situation. Worse, she cancelled my allowance to cover the difference between what

I earned cleaning silver and the cost of the notebook. That meant no candy, Cokes, English muffins, or movies for that week. She meant to get my attention, but it never worked. She just made me mad.

◆ ◆ ◆

Eventually, after they cancelled my allowance numerous times, I convinced myself I should steal from my parents. I knew there could be no moral justification for this, but driven by resentment, I rationalized that my mom and dad were unjust. They seemed to think I lost things due to inattention, and in a way they were right. My mind simply wouldn't focus. My attention wandered wherever the vectors of my existence took it. Yet I couldn't offer this lame excuse to my parents, both of whom were precise people.

God knows, I tried not to lose stuff. The belittling of my intelligence every time I lost a notebook, a hat, a schoolbook, my gloves, or any number of other things, was intense. My parents nicknamed me "Jughead."

I might have stolen from them just out of anger, but I had another strong motivation: I craved sugar. Of course, all children want sweets, but I had an addictive need. My mother kept a box of assorted cookies in the kitchen and allowed me to have two after dinner — but that didn't come anywhere near answering my lust. The need for sugar ruled me. Sometimes I'd clip an extra cookie, but since my mother kept a careful inventory, she'd quickly ferret out my crime and think up some sort of additional punishment. I'd occasionally resort to lumps of brown sugar, but I knew I invited retribution if the supply got too low.

At the time, stealing from my parents felt as justified as Manifest Destiny. Just as America had nothing but forests, my parents had nothing but money. My childish mind believed I had an absolute duty to make myself happy. This exact line of thinking would eventually lead me to alcoholism, but even if I'd recognized candy as a "gateway drug," I don't think I would have stopped.

My mom's purse sat on the front hall table like a fat partridge. Her wallet brimmed with quarters. At first I nicked only silver, and she never noticed. Soon, however, I graduated to currency and, of course, I got a little too greedy.

The day my avarice got me, my mind swam in an ocean of ice cream and soda, and I had not a cent to transform my urgent need for sugar into reality. Waiting for Mom to go upstairs, I quietly opened her purse. There, I saw several twenties, a couple of tens, but only a solitary dollar bill. That worried me, but nonetheless I swiped it.

A short time later, Mom reappeared.

"Bill, isn't today the day you were supposed to bring your UNICEF money?"

(Nearly every family in the Bronxville schools pledged support to the United Nations International Children's Emergency Fund.)

She opened her wallet, saw the dollar missing, and grunted with surprise. Then we locked eyes. She knew she had me.

"Okay, give it here!"

"Give what here?"

Roughly, she grabbed my arm just above the elbow, and as we headed into the kitchen, she said, "William Seaton McBean, you're going to sit right here until you tell me what happened to that money!"

"But I'll be late for school!"

"Too bad!"

I knew stealing would convene a session of "family court." When I did something and Mom caught me, she'd inform my father. Faced with my categorical and unending denials, he'd convene a "court" in which Mom was the prosecutor, he was the judge, and I was the defendant, appearing *pro se*. A conviction for theft would unbuckle my father's belt.

As Mom wiped the kitchen counters and scrubbed the cast iron frying pan, she eyed me accusingly. A few minutes later, she decided on a new tactic.

"I hate doing this, Bill, but I'm just going to have to go through your pockets. Come with me."

For some reason, forcing me to disrobe in the kitchen seemed improper to her — my lucky break. As we walked up the stairs, I lagged behind a little and managed to transfer the dollar from my pocket into my underpants.

When we got to my room, she said, "All right, take off your pants." She became tense with concentration, her pink face laced with capillary breakage. Her strawberry blonde hair, set in a short permanent wave, resembled a helmet.

Slow and sullen, I complied. When the search turned up nothing, she snapped, "Take off your underpants."

A flash of inspiration saved me. I covered my groin with my hands and looked bashful. Her eyes showed indecision and then she capitulated.

"Oh, never mind!"

The theft of the dollar launched a long and successful campaign of larceny, and although Mom surely knew I victimized her, she never again had the nerve to call me on it.

◆ ◆ ◆

Literary people like to say writing a memoir ultimately means being willing to look in a mirror, for the memoirist needs to face the truth about himself. Although I quit stealing after I left my home in Bronxville, I certainly didn't become honest. Instead, my dishonesty expressed itself in ways less likely to bring me grief.

I felt not the slightest shame about stealing from my parents. Nor can I explain away my larceny by saying I suffered from the chaos of an alcoholic household. Although my parents specialized in shaming their children, our home couldn't be called chaotic. Dad didn't beat Mom. Although he probably had been drinking when he beat his children, the man hitting me with his belt neither slurred nor stumbled.

Avoiding responsibility as a child set me up for a life of lying to avoid the consequences of bad decisions. Now, as I try to find psychological and biochemical explanations for my behavior, it feels very much like dodging responsibility, which in turn makes me feel guilty. But do I feel guilty because that's a characteristic trait of most adult children of alcoholics?[18]

It's impossible to know, just as it's impossible to know if my memory of my childhood is accurate. Mary Jo, my chief confederate, says she doesn't remember the "two moons" incident. She does remember — vividly — the dump surprise. When she brings up anecdotes that lodged in her mind — snippets of life in which I was present — I either don't remember them or remember them vaguely.

In truth, I can only say I vividly recall the anecdotes used in this memoir. They represent my best recollection of what happened. I was an "eyewitness" to my childhood, but experts often say eyewitness information is the least reliable kind of evidence. Maybe that's why literary types call memoir "creative nonfiction."

CHAPTER 9: FIENDISH

In real time, I understood very little of the "behind the scenes" drama of my parents' marriage. They consistently presented a united front to their children. Yet I knew a lot of horse-trading went on when they had the kitchen door shut.

My mother wanted my dad to be more than a breadwinner. She asked him to be actively involved in the raising of his children. There were days when she must have regretted her "modern" approach, because Dad's child-rearing practices fused sadism and satire. He blended them as freely as he mixed Scotch and water.

The Sunday Morning Memau represented sadism.

One Sunday in December of 1956, I awoke to the tolling bells of a nearby church, my nose pinched by cold. We all slept with a good supply of fresh air, but on this particular night I overdid it, opening both my east and west windows. When I glanced at the foot of my bed, a small snowdrift covered the bright stripes of my Hudson Bay blanket.

I knew I should clean up the mess quickly; if my mother saw it, she would be "beside herself." Yet I burrowed down into the warmth, wanting this delicious state of affairs to last a few more minutes.

Then I heard the latch of my door click and the sound of scurrying feet.

"Could I get in bed with you?"

Mary Jo hugged herself and hopped up and down to ward

off the cold.

"What's the matter with your bed?"

"Nothin,' 'cept I'm scared of the Memau."

An embroidery of the Memau, done by my mother following Dad's 1974 death. It's based on Dad's drawing. The head was blue, the beak yellow and the forked tongue red. Blood drips from the creature's mouth.

A vicious thug, the Memau victimized the McBean children every Sabbath from 7:00 a.m., when we got up, until 10:30 a.m., when we left for church.

An agent of our father, the Memau, a brutal hand puppet, existed to assault children. It attacked the tender flesh under the chin and pinched savagely. As the Memau pillaged, Dad would emit the puppet's high-pitched feeding cry: "Me me me me me me me me!"

Occasionally, he would issue advance warnings. He'd draw a picture of the Memau (essentially a stick figure with a bulbous head, mean little eyes, and a long, curled tongue) and put it where one of us would find it. Minutes before showing up at my bedside, Mary Jo had found the heinous creature under her pillow.

None of us liked the Memau, but Mary Jo least of all. She began talking apprehensively of the creature's attacks as early as Thursday, and for the next three days her distress mushroomed into a state of neurotic anxiety.

She knew that when she left my room, Dad would be around every corner, hidden behind every shadow. His malicious intent imbued the air with fear.

In years past, I would typically be the first one to get it, but now I could fight back. My resistance led him to pick on Anne, but she got mad and started screaming at him. The twins, Susan and Joan, were too young to terrorize. But Mary Jo presented his favorite kind of target. When he'd approach her, eyes wide and shining, lips twisted into a peculiar smile, one hand behind his back, Mary Jo whimpered so pathetically, only a devout sadist could have found it amusing.

All of us — even Mom – asked him to knock it off, but he'd just call the Memau an independent evil spirit that grabbed control of him and forced his fingers to attack. He claimed to be powerless to stop it.

Of course, no one understood Dad's true reason for enacting this weekly torture. It could be that he thought we liked the game, that it was some sort of combination of tickling and "no bears are out tonight." More likely he enjoyed scaring Mary Jo and found her unstrung shrieks hilarious.

If he did indeed derive humor from the hapless, then the sight of Mary Jo in my bed that morning would have caused his mirth to become full-blown. She quivered beside me, completely under the covers, like a puppy enduring a thunderstorm.

We didn't speak. My open storm window rattled as a gray winter wind shook our silence. Then we heard Dad mounting the steps to the third floor toward Mary Jo's bedroom. He reached the top of the steps, opened the bedroom door, and stopped. He turned around, came back down the steps and again halted. Then he went down to the kitchen, where we could hear muffled talk with Mom. A minute later, we heard his tread returning to the second floor. He headed down the hallway to my room. We could hear him obsessively combing his fingers through the coins in his pocket.

He opened my door and peered into the room.

"Bill?"

"What?"

"Do you know where Mary Jo is?"

"No."

"Humpf. You better get up. Your mother has breakfast almost ready."

When he left, we whispered our plan. We'd go downstairs together. Mary Jo would claim to have been in the bathroom when Dad was looking for her. He might not entirely swallow it, but it wasn't the kind of lie that would cause repercussions. Once we were at the breakfast table, the chances of attack were reduced because Mom insisted on decorum at meals.

We came downstairs, rigid with apprehension. Dad sat in the living room engrossed in the *New York Times*. He didn't even look up as we passed, but I didn't buy it. He knew we'd taken countermeasures, and his nonchalance told me he would not be defeated by such a callow lot.

We ate our waffles and sausage slowly, knowing that the time between the end of breakfast and departure for church represented his prime attack window.

Nonetheless, when we left the table, he didn't move.

The newspaper apparently had his total attention. When we went upstairs to change into our church clothes, Mary Jo escalated.

"What's he doing?" she asked, tears popping from her eyes. "Do you think he's coming?"

I told her she could stay with me while I dressed, and then I'd come with her up to the third floor to stand guard while she put on her fancy dress and patent leather shoes. She jittered with apprehension, so I had to find most of her stuff for her.

Finally, about five minutes before it was time to go, we crept downstairs and into the central hallway. We could hear running water and the clank of cutlery as Mom did the dishes, but Dad had disappeared.

"You kids get your coats on," she called to us.

Mary Jo, eager to leave, ran to the closet. When she opened the door, she shrieked.

"Me me me me me me me!"

Mary Jo screamed like she was being torn apart by a wild animal.

"Daddy, don't, oh, please, please, Daddy, don't!"

He grabbed her and pulled her into the closet. He had her on her back, among the family's galoshes. I couldn't see her face; I could see Dad's right arm, moving in fierce rhythm with his hand, which was tearing at my sister's throat.

Mom left her dirty plates and rushed toward the noise.

"Peter, for criminy sakes, stop this nonsense right now!"

Dad came out of the closet and feinted toward Mother,

still uttering the Memau's cry. She wound up like she was going to smack him, and he withdrew, cackling.

"Why, Peter? Why do you insist on creating pandemonium every Sunday morning?"

"My dear, I'm just doing as you've repeatedly requested: I'm being a part of their lives."

Dad found Mom's frustration and anger nearly as funny as he found my sister's fear. He had no intention of letting her influence his behavior.

We drove to church, and Mary Jo cried the whole way. Once we arrived, Mom had to spend an extra five minutes with her, getting her tears wiped, her nose blown, and her breathing normal.

◆ ◆ ◆

This portrait, taken by the author, was shot about nine months before his death at 55. Although he made the face frequently when younger, he was in a state of alcoholic decline, so this Haut had to be coaxed from him.

Dad used a trademark face called the "Haut" as his contribution to satire.

He invented the Haut with one of his friends in 1938. He intended the face to disarm people who took themselves too seriously.

This visage wasn't a device that could be employed by the young. To be effective, the practitioner needed to have a good deal of meat on his mug: at least jowls, preferably dewlaps and waddles.

The Haut was accomplished by jutting out the chin, drawing the lower lip up sharply, and bugging the eyes. It order to be successful, the face-maker needed to exude self-satisfaction.

Advanced Hauting required mimicry of smugness in language as well as visage. In response to some overwhelmingly self-important person, one might Haut and say something like, "Well, I'm an expert in metaphorical physics."

People who didn't really understand my dad would say Hauting represented his sardonic cast of mind. I always thought that laying a Haut on someone — especially a Haut that wasn't accompanied by verbal mockery — was pretty much like giving them the finger. The face hid an unending supply of rage.

In a letter written in Germany in April of 1945, Dad said he found an air rifle and amused himself shooting chickens. It wasn't long before he became bored by hearing their alarmed squawks:

As I pursued this pleasant sport this afternoon my roving eye spied a frau with a most ample posterior riding a bicycle down the road. The bicycle was loaded down with sacks of food and the lady was dressed in slacks which strained tightly over her flesh. I am sure my eyes protruded in much the same manner as the black house boy in "You Can't Take It With You." I displayed none of the restraint of the houseboy. My muscles were as putty in the grip of a powerful impulse. I pumped the gun, aimed dead center on the slacks and fired. The results were beyond my fondest hopes. The bicycle went one way, the sacks another and the frau straight up emitting an ungodly shriek. I don't know where she came down because I was doubled on the floor with paroxysms of mirth. I thought I would surely strangle... At last I have found the perfect weapon for the discomfiture of the Herrenvolk.

I imagine, as the outraged woman got up from the road and looked back at him, he Hauted at her.

Dad came into World War II Hauting. It was nonsense he developed while attending Bronxville High School. The sadism, however, manifested when he returned from the war. After it became evident in our household, all five children knew a family secret had been born. Yet Bronxville was full of World War II vets. We couldn't have been the only home harboring such problems...could we?

CHAPTER 10: BUTCH

Not one of my childhood friends talked to me about their dads' war experiences.

Certainly, there were other fathers who suffered as badly as Dad, and I'm sure those families kept their secret as well as we kept ours.

But the Bronxville schools weren't filled with low-functioning, anxious, neurotic children like those from the McBean clan. Normal, happy kids abounded.

So what factors kept our contemporaries on center stage and swept us into a corner?

One obvious answer: many American military personnel never saw combat. Twenty-five percent never left the US, and 50 percent of those overseas were never in a battle zone[19].

Some Bronxvillians didn't see combat for another reason: even in the hyper-patriotic days following Pearl Harbor, the well-educated often made sure they stayed out of harm's way. They knew they had to serve in the military, but why not as an attaché in Washington, as a military intelligence analyst or as an editor for *Stars and Stripes?*

But not my dad. He had a streak of rural patriotism in his soul that was as pronounced as the black-dirt cornrow furrows of his native Midwest.

Fresh out of Dartmouth, he made a point of enlisting in the 35th Division because he wanted to go to war with Nebraskans. Having moved to Bronxville from Omaha at fourteen because of his father's promotion, he felt a monumental disdain for his cosmopolitan surroundings. Many times he exclaimed to me, "Can you imagine fighting the Germans with a *New Yorker* watching your back?"

Following the advice of his father, my dad angled for the "safe" job in artillery because those operating cannons worked thousands of yards behind the front lines. Since my grandfather trained as a World War I army artilleryman, but never saw action, he might not have thought to tell my dad a horrific fact about launching shells against one's foe: the second enemy spotters saw the white puff of smoke from your gun, they sent shells from their own cannons down on your position.

This constant exposure to death carried over to life in Bronxville in ways that were often unpredictable. Dad occasionally got himself into terrible situations because he instinctively reacted to threats with violence.

For example, the day his blood feud with rodents turned against him.

A few years after the rat incident, Dad had his annual spring conference with the arborist hired to care for the trees on our property. Because he spent his teen and college years in the house where he now cared for his own brood, I think Dad saw the trees as a fiduciary responsibility passed on to him by his father. He also loved their majesty—especially the tulip trees. He admired their dark, deeply etched trunks that seemed like powerful engines trying to grasp the gray water vapor that swept in from the ocean. When their flowers, resembling light green pine cones, began to rattle down with the winds of encroaching fall, a sweet cucumber smell filled the neighborhood, giving Dad such a contented feeling, he didn't even mind cleaning them up.

However, on this particular day the arborist wasn't

there to talk about the beauty of trees; he came to work my dad for money. Tree trimming can be dangerous, he said. Not only could a guy take a tumble or get hit by a falling branch, but there were always rabid squirrels to consider.

"You can always tell when them things got rabies 'cause they come right up to ya," Dad later said, mimicking the man's Downeast accent. According to my father, no one worked a mark harder than a displaced State of Mainer.

Dad later recalled he didn't pay the man a premium because of the rabies scare, but he did remember the anecdote a few days later when he glanced out the kitchen window to check on Susie and Joanie, who were playing in the sandbox on the back terrace. There he saw a black squirrel chittering away at his daughters on the side of the sandbox.

Quietly, Dad opened the back door and asked the girls to come inside, "right now, please." Then he grabbed the hedge clippers, which happened to be sitting on the kitchen counter, walked outside and dashed the life out of the vermin.

When he turned around, he saw his middle child, Anne, with her hand over her mouth.

"But, Daddy, that was Butch!"

As in Butch, the pet squirrel belonging to the old woman who lived in the small white clapboard bungalow two doors south of us.

Slowly, Dad scooped up the body and put it in a brown grocery sack. Without saying a word to anyone, he walked down the street to tell the poor widow what he had done.

He wasn't allowed to be alone in his misery.

"Daddy killed Butch! Daddy killed Butch!" chanted all five of his children, prancing down the street after him.

"I don't remember him getting mad at us for that," Anne told me recently, "but I do remember him feeling really bad about killing the woman's pet."

◆ ◆ ◆

The Butch incident must have made my father freeze inside, like his emotions were brim-full but just couldn't spill over.

The "frozen" phenomenon is detailed in Dr. Scaer's work. His discussion of PTSD includes the long-established principle of the fight-or-flight response. He pointed out that with most animals, human beings included, if neither fight nor flight were possible, the animal often chose the "freeze" response. The critter played possum, or rolled over on its back and exposed its stomach, or pretended to be dead. In theory, a predator will lose interest in a victim that refuses to struggle.[20]

Animals that ran into real trouble with trauma — in lab experiments, at least — were those that weren't ever released from the "freeze" state, the ones that were clasped in a perpetual state of fear and never saw the opportunity for fight-or-flight open to them. Those creatures, when freed to the outer world, generally couldn't cope and soon died.[21]

Dad had no way to escape his frozen state. Alcohol numbed him but did nothing to address the central problem. He wouldn't go to therapy for fear of endangering his law license. There weren't any drugs to address his difficulties. His role as a father, breadwinner, and attorney froze him into a very defined role from which he couldn't escape.

Mary Jo and I saw our opportunity to flee and took it as quickly as we could. Mary Jo, who got the belt every bit as much as I did, went to college in Colorado and returned as seldom as possible. Although Anne had problems with Mom, she never had the academic problems that washed through our household. That's not to say she was unaffected: omnipresent anxiety prevented her from getting a driver's license until she was 26 and delayed her application to graduate school until nine years after college because she convinced herself she was too "stupid." Susan died young, and our sister Joan suffered for years from various illnesses. Susan and Joan, fraternal twins, were the ones who never got away. They witnessed the end stage of our parents' alcoholic defense against World War II.

Mary Jo was a depressive; I had an anxiety disorder and suffer bouts of major depression. Therefore, both of us, by definition, have problems with the stress hormone cortisol. An excess of cortisol can also cause learning problems,[22] which may explain why four of five McBean children were marginal students, although all showed academic competence after escaping 72 Summit Avenue.

Call it the psychoneurotic wave, call it the transgenerational transmission of trauma, or call it too much cortisol — but something had made our family obviously different. Not different in a good way — different in the same way those "frozen" animals were dissimilar to their "unfrozen" counterparts. We couldn't function.

CHAPTER 11: FORGERY

My effort to avoid punishment may have reached its apogee as I entered the spring term of seventh grade.

The Bronxville School's excellent music teacher, Murray Linden, garnered the nickname Murballs because his eyeballs were abnormally large — at least as big as whopper marbles. On the not infrequent occasions when he became angry, his eyes tended to show a lot of white, making him look like a crazy alien.

His penchant for rage amused many of my cohorts, and they did what they could to provoke him. His music room sat below the big gym. The gym floor had removable brass covers designed to protect electrical outlets. Under one of those covers, however, there was no outlet — just a hole opening directly into Linden's music room below. The mischievously inclined could put their mouths directly on the hole and croon "Murrrrrballlls, oh Murrrrrballlls."

Before long before he stood in the gym, his eyes rolling back, screaming at the top of his lungs. "Okay, which one of you boys did it? Who was it? Who was interrupting my choir practice?"

About fifty boys looked back at him, each with a blank expression.

In eighth grade, he assigned me to write a five-page paper on any work I chose from the classical repertoire. I couldn't imagine going through the drudgery of listening and relistening to some symphony and then writing over a thousand words about it. In those days, I found it taxing to write a hundred. When I failed to turn in the paper, he gave me an "F" in the class.

I brought lots of Cs and Ds home to Mom and Dad, but never an F. If I brought home an F, I'd never see my radio again. I'd have no chance of ever going to Teen Center. My allowance, already paltry, would once more be cut off. I couldn't deal with it — and I didn't have to because I had a plan.

The school instructed students to show their report cards to their parents and to bring them back with parents' signatures affixed.

At first I thought maybe I could trash the report card and say I lost it. Maybe I could go through that routine several times before breaking down and admitting my failure. I knew, however, what the penalty would be for that strategy: more scorn, derision, and sarcasm. Evasion of all responsibility was my real goal, and I could accomplish that only by changing the grade.

Pickwick Stationary stocked a product called ink eradicator. It came in a little bottle with an eyedropper lid. The directions said, *Apply one drop on area to be eradicated and then blot. Works on all types of fountain pen ink.*

I looked at the ugly, bold F Murballs had placed among my Cs and Ds, and I wondered if it had been made with a fountain pen. It occurred to me that if I botched this, my sorrows would be greatly magnified. Yet I knew Dad was going to decompensate when he saw the "F." It wouldn't be the standard sneer or expression of disgust. It would be a full-bore abreaction.

So I decided I had to try it.

I sneaked the report card into our house and up to my

room. I squeezed a drop of the fluid onto the F and quickly blotted it. The F still screamed from the page. I decided I needed to try another drop and let it sit longer so it would have more time to dissolve the ink. I gave it ten seconds and thought I saw some kind of reaction. I blotted again, saw the result, and winced. Instead of disappearing, the F became veiny around the edges. Worse, the report card paper began to disintegrate. Clearly, Murballs hadn't used a fountain pen.

At this point, a cagey criminal might decide to revert to plan A — losing the report card. I lost so many other things, no one would doubt me. However, I chose plan C: making the F into an A with a black ballpoint pen.

I didn't produce a very convincing result.

As I pondered my botched forgery, Mom walked into my room without knocking. I furtively shoved the report card under a close-at-hand book.

Mom, her face sharp with suspicion, snatched the report card from its hiding place. With an irritable flick of her hand she opened it and eyed the grades. Her perusal stopped at the malformed "A." As she focused on it, I tried to move the ink eradicator from the desktop to the floor behind me, but she spotted my attempted guile and snatched it out of my hand.

She looked at the bottle, drilled me with her piercing green eyes, and stomped her foot. Her left foot. The one she always stomped.

"I swear to God, Bill, this is the living end. Your father will be informed of this, and you will be very, very sorry."

She turned on her high heel and left the room.

My success as a criminal — which had enjoyed such a brilliant start with the dollar-bill theft and had since diversified — primarily into shoplifting, vandalism, and torturing the local gendarmes — led me to believe that I could connive my way out of any mess, but this incident showed me otherwise. Now I had to go through the ritual of waiting to see if Dad would beat me.

The agonizing minutes prior to the beatings never varied.

I'd lie at the foot of my bed and gaze out my west window, the one with a crow's nest view. From it I could see through the rattling branches Avon Road on the slope of the opposite hillside, and I could trace the yellow lights of the bus carrying Dad home from the train station.

Many times, I saw him coming a full ten minutes before he'd hit the front door. I saw the street up which he'd walk from the bus stop. He carried a rolled-up paper in his right hand. Rhythmically, he whacked the newspaper on his thigh as he ascended the twenty-five steps from the street to our house.

He'd call, "I'm home," as he walked through the front door. Then the sound of ice cubes falling into a highball glass and murmured talk with my mother.

A few minutes would pass before he began the ascent to my room. By the time I heard the change rattling in his pocket, my respiration would have increased so much that the atmosphere in the room was mainly water vapor and carbon dioxide; the swampy fear would put me into the sharp narcotic trance a mouse must feel when it gets dropped into a snake's cage.

Frozen.

He would open the door and stand there, looking down at me, silent. I'd turn my head away but listen intently, and I'd wait for the sound of his belt being unbuckled.

Something about the way he beat me felt particularly cold and informal. He never uttered a word of regret or explanation. He never made an effort to warn against the pain of laceration and certainly never said anything as vapid as "this hurts me more than it hurts you."

After the sound of leather straining against brass fitting, he'd say, "Take down your pants and lie face down on your bed."

"How many?" I'd ask.

"Until I get tired of it," he'd say.

From experience, I knew it would be from eight to twelve. I'd wonder, *Would it kill him to just tell me?* But I also knew the punishment included the torture of not knowing.

On the day of the Murballs fiasco, Dad surprised me. He didn't come upstairs.

"Bill, get your ass down here!" he yelled in his command voice from the first floor kitchen.

"So on top of everything else, you're a crook."

"I'm not, I'm..."

"You're not? This is forgery, *forgery* of an *official document.* The only thing saving you from doing jail time is your status as a juvenile."

I wanted to counter that if I wasn't a juvenile, I wouldn't be getting a report card—but I worried about his temper.

"Bill, you've been telling a lot of shifty little lies lately, and I can see now you've taken the first step on the path to being a career criminal."

I tried to say he was exaggerating, but he said, "Hush

up!"

He looked at me for a long moment. I met his eye, looked at the floor, and met his eye again.

"You make me sick!"

Occasionally, Dad did try to connect with me.

One weekend when I was eight, I engrossed myself in a Superman comic book, completely immersed in a world where reporters had super powers. Abruptly, Dad entered my bedroom. Usually, an unannounced appearance meant his gorge was full. But on this particular roseate evening, he didn't appear to have an agenda. He wore his brown plaid sports shirt. His breath smelled of beer and onions, so perhaps he'd been watching baseball. He placed one hand on my knotty pine bed frame and the other beside me on the bed, hovered over my prone body, and peered out my west window into the twilight. I had fallen on my comic book because I didn't want to be ridiculed, but he ignored my fascination with the Man of Steel. For a few moments he said nothing, but then, softly, almost as if offering intimate advice, he said, "You've got a strong position, Bill. You've got the high ground. From here, you could get the enemy zeroed in and raise all kinds of hell."

He looked at me, waiting for a response. I had no idea what he was talking about, so I said, "Yes, sir," and he left.

Dad obsessed about artillery placement. Every time we went anywhere overlooking a populated area, he'd refer to it as "an artilleryman's dream." And often, when we'd arrive at a destination in a deep valley, I'd see his eyes scanning the ridges above us, and I now know he felt like a target.

His battlefield letters written in the late summer of 1944 reflected this preoccupation with high ground. As the Cannon Company and the rest of the 134th Infantry Regiment rushed eastward toward Nancy and the terrible fighting at the Moselle River, joyful crowds lined the roads in every village.

The German army retreated in disarray, and many of Hitler's surrendering fighters looked ragtag and starved. Germany, which relied on horses to pull artillery and supplies, couldn't react to American forces equipped with Jeeps and two-and-a-half-ton trucks.

Glory accompanied the US Army's arrival into tiny French villages.

August 22, 1944

These Frogs are crazy. They mob us, paw us, steal our food and gawp by the hour... Long lines of them stand along the road... and yell for candy and cigarettes... One enthusiastic French lass threw me an egg while traveling 30 mph, and with my usual skill I muffed it and caught the whole thing square between the horns and finished my triumphal trip through town graciously nodding to the populace and dripping egg yolk from cowlick to corns. Another equally enthusiastic French lassie offered me a drink out of a long brown bottle. I, thinking it no harm, drank the whole glass at a gulp and landed halfway across the road. It turned out to be Cognac and not cider as I expected. My toes cramped up for a while and my eyes ran tears profusely, but I weathered the storm.

He frequently commented on women: when he detected virtue, they were "lassies," but when he thought them capable of seducing an American officer, they were floozies or worse. For almost a month, his letters showed little sign of strain, but on September 20, 1944, his correspondence again became terse:

Things have been hot as hell around us. It begins to remind me of St. Lo again and I thought all that was past... The German artillery has also showed its head again so the holes are going to record depths.

The 35th Division and the rest of the American Third Army now felt the desperation of the German army's defense as the Allies closed in on the Fatherland's southwest border.

The Nazis set up their force on hills around the fortress-like city of Nancy. Some of the heaviest fighting was concentrated around a knob-like hill called Pain de Sucre that commanded a clear view of the surrounding terrain.

As the US Army tried to dislodge the Germans, it came under intense shelling and machine-gun fire, but the Allies won that promontory September 18, 1944, lost it September 19, and then won it again later that day. The battle featured two dead-of-night Nazi raids[23] that must have been the very fabric from which PTSD was woven.

It's difficult to know exactly where Dad was located during that specific time period, but on September 21, he wrote:

Two nights ago the Krauts were dropping a lot of heavy stuff around us and were sneaking up pretty close in the bushes to let fly with their burp guns.

It's impossible for me to believe that the Germans in the bushes with the burp guns didn't create anthills in his mind just like his echoing nightmares created anthills in mine.

Yet in a letter to Mom on October 3, 1944, he said:

The war hasn't changed me much as far as I know. It has given me plenty of misery and some god-awful scares, but I don't expect to be permanently marred in any way. I fear that I will be just as silly at times and just as nasty at other times as I ever was.

Yet some people in his family could sense something amiss just by reading his letters. For one thing, they contained too many references to alcohol.

When his father expressed a fear at the end of one of his letters that *I might run hog wild on Cognac and Champagne*, he wrote October 4, 1944:

No danger. My drinking is done in widely separated nips. I have no intention of running wild over here. I can't take this eat drink and be merry for tomorrow we may die stuff very seriously. I think that if I am going to sow wild oats I will wait until I get home.

◆ ◆ ◆

On the night Dad meted out punishment in the Murballs affair, he didn't beat me, which amazed me because I certainly expected this offense to unleash an unprecedented fury.

Instead, he dealt with it as an embarrassment to the entire family.

I stood in the kitchen, and he sat in his accustomed place. Before issuing his final verdict, he picked up the report card, looked with disdain at the altered grade, and threw it back down on the kitchen table.

"Well, the first thing that needs to be done is this: tomorrow morning, you and your mother will go to the principal's office and you will confess your illicit behavior. You have put your mother in an excruciatingly embarrassing position. I hope you're happy with yourself."

"Not really," I said.

"Needless to say, you're grounded. Indefinitely."

I said okay, and he told me to get out of his sight. I did

and stayed out of his sight — as much as possible — for weeks.

Of course, I had no such option with Mom. We went down to the school the next morning. I confessed contritely to the obese, blond principal — a transplant from Topeka — who gave me a lengthy talk about the importance of honesty. We then visited Murballs, who instead of living up to his reputation, put on a display of magnanimity. He told me to write a paper on Beethoven's 4th Symphony and gave me a deadline of a week. I went home and listened to the damn thing about four times, produced five pages of doggerel, and got a C.

Although confined to my room much of the time, angry and morose as an adolescent can be, my second year of puberty made me bullish on life. I increasingly noticed the young women walking the halls of Bronxville High School. Rating my chances among the fifty females in my class occupied much of my time. I knew I had no shot with most of them, and many held no attraction for me. But for the first time in my life, there appeared to be one girl with whom I had a chance.

CHAPTER 12: LITTLE DOUCHE BAG

In my sophomore year in high school, Karen K wrote something amazing in my yearbook. She didn't just say, *It's been a great year, see you next fall* or *It's been cool sitting next to you in History, wasn't Mr. Joel a riot?* She wrote: *Billy the Kid — hope you have fun this summer. Remember to stay away from dangerous places such as 'haylofts' etc., Love, Karen.*

I read her inscription and looked at her. She had auburn hair, green eyes, and the most luscious pink tongue.

I don't know what it means when a high school girl writes the word "love" today, but in 1962, that four-letter word meant it was *on*. No other girl had signed my yearbook with anything like affection. As far as I knew, the word "love" hadn't appeared in any of my friends' yearbooks, although I certainly didn't have access to the coolest yearbooks on campus. In any case, Karen's message seemed like a big, bright, hot, red neon invitation.

For the next few days, I wobbled like a top. I generally felt like an outcast, so Karen's note was a jolt. Her words, potentially, had enormous importance. If I had a girlfriend, it would mean instant credibility. I'd have someone to hang out with, to go to dances with, to sit in the soda fountain with. It would mean I was *likable*.

I had her phone number but lacked the confidence to make that rotary dial whirr. I don't think I could have called her if I had a gun pointed at my head. Plus, what was I going to say to her? "I really dig you, Karen, but I'm grounded."

Instead, I stalked her in my brief periods of freedom after school. I walked to the drug store where I knew she hung out, and looked through the window. When I saw her, I ducked out of sight and scampered home.

During this period, my constant tormentor, J.P., began his spring offensive. At the time, I had no idea why J.P. picked on me. A big, well-liked varsity athlete a year older than me had much better ways to waste his time.

Early one day about a week after the yearbooks came out, as I made my way through a clamor of students climbing an echoing stairway at school, I felt him behind me and then his hot breath on my ear.

"I'm going to get you, you little douche bag," he hissed. "I'm going to get you, and I'm going to pull your pants down and shove rocks up your rectum."

He was thirty pounds heavier and five times nastier than anyone else I knew. He and his buddies would fall in behind me as I walked up Tanglewylde Avenue toward home, and as soon as we left school, they would descend on me like rabid orangutans.

I, however, had a plan.

Instead of leaving school by my normal route, I left via the Pondfield Road door. I intended to walk south of the business district, where J.P. might be hanging out, and then eastward toward my house. It would take a half-hour longer, and because it rained that day I'd get soaked, but it beat getting caught by J.P.

I managed to escape the school grounds undetected. As I walked past the tall gray spires of St. Joseph's Church, my mind roamed out of the realm of fear and almost immediately into the sphere of the carnal. My thoughts shifted to the delicious pink mouth. I had a strange idea that if I saw her today, I might be able to talk to her.

There were two soda fountains in Bronxville, the popular Bellis Drugs, where I had a better-than-even chance of running into J.P., and Steinman's Drugs, where Karen often met with her girlfriends. Showing up at Steinman's posed a risk — you could meet anyone anytime in our tiny village. But temptation overwhelmed me.

I started thinking of cool things I could say if I saw her. I attempted different inflections of "hello" several hundred times. Or perhaps, like the Big Bopper, I could say, "Helllllo baaaaby." But probably not.

As I came around the corner and began walking west on Pondfield Road, I saw her, walking into Steinman's, just twenty yards ahead. Although now all bundled up against the weather, I had seen her earlier in the day. She wore a very flattering red sweater, a little plaid skirt, and red knee socks. I prepared my most winsome smile for her, but then I spotted J.P. I had let my guard down, and now I'd pay the price.

J.P. stood by the curb with two of his thug buddies. He had deceptively handsome features that disappeared when he turned vicious. He wore his blue-on-gray letter jacket and smoked a cigarette, in spite of being "in training" during baseball season. He spotted me a second after I saw him.

"Weeelll!" J.P. said. "I was afraid I wasn't going to run into you this afternoon!"

I wanted to take flight, but because of Karen's presence, I had to stand my ground. J.P. scooped a handful of wet leaves from the sidewalk and tried to smash them into my face, but I blocked it and managed to shoulder him off the sidewalk.

His look of indignation quickly turned to fury. He rose

up over me and landed on me with all his weight. I splashed into a two-inch deep puddle. He straddled the puddle and using both hands infused water into every pore of my body. He washed my face with puddle water. He splashed it down my neck. He funneled it down the back of my pants.

As I struggled to free myself, I saw Karen looking at me and then disappearing behind the green glass of Steinman's front door. Her face was unreadable, showing neither scorn nor sympathy. I wondered if she was going to watch the proceedings from inside.

For a moment, I irrationally entertained the hope she might intervene and tell J.P. he was a big bully. Then, perhaps, she'd take my hand and buy me a cherry Coke and an English muffin. The mother I never had.

J.P. staunched that reverie when he did something that turned me from an angry young man into a hysterical infant. As he allowed me to stand, he grabbed my baseball hat from the pavement, where it landed during our struggle.

I'd much rather have had a bloody nose than be parted from that hat. I'd lost three other hats that year at $1.25 each. I currently owed the 'rents $12.65. I already deferred my dream of asking Karen to the movies until August, and losing this hat would set me back further.

Thinking Karen might be watching, I decided to go down fighting. I set my schoolbooks on top of a trashcan and turned to confront my tormentor.

"Goddamn it, J.P., give me my hat," I said, advancing on him.

"Wooo, big Billy's getting mad!" The chorus of thugs chortled.

J.P. held my hat in the air, well away from my reach.

"I'm not kidding! Give the hat back!"

"Or what, big bad Billy?"

Abandoning caution, I took aim at his porcine snout and let loose with a punch that should have drawn blood.

Had it connected.

Had it come even close.

Instead, J.P. leaned back, and I flew by and landed on my hands and knees.

I could imagine Karen, on the other side of the green window, her little pink mouth tittering into her hand. Or maybe she slapped her knee — by this time I didn't care. Outraged, I focused solely on getting my hat back, no matter what.

The trio of bullies tossed my hat back and forth as we crossed Pondfield Road, me yelling and swearing, them having the time of their lives. We descended into Garden Terrace, and within a minute or two, they had me isolated — which had been their goal all along.

They grabbed me, picked me up, and threw me through a hedge, then walked off laughing with my hat still in their possession. I lay there on the ground, groping for my glasses in the mud with grimy hands, my eyes fixed on the disappearing hat. Even more expensive than a knit cap, it represented five times my weekly allowance.

I walked home, my mind stuck in its woe-is-me cycle. Thirty minutes later, halfway up the steps of my house, it occurred to me that I left my books back at the drug store. Terror pressed its thumbs into my Adam's apple. I might have lost twenty dollars worth of books! The hell with Karen. I'd never have the coin to take out any girl ever!

My mother would kill me for being so late, my feet were

already frozen, and my nearly new Bass Weejuns ruined, but I had no choice. I walked back to Steinman's and found the books, not where I left them, but in a nearby puddle. They were soddened through.

When I finally got home, the dame of the McBean clan greeted me.

"William Seaton McBean, you are late!"

Then she noticed I was waterlogged and covered with sidewalk sand, leaves, and twigs.

"What happened to you?"

"I fell."

"You fell? How many times?"

"I don't remember."

Then she looked at my books.

"Oh, Bill, for criminy sakes, these are ruined!"

"Can't we dry 'em out or something?"

"I suppose we'll have to try," she said, disgusted. "But you're sure to get charged for the damage, and I'm just as sure *I'll* end up paying for it."

"I'll pay you back. I promise."

She snorted. "Go upstairs and change your clothes. Then come directly back here and do what you can to salvage the mess you created."

Unthinking, I attempted to hand her my sodden pile of books.

"Get those away from me!" she shrieked. "You march those down to the basement right this very minute and put them where they won't make a mess that I'll have to clean up!"

I began to wander away, but she hadn't finished.

"Where's your hat?"

"I dunno."

"Bill, how could you! That's the fourth hat this school year!"

"I know that," I said with as much testiness as I dared.

"Well, retrace your steps. Where do you think you lost it?"

For a split second, I thought about telling her the truth, but she had gotten me in trouble with Dad so many times that I found the thought of her sympathy unbearable. Also, she might call J.P.'s mom, which would mean I'd get pounded into a pulp the next day.

"I don't have any idea."

"What do you mean, you don't have any idea! Do you just wander around out there in a daze?"

"I dunno."

"You are *impossible.*"

CHAPTER 13: THE BURGERMEISTER

Dad said he "hated just about everybody." Although he was being facetious, there's no doubt the fighting in Europe left him deeply embittered. The process of alienation began at St. Lo and intensified as his company trudged toward the Ardennes Forest.

This gun station was firing about 1,000 rounds a day when this photo was taken. Note the large ammo supply just to the left of the kneeling figure.

In November of 1944, the skies excreted unholy amounts of water, and then it got cold—cold enough to snow, but not cold enough to congeal the awful manure-and-mud composite that made up the roads. The thoroughfares became great wallows that sucked the howitzers under and stopped all forward progress.

As the soldiers struggled to free their weapons, they knew they were stationary targets for enemy artillery. Aware of their sitting duck status, the men jumped into muck up to their knees and heaved at the guns with frantic urgency.

Some small solace could be taken from the German habit of laying down artillery shelling by set patterns, so sometimes the troops heaving at the howitzers could guess when they were in jeopardy. Mortar fire, however, seldom came with a calling card.

Sometimes it took hours to free the howitzers, and the men would come away from the experience miserably cold, dirty, and wet, only to have it happen again a few hours later. And of course, only Eisenhower got to change his clothes.

Dad's executive officer status meant he didn't swim in the ocean of muck with the cannons. He couldn't escape the cold, the wet, and the mud, though. That was impossible.

Appropriate waterproof clothing, available to the officers, couldn't be obtained by ordinary GIs. The bulky GI-issue winter overcoats proved a hindrance to men for whom agility could be the difference between life and death. Most soldiers settled for the waist-length Eisenhower jackets enhanced by several sweaters, the *Combat History* said.

The army also plagued its soldiers with poor advice: it told the men they could avoid "trench foot" (which often led to gangrene) by removing their boots and socks daily and exercising their toes. The men found that when they took their boots off, their feet swelled so much they couldn't get them back on.[24]

Between the boot problem and quality of the winter clothing, the cold proved to be a great ally of the Germans. Swollen feet, hypothermia, and exposure sent hundreds of American soldiers to the rear.

Dad had immunity from many of these problems because of his officer status and because he had a portable stove. Warm feet and dry socks may have been his greatest luxury, but if combat conditions relegated him to a foxhole, he suffered with his enlisted subordinates.

Camouflaged gun emplacement somewhere in France.

Although he tried to spare my mom most of the graphic details, his nerves obviously became increasingly frayed as the Cannon Company got closer to Germany.

November 24, 1944:

I am getting jumpy. And my attention and memory aren't worth a damn anymore. Everyone here shows the same symptoms. A door slams and we practically go through the ceiling.

His letters never stated the exact nature of his worries, but the *Combat History* said the men of the 134th Infantry Regiment were tasked with routing Germans from the tightly woven forest northeast of Nancy and from the nearby Saar River Valley, a German industrial hub.

The Germans planned to stop the Allies at this point and inflict such terrible punishment on them that politicians from England, Canada, and the US would sue for peace.

St. Lo, Mortain, and Pain de Sucre had been terrible, but they were now operating in the dead of winter in Northern

Europe. That made digging deep holes difficult or impossible. It meant a whole new level of misery. The fighting would be just as intense, but hands and feet would be numb, they would become chapped, and they would bleed, and there would be no respite from this condition for months at a time.

◆ ◆ ◆

I focused on four days — two that Dad all but omitted from his correspondence, probably to spare his family from worry, and one that he included, which most men most decidedly would have left out.

The first was November 13, 1944, the day the first serious snowfall hit northeastern France. The Cannon Company fought in the villages of Achain and Pévange and backed the regiment's effort to remove the Germans from Rougemont, an imposing edifice that hung over the two hamlets. The Germans naturally positioned their artillery on Rougemont. In the early morning the mountain wore a stunning white mantle; following the day's battle, it wept tears of red.

The house-to-house combat below Rougemont featured many stories of personal bravery. One soldier, who on his own killed twenty-five Germans and took twenty prisoners, got the Congressional Medal of Honor. Heroic acts may be the grist of foxhole bonhomie, but the day's casualty figures appalled even the bravest soldiers: more than two hundred injured or killed with fifty men evacuated because of exposure. The men forever remembered that day as "Blue Monday."[25]

The German cannons had a height advantage of over one thousand feet for most of the day. The German artillery spotters only needed to wait for the poof of smoke from Dad's guns to zero in on the Cannon Company's location. That they didn't all die is a testament to Dad's guile, gristle, and perseverance.

Dad described a second incident in a letter dated November 26, 1944. It involved that most dangerous of all assignments: scouting.

Somewhere in Germany

Early in the morning, I started to reconnoiter for new gun positions. My troubles started about halfway to my destination when we passed a spot where a battery of horse-drawn German artillery had been caught on the road by our heavy guns. Parts of Germans and parts of horses were scattered all along the road for several hundred yards. We were caught in a convoy and forced to drive right over all the corpses and listen to them crunch under our wheels. I got half sick right then and stayed green for the rest of the day.

Upon arrival in the town which was our destination, I was standing by the side of the road waving my arms and yelling at my subordinates when an ambulance full of medics hit a mine right in front of me. Ambulance and medics went sky high and I found myself confronted by six maimed men, flopping and gasping in the road like so many fish just jerked out on the banks. One boy had his whole backside blown off and his screams were probably the most awful sound I have ever heard. I think I shall probably have permanent green spots from that sight.

Twenty minutes later the Krauts threw an artillery barrage into the town and I dove headfirst into a cellar full of bicycles where I spent the next twenty minutes tangled up in the bikes waiting for things to settle down and trying to untangle myself… All in all it was quite a day. I hope that tomorrow is a little quieter. The men in the rifle companies see spectacles such as this every day. But being a comparative rear echelon man… I am not quite hardened enough.

I know I shouldn't be writing tales such as these to you, but at times I feel a tremendous compulsion to tell you what it all really looks like. I will try not to do it too often.

This place looks like a Hollywood war set tonight. Every other house is afire and the streets are full of loose stock. Many of the animals are wounded and dragging themselves about. It will be a mercy if some GI makes a steak out of them. The remaining civilians are huddled in a mass under the church. They are pitiful specimens — all citizens of the New Order. I hope they are satisfied with the fruits of their goose step and Horst Wessel. Most of them are in a panic, as they believe that they are all going to be shot by the Americans. Might be a pretty fair idea at that.

A huge mail came in and I waited expectantly. Never dreamed I wouldn't get a letter. Expected at least three, but got only 0. Better luck tomorrow, perhaps.

This epistle marked the beginning of Dad's conviction that German civilians should be subjected to collective punishment. It also represented the start of a churlish state of mind that I believe adopted sadism as its default mode. He began to enjoy seeing people suffer, a state of mind he eventually inflicted on his family.

The third incident, one most men would have left unmentioned, was in a letter in December 1944. It was in response to a letter in which he said he was nominated for a Bronze Star but not approved. Mom apparently expressed anger at this decision.

December 3, 1944:

I'm glad you think that I'm nice, but I'm really not as nice as you think. You should see some of the nasty things I do every so often. I put a dead rat in the supply sergeant's bed the other night.

That story lends a malevolent sheen to the fourth incident.

Dad, center, poses with Nazi flag in Habkirchen, Germany

On December 12, 1944 the Cannon Company pulled into Habkirchen, Germany, a town the men would later refer to as "Hell's Kitchen." It was the first town in Germany, across the Blies River from France. Soldiers of the Reich fought stoutly to defend it, subjecting all units of the 134th Regiment to heavy and continuous shelling.

The village had supposedly been cleared of German troops, but in reality, the Nazis had retreated into the woods and during the night moved in to retake Habkirchen. Under attack by an enemy using mortars and machine guns, Dad's artillerymen suddenly became front-line soldiers under siege. To fend off the assault, the Cannon Company, along with the 161st Field Artillery, used howitzers to fire directly into the German lines. The sound of howitzer shells ripping through the forest, taking down trees and destroying everything in their path, presented a very convincing argument, for the Germans retreated.

In his letter of January 12, 1945, Dad said he directed the battle of Habkirchen from the basement of the burgermeister's (mayor's) destroyed home. When orders came to pull out, the burgermeister and his family begged to be taken along, saying the Germans would certainly shoot him for his hospitality to American troops. Dad refused, saying American combat forces couldn't relocate civilians. The next morning, however, the burgermeister and his family stowed away in the company headquarters cargo truck.

The Cannon Company convoy, headed back into France, had to cross a lengthy, vulnerable bridge to get there. The bridge had been under heavy bombardment, so Dad, riding in the lead Jeep, ordered the convoy to take the bridge at full speed and to meet at an assembly point on the other side:

About the time we hit the bridge the shells began coming in again and the burgermeister's family began to howl and tried to bail out but the speed scared them and they just howled. The driver of the truck was badly unnerved by the shells and the sudden screams from the rear end practically sent him into the river.

When the convoy reached the assembly area on the other side of the bridge, the soldiers discovered one of the burgermeister's daughters *had a shrapnel flesh wound in her rather plump posterior. The men found this highly amusing and all wanted the privilege of administering first aid.*

The girl was bandaged up and the family left by the side of the road.

By that point in the war it seemed obvious, from reading the letters, that Dad had decided to keep his sanity by adopting a twisted sense of humor. In the years following the war, my bet is that Hell's Kitchen festered in Dad's brain. I imagine he thought about the burgermeister and his family years later and knew they were probably executed by the Nazis. This incident — or ones very much like it — scarred his mind, hurt him every day at his law office, every evening when he tried to be a father, and every night, when he prayed his full measure of whiskey would be enough to keep his memory etherized.

The Cannon Company, along with the rest of the regiment, got called into the Battle of the Bulge the day after Christmas following a two-day holiday feast in Metz, France. Prior to that, the division had been on line for 160 continuous days.[26] Dad's letters didn't reflect this hardship, nor did they insinuate the danger of the coming battle, which would end up causing seventy-five thousand casualties.[27]

Dad in an undated photo, probably in Germany

When the Cannon Company arrived in the south end of the Ardennes Forest in late December, the beauty of the battlefield struck Dad.

December 28, 1944:

We moved into position a few nights ago in the bright moon-

light. And I enjoyed the whole business for a change. Felt just like I was back in Vermont. Cold dry air made me feel like a young colt. A little later I heard a shell whine over, though, and my appreciation of nature vanished like spit on a hot stove.

Snow certainly puts a prettier face on war. It covers up all the dead men and animals and coats the ruined buildings over. What an improvement over mud it is.

By the time the Cannon Company arrived, the Battle of the Bulge had been on for two weeks and was to last another month. The Nazis wanted to capture the vital supply center at Liège, Belgium and the indispensable port of Antwerp. The thrust of the enemy military made a sixty-mile deep bulge in the US front line, giving the conflict its name. Only once, in a letter dated January 26, 1945, did Dad give any hint as to what he was doing during this infamous conflict: he served as an artillery observer.

That meant he served as the tip of the spear. His was the most dangerous, most forward position of his unit. He and his driver, two men armed with M1 rifles and sidearms, crept up near the front line; two men and a Jeep, depending solely on guile for their survival, reported back to the fire control station about the accuracy of artillery strikes. Those radioed reports were monitored by the Germans, so quite often the moment they transmitted the Germans knew they must be nearby and started looking for them.

Even when reconnaissance units used field telephones, they were still in danger because radio operators were always present as a backup. Enemy spotters using binoculars could pick out the radiomen because of the height of the antenna. The second the Germans detected the recon guys, shells screamed down on them.

Only the weather stopped the war machine from grinding up cartilage and bone. For much of the time, fog and heavy snow covered the battlefield. Yet even when the gales shrieked, Dad's howitzers boomed, sending shells down in areas where the army guessed the Germans had amassed troops. Lieutenant McBean had no problem firing his guns, but when it came time to move the cannons, the snow proved a formidable obstacle. For the Allies and the Germans alike, slick conditions proved a constant problem. Towing howitzers proved nearly impossible. Even tanks slid off the roads.

During the Battle of the Bulge, there must have been dozens of mind-bending moments, but because of the widespread publicity the hostilities received, Dad went out of his way not to worry his family. His letters occasionally described the plight of German civilians and sometimes related a humorous anecdote, but they primarily assured his family that he hadn't been killed.

Given the horrific losses, the 134th Infantry Regiment fared relatively well: 140 killed, 1,011 wounded, 298 missing, most of whom were killed.[28]

In all of this grimy, bloody, ice-encrusted conflict, opportunities for mishaps abounded: mayhem rushed a nose-count, or imminent destruction caused trucks to pull out before everyone climbed onboard. Yet if there's one thing I'm sure of about my dad, it's that he took responsibility for each of the men under his command. I'm certain he tried to take care of them as well as he protected me that day in the tiny bathroom of the tourist cabin in Nova Scotia.

Although I have no way of proving it, it seemed to me the same horrific images that gave Dad repetitive nightmares also imbued him with rancid feelings about humankind and put him on a constant search for new enemies.

Even while in Europe, he wrote bitterly about strikers and pacifists back home. After he got out of the olive drab, he had the Russians to hate. And the Blacks. And the Catholics. And the Irish.

The advent of rock 'n' roll gave him something special to hate. He thought some anti-American force — probably the Communist Party – had put "ni--er music" in the hands of white matinee idols for the purpose of undermining the morals of the country's youth.

"It's as clear as the nose on your face," he said.

I exhibited some serious learning and social difficulties at the time. My parents didn't know what was wrong with me, but they suspected the new music might have something to do with it. Dad knew I listened to it when he wasn't home because once, when he turned on his bedroom radio to soak up classical music while shaving, he got blown out by Little Richard's "Long Tall Sally."

Dad also had other worries about rock. He read a newspaper story that said rock 'n' roll encouraged children into early sexual experimentation.

He tried to talk to me about the craze.

"Bill, it's jigaboo music. There's nothing to it. It's just melody and a drumbeat. Like in the Vachel Lindsay poem:

...Along that riverbank

A thousand miles

Tattooed cannibals danced in files;

Then I heard the boom of the blood-lust song

And a thigh-bone beating on a tin-pan gong.

It's primitive!" he declared.

Dad could quote from dozens of poems. He could be eloquent about things he disliked, and he very much disliked Black people. He quickly saw the link between Blacks and rock and began to wonder how Patrice Lumumba, the communist leader of the Congo, fit into the picture.

At the time, I feared Black people as much as he, but I couldn't believe rock 'n' roll had anything to do with "Negroes." Elvis wasn't Black; I knew that. For my father to condemn Elvis in such a vehement fashion gave me the best evidence yet of his malice toward me.

I didn't fall in love with Elvis right away. I found his first big hit, "Hound Dog," more than a little puzzling. My ten-year-old mind wondered why catching a rabbit was such a big deal. And why would Elvis say his dog claimed to be "high classed?" (Had I heard Big Mama Thornton's 1953 version of the song, the tune probably would have made more sense, since she intended the song to be sung by a woman to a man.)

The second Elvis song I heard, "Heartbreak Hotel," mesmerized me. It concerned a group of people — call them disenfranchised if you want to be nice, call them losers if you don't — but even at ten, I understood his message. I felt like I was living in some sort of luxury hotel where I was a welfare recipient who was allowed to stay out of obligation. I *was so lonesome I could have died.*

Mom, at least, had some common sense about how to deal with children. Occasionally, she tried to persuade Dad to moderate his views on rock. I heard her reminding him that their parents hated Benny Goodman.

Thus, they tolerated my intense interest in the Billboard Top 40 for a time. Dad tried to restrain himself, hoping rock 'n' roll wasn't here to stay.

Encouraged, I stepped up my campaign to get greater access to the music. Everybody at school talked music constantly, and I was largely shut out of the conversation because I didn't have access to "all the hits all the time."

In the weeks leading up to my tenth birthday I'd begged my parents for a radio. What I really wanted, however, was to be a "hit" myself. I wanted to be at the hub of the rock 'n' roll world, and to achieve this, I needed not just a radio, but a transistor radio. These small cordless devices had just come on the market, and they were in the hands of very few children.

I saw myself at the epicenter of vast, spontaneous dance parties. There I was, hanging out in the schoolyard after the final bell, radio in hand, listening to the latest Elvis hit. People gathered around me, hoping I'd share a note or two.

My angst over not being tuned in amused my mother. Each time I'd fervently renew my request to join the transistor generation, she chortled like a pigeon and said, "We'll see what we shall see."

Finally, my birthday arrived. As I ate Rice Krispies with my sisters, my parents walked in with a large gift-wrapped box.

"Bill, you'll be getting most of your presents at your birthday party Saturday," Mom said. "But we didn't want you to have to wait another day for this!"

Both of them stood there, beaming at me, all altruism and light. I, however, knew I wasn't getting my heart's desire. The box was too big.

Lethargically, I removed the giftwrap and found a cream and brown Zenith AM table model. For 1956, it represented the highest quality "beginner" radio available, and I should have been very grateful. But I felt crushed.

My parents anticipated my dissatisfaction.

"Bill," Dad said, "you didn't get exactly what you wanted for three reasons. First, just because other Bronxville brats have the latest gadget doesn't mean you're going to have one. We don't play 'keep up with the Joneses' around here.

"Second, the cost of those little things is prohibitive. The day I spend $25 on a child's birthday, I hope somebody shoots me.

"And last, you and I both know what would happen if we gave you a transistor."

He looked at me with his eyebrows raised, waiting for me to state the obvious.

"You were afraid I'd lose it."

"Yeeees!" my old man said, chuckling.

My parents made a huge compromise when they gave me a radio. I'm sure Mom pressured Dad into it, and he gave way grudgingly. The gift didn't mean he acquiesced on rock. For him, it continued to represent the crumbling of American civilization. Many parents during the fifties shared my father's animosity. Yet most saw the wisdom of not going to war with the children about it.

Although the radio seemed like a peace offering, my dad never really wanted peace, and neither did I.

CHAPTER 14: ELVIS

Just as my father scanned ridges for gun positions, he continually looked for slippage in our country's morals, and for evidence that our will to fight Communism had faltered. On the moral side, he saw the "Elvis influence" multiplying like bugs on a pond. On the geopolitical side came Sputnik.

The morning in 1957 when Russia launched its beeping little satellite may have been the only time I ever saw Dad truly outraged when I wasn't the cause of his ire. After hearing the news on his bedroom radio, he began roaring.

"Those goddamned incompetent sons of bitches!"

I encountered him as he bulled out of his bedroom.

"The commies have beaten us into space!" he screamed to my mother from the second-floor landing.

I was two feet from him, but I didn't say a thing. I thought, *What space?*

As he careened around the corner to go downstairs, he slammed into the hamster cage, causing cedar chips to fly into the air and very nearly giving our dear pet a hard landing.

He clambered down the stairs two at a time, screaming the news to Mom. Then he stalked out the door in search of the *New York Times,* which he snatched off the front steps like a life raft, even though he had often said he didn't believe a word in it.

For five minutes, he stood outside in his pajamas and read about the great Soviet accomplishment. He might have remained there longer had not rotund Dick Middleton, the only Democrat in the neighborhood, walked by with his toy poodle named Dwight.

"Good morning, Peter!"

Dad shot him an assassin's stare and came inside.

He took the paper to the breakfast table but didn't touch his food and didn't bother to get dressed or shave. When he finally finished reading the newspaper's extensive coverage, he realized he had missed his bus and his normal commuter train. He made it into work an hour and a half late.

◆ ◆ ◆

Dad already hated Russians because of the Red Army's infamous rape campaign after it occupied Germany in 1945. That the Soviets had infiltrated the rock 'n' roll movement stood in his mind like a granite statue.

Elvis's 1956 appearance on the *Ed Sullivan Show* confirmed his suspicions.

We both viewed The King's appearance as climactic. For me, it meant the voice of the American youth underground had arrived on the country's biggest stage. For him, it meant that a show he had long watched and depended on for quality entertainment had compromised its integrity.

Although I loved the sound and the wildness of his act, Dad believed Elvis was doing more than bringing rock 'n' roll music into the American mainstream. He brought sexuality into the open, and that revolted him. There had certainly been sexy performers in the past, but Elvis seemed to incorporate the visceral joy of sex in his stage act.

Our family watched Sullivan every Sunday night. It exemplified wholesome family entertainment the tight harmony of the Lennon Sisters and the warmth of Rosemary Clooney. But Sullivan knew he needed to stay up with the times, and when a couple of other variety show hosts invited Elvis, Sullivan gave in.

Our thirteen-inch black-and-white TV was in the dining room, and we sat around the table so we could all see the screen. The only light in the room came from the TV. Our faces looked like silvery masks floating in a dark universe.

Dad reacted in an even more visceral way than I believed possible. Elvis opened his performance with "Hound Dog." His legs started gyrating, and when that happened, the girls in the studio audience began screaming. Even though the camera quickly moved away from his legs and into a tight head shot, Dad had seen enough. He got up and turned the TV off.

"I will never allow that kind of filth in my house," he pronounced. "Is that understood?"

He used his Army "command voice," and it filled every corner of the dining room. I looked at him, his face contorted and red, his manic, bloodshot eyes shifting between me and my sisters. His vehemence astounded me. He seemed desperate and slightly mad.

I had expected the standard fare in our household — sarcasm. I thought he'd watch the segment and then say something like, "Well, he's certainly no Caruso!" But he had turned the TV off! Like he truly believed if we watched another second, a seam of evil would rend our lives and move us to the wrong side of the River Styx.

I asked my mother, after he had taken his highball glass upstairs, what gave him the right to do what he did, and she said, "It's his TV." I thought, *Ooooh, so that's the way we're going to play it!*

Dad's fit of pique shouldn't have been such a telling moment, but it turned into that because I thought even if he hated Elvis, he should have seen how much I loved him and paid that love a little respect.

The next day at school, everybody talked about The King's performance. One of my friends had a pretty good take on the crazy way he moved his legs, and we all screamed. I don't remember what I contributed to the conversation, but I certainly didn't tell anyone that Dad had turned off the TV. That would have been like telling about his nightmares — like admitting he was crazy.

◆ ◆ ◆

I often compared Dad to other fathers.

Prior to junior high school, Bronxville had two Little League teams, and I played — inadequately — for one of them. The captain of the team was Bob M. He pitched and his dad coached. I got to see how Bob M.'s dad worked with his boy. When he pitched well, which was most of the time, he got a low-key "attaboy." And when he got hit hard — as happens occasionally to all pitchers — Bob M.'s dad would be warm and analytical. Did Bob think his curve wasn't breaking? Did he have problems with pitch location? Could the opposition be stealing the catcher's signs?

Thinking about Bob M.'s dad got me wondering why my father couldn't have taken a more intelligent, strategic approach to the rock 'n' roll "problem." Obviously, Elvis's long-haired, pretty-boy look and the girls' screaming revolted him, but why couldn't he be cool and contrarian about it? He could have pointed out that Elvis offered nothing more than a crooning heartthrob with a few tricky dance steps. He might have said Elvis would have been nothing without his accomplished backup group, the Jordanaires, which represented the great American tradition of gospel harmonizing. That would have equipped me with some lines for school the next day, and while everybody else raved about him, I could have risen slightly above the fray. How cool would that have been?

I think Dad's intoxication made this impossible. Yet in other situations, he acted unflappable and politic. I occasionally went with him to his law office when he had to work a half-day on Saturday, and I observed him at large family gatherings. Smooth as a sea-washed stone.

After Dad turned off the TV, my homework awaited, but instead I flopped down on my bed and turned on my little Zenith to a very low volume, so if my parents listened by the door, they wouldn't be able to hear. My little radio had quickly become my connection with the outside world. As I lay in the dark, illuminated only by the orange glow of the radio's vacuum tubes seeping through the back panel, I felt like I lived in a dictatorship and listened to Radio Liberty. It represented the independence I craved, even as a boy of ten. This insane world of rock 'n' roll had nothing to do with reality and everything to do with emotion. It made me laugh. It made me dream. It made me think about deliverance.

Ironically, with the exception of the communist connection, Dad had Elvis right. He was a pretty boy. The screaming girls were absurd. And he did lead me and millions of other white kids to an appreciation of African-American music.

Soon after Presley came Ray Charles, Jackie Wilson, Little Richard, and Screamin' Jay Hawkins ("I got a *spell* on you, cause you're mine, *OH YEAH YOU MINEEEEE!*"). Sometimes my passion for this form of insanity would get out of control, and

I'd turn it up, turn it up until my little Zenith danced on my bedside table.

Then Dad ducked his head into my room and roared, "Knock it off! Just because you've obviously lost your mind doesn't mean you have to take the rest of us with you."

Almost as popular as Elvis and every bit as influenced by Black musicians was Buddy Holly. In Bronxville, we knew absolutely no Black people unless they were in service to our families. But we loved Holly because he obviously picked up on the rhythmic wiles of Black artists like Bo Diddley and used them to express universal musical truths. This early blending of cultures, I think, led many rich suburban white kids to support the civil rights movement. That's probably what Dad saw coming as well, and in that respect he was truly prescient.

Societal trends Dad saw clearly, although his spin invariably saw a negative outcome. He saw integration of Blacks and whites as bad without ever trying to imagine what the upside could be. Yet when it came to dealing with the undercurrents in his own family, he failed utterly. In me he saw a miasma of poor grades, forgetfulness, deceit, and rebellion. He felt responsible for changing the course of my life but understood only one method for getting that done: the carrot and the stick. He made it clear the carrot was always available, but his overuse of the stick made me want to tell him what he could do with his carrot. For by this time, anger filled my heart. It would have been nice if I could have emulated my father, but given what'd happened, that turned out to be impossible. Instead, I chose as a mentor a nineteenth century child with an alcoholic father: Huck Finn.

CHAPTER 15: INCOMPETENCE

I discovered Huck not through my own literary curiosity, but rather from a newfound confrere, Tommy C.

Although I read books, I did so because I remained confined to my room. I didn't yearn for literary excitement. I craved adventure. I wanted to be bad, and in the field of bad, Tommy C. was a leader.

A red-headed kid with freckles on his nose, Tommy seemed very much like the little boy my mother said she wanted before she conceived me — except she wouldn't have wanted Tommy. He was an innovator in the field of naughty.

I wanted to hang with Tommy because by now I felt pretty cynical about the value of behaving myself. I just didn't understand the upside. I apparently couldn't get the school thing and would continue to get punished for that. I didn't possess a lick of hand-eye coordination, so that eliminated sports.

Tommy didn't do sports or traditional academics either, but he had an imagination that focused on insurrection. He saw every day as Bastille Day. Consequences were for people who got caught.

One day, after the final bell rang at school, Tommy casually mentioned he'd read Twain. Unlike other children, we didn't have anything constructive to do, so on that smoky fall afternoon, he led me to his camp in a forest of rhododendron bushes. There we planned to transform Bronxville into St. Joseph, Missouri.

Huckleberry Finn didn't come up on the curriculum until seventh grade, yet Tommy, understanding it to be a guide to overthrowing parental rule, slipped it off his family's bookshelf and perused it a year early.

"Huck's dad was no good," Tommy explained. "He was always getting drunk and thrown in jail. So Huck decided to take off. He made himself a raft and floated down this river. He brought his best friend, Jim, with him. So I guess that's you."

The occasion represented the first time anyone had chosen me for anything. Had Tommy proposed joining the American Communist Party, I would have been game.

Reaching his camp seemed like stepping into an enchanted vale, even though he picked a location near the school and just down the street from his house. One moment you were walking down a sidewalk adjacent to a thicket of rhododendrons, then you simply stepped off the sidewalk into the bushes and saw that the foliage wasn't an impenetrable copse but in fact fashioned a tent. As you made your way in, thin trunks needed to be pressed aside, but within a few feet you came to a dim and quivery clearing that smelled like nutmeg and cinnamon, the leaves so thick you couldn't see the sky, or houses or anything other than shifting foliage.

We sat down on a soft floor of dead plant life. Out of his pocket, Tommy produced a corncob pipe.

"Huck smoked a pipe just like this one," he said.

Puffing on the shavings from Tommy's pencil sharpener became our first adventurous act. He declared that since poor river boys had no way of getting tobacco, we'd have to make do.

With a rakish gesture, Tommy fired a kitchen match against a stone and applied the flame to the pipe. White plumes and the smell of burning wood wafted through our defilade, and we at once walked the road to independence.

After the choking and sputtering abated, we put our minds to other assaults against convention. As wedges of orange afternoon sunlight found their way through the oblong leaves, we agreed a river needed to be part of our plan.

The Bronx River, a stream entwined with burly oaks and sugar maples, its banks flocked with ironweed and goldenrod, flowed nearby. It blessed the eyes but assaulted the nose. The river carried our town's effluent toward the East River in those years before environmental laws. It certainly wasn't raft-friendly, but it did beckon boys in search of danger, for over the river ran an old, oxidized railroad bridge.

In the 1950s, the Harlem Division of the New York Central Railroad (now referred to as Metro North) served Bronxville. The railroad cars, painted olive drab with gold trim, carried our dads to work. The trains drew energy from an electrified third rail. High-pitched whistles screaming, they crossed the bridge several times an hour.

Climbing onto the bridge would be our first challenge, Tommy decided. He planned to place a penny on a non-electrified rail to see what damage the train inflicted on it.

We found, however, that access to the bridge wasn't going to be easy. A twelve-foot chain-link fence topped by barbed wire blocked our way. We needed to cross the river so we could climb to the bridge by the opposite embankment. Places along this free-flowing latrine offered midstream rocks that made a crossing barely possible, but any slip might result in shit-shoe, or worse.

I considered it highly unlikely I could hop gracefully over three rocks to the safety of the far bank. If I fell, it would be a very long walk home and a hostile reception once I arrived.

"Oh, come on, it's easy," Tommy said. "Watch me."

His freckled countenance fell quiet. Eyeing the three rocks in the river, he coiled and, quick as hopscotch, landed on the far side. Then he put his hands on his hips and stared at me.

The more I thought about it, the less I wanted to do it. I just knew I would fall in. No danger of drowning existed, just great risk of fecal involvement. I gagged, I choked, and then I began reframing.

"Why don't I be the look-out?" I asked.

"You are such a chicken."

"But what about the cops?"

"They never come down here."

"They do. I saw them when I camped here last week."

Tommy hadn't attended the campout, so he couldn't contradict my lie. He looked skeptical and shifted his weight to his other leg.

"If I see anyone coming, I'll whistle."

Tommy waved dismissively and stumbled through sandy soil up the embankment to the trestle. A short time later, a train came. Tommy picked up the realigned coin and returned to the other side of the river.

Without a word, he began walking toward home.

"Hey, wait a minute, let me see!"

"The heck with that. You're chicken. I'd rather show it to my mother."

"Oh, come on!"

Tommy continued walking at a brisk pace, and when it came time for me to turn down my street, we said distant goodbyes. The next day, I saw Tommy showing the coin to a group of boys and then pointing at me. A group jeer followed, and I got away from them as quickly as possible, losing myself in the crowd.

Within a few days, however, Tommy caught up with me as I walked home. He had a new project: making slugs for use on vending machines. Did I want to see the manufacturing process?

That afternoon we went down to his basement, which doubled as his workshop for mischief. He had swiped a few of his dad's shotgun shells and pried them apart with his pocket knife. The black powder he carefully funneled into an old pill bottle and set aside for later use. The shot he placed in a beat-up metal measuring cup, which he placed on the glowing coals of his family's ancient furnace. The lead shot quickly liquefied, and he carefully poured it into a clay mold made with an Indian head nickel. When it cooled, Tommy had a coin that looked a little bit like a legitimate nickel but weighed much more. When we dropped it into a Coke machine, we heard the sound of angry springs followed by a dull clunk into the coin return. The machine wasn't fooled for a second.

This failure gave me a sort of quiet satisfaction, but it didn't discourage Tommy, who announced rocketry as his next quest. I observed we had gotten rather far from Huckleberry Finn, but Tommy said Huck would have made rockets if the basic materials had been available to him.

We went to the hardware store and bought one-half-inch diameter aluminum pipe. Back at Tommy's workshop, we sealed one end of the pipe with candle wax, loaded the other end with the black powder, and then used paper to crimp the fuse. The fact that our invention could easily have turned out to be a pipe bomb never occurred to us.

A wooded outcrop above the school, about three hundred feet distant, served as our testing center. Our goal was to hit the school with our rocket. An angle iron salvaged from Tommy's garage and propped up with a stick became our launching apparatus. Our first attempt ended when the pipe made a snake-like hissing sound, tumbled off the launcher, and chased us this way and that until it ran out of fuel.

I looked at Tommy, sneering, as if to say, "Second failure in a row. Now what?"

But I didn't have to ask the question, for Tommy had already analyzed the debacle.

"More powder."

We had several more disappointments but continued to make modifications. Candle wax was replaced by a clay-putty combination. We tamped down the powder so we could get more in the pipe. Finally, we came up with a rocket that just had to work — it had to, or we swore we would move on to other forms of juvenile delinquency.

We returned to the promontory over the school and carefully aimed the launcher toward the neoclassical brick bastion. Gingerly, Tommy lit the fuse and jumped back. The rocket shushed straight out of the launcher into the blue sky. For several seconds, we wondered if we'd ever know where it went, but then we heard the mellifluous sound of shattering glass.

Our goodbye that afternoon was suffused with joy and optimism. As I walked toward Summit Avenue, I thought of other targets, but the closer to home I got, the more my real-life responsibilities intruded. I remembered I had pledged to wear my orthodontic retainer all day, but because it had been recently adjusted, it hurt like hell and I'd taken it out. When I reached in my pocket to find it, it wasn't there. I felt like my blood pressure dropped by half. I became etherized by fear. Retainers cost fifty dollars each, and I had now lost five of them. When added to the cost of lost school books, hats, and gloves, this latest misstep meant I now owed my parents well over three hundred.

I lowered myself to the curb, put my head between my legs, and pondered my hopeless condition.

I had few options. Since I had already lost so many retainers, Mom asked to see it every day when I got home from school. No lie I might tell would be creditable. I couldn't steal a new one, and I couldn't independently get another made. All I could do was turn around, go back to school, and try to find it.

It was about 4:45 p.m. when I began my trudge back to school. I had a couple of ideas about where it might be, but the custodians chained the doors at four thirty, just before they laid down lines of pungent sweeping compound. I had tried to get in at this time of day before, and even on the few occasions I got a janitor's attention, they'd shout, "School's closed, be gone with you, boy!"

The school had something like twenty doors, and all of them were locked and chained. I saw the shadows of a few janitors, but none even hesitated when I banged on the door.

Downcast and about to give up, I turned home and almost bumped into Mrs. Tucker.

"Dear heart, whatever could be the matter?"

The matronly French teacher continually reminded us it took fewer muscles to smile than to frown. Tears lurking in my eyes, I told her what had so upset me and she said, "Well, this afternoon is apparently when the well-intended were meant to find each other. I forgot a pile of exams I need to correct tonight, so you will have a brief opportunity to find your retainer while I get them."

I swore to Mrs. T. that I knew just where I put it, and I kind of did, but when I got to Mrs. Pitella's English class, it was nowhere to be found. Desperate, I thought of where else I might have left it. Maybe I took it out in the library, but it wasn't there either. I searched the teachers' desks and ransacked closets that might be used for lost-and-founds, to no avail. I began thinking about my conversation with Dad.

When I finally met Mrs. Tucker by the faculty entrance, she seemed genuinely disappointed by my failure but thought maybe I exaggerated my plight.

"Surely, Bill, your parents realize mistakes happen. Certainly they can't be harsh with you over a simple case of boyish carelessness? Do you think it might help if I called them on your behalf?"

At this point, I had the choice of telling the good woman I'd lost five retainers — and watching her face fall — or of telling her everything would be fine. I chose the latter course.

As I walked home, I resolved to tell Mom right away. Irrationally, I figured if I told her immediately, there was still some chance she might let me go to the Saturday matinee.

When I walked in the kitchen, Mom's eyes bunched up and her mouth tightened. More than an hour late — again! Before she could say anything, I told her I had just spent an hour at the school looking for my retainer, and she could ask Mrs. Tucker if she didn't believe me.

Mom had a glass of sherry in one hand and a smoldering L&M in the other. As she placed the cigarette in an ashtray, she hissed, "And did you find it?"

"We really looked for a long time — even looked in trash cans and stuff, and..."

Mom smacked her hand on the black and white marbled linoleum kitchen counter. "William Seaton McBean, you are the living end! How could you possibly be so careless? Do you think we're made of money? Good God!"

"Mom, I'm really sorry."

"If you'd be good enough to get out of my sight, that would be a great relief!"

Sometimes, when she said this kind of thing, I thought it might be better for everybody if I just took off. She obviously didn't like me, and I sure as hell didn't want to be around her. But my feelings about my mother, which ranged from distaste to contempt, were manageable.

I felt differently about Dad. When he became angry, I got emotional rickets. If he showed contempt, my self-worth immediately shriveled. Mom supplied him with information, causing me to dislike her intensely. A direct relationship existed between the intensity of my mother's anger and the power of my father's sadism. Mom's anger was generated from her job as family budget manager. I probably caused major shortfalls. It incensed Dad that a great genius like himself spawned a boy of very little brain. I think he felt justified in taking shots at me just because I acted dumb.

"I wasn't surprised that you would lose one retainer, Bill. After all, you've lost at least one of everything we've ever given you," he said that evening. "What I'm wondering is if losing five of these things comprises some sort of middle-finger message for your mother and me, or if it's simply what it appears to be: rank stupidity."

I continued eating my dinner. He'd asked a rhetorical question, and I knew he'd soon plunge in the dagger.

"Almost anyone, even a kindergartener, manages to look around him before he leaves and asks a very simple, rote question. Do I have what I came here with? Am I missing anything? Most people manage to form this habit from a very early age. Why not you?"

Had I a reasonable answer to that question, we wouldn't be having this conversation. I didn't know what to say. My silence flipped him into command-voice mode.

"I said, *Why not you?*"

"I do have that habit, Dad, but I just get distracted more than most people, I don't know why."

"Distracted?"

"Right."

"Bill, we know that you have above-average ability. You're not a simple boy. And yet you lose things at a rate that would indicate that you *are* simple. Five retainers. Four hats. Several pairs of gloves. School books galore. Wallets. Anyone could extend the list. Bill, what is wrong?"

"Everybody's got problems. I lose stuff."

"Do not get flippant with me!" he bellowed.

"I'm not being..."

"Button your lip and listen. Your days of losing retainers are over because my investment in your mouth is at an end. I've tried to give you a leg up on life by making you look decent, but you apparently don't care. That does not, however, mean that your debt to me for the loss of the retainers is wiped clean.

"Now, we need to redesign your payment program. The cancelation of your allowance plus the work program we've designed around the house isn't amortizing the debt quickly enough. Tomorrow you will get a paper route. You will give me a hundred percent of the proceeds of that effort until your debt — get the exact number from your mother — is repaid.

"And Bill, just so you know, I don't buy this business about you getting distracted. When it's something you're personally interested in, you pay attention just fine. Have you ever lost your sacred movie money? Money for Teen Center? Have you ever misplaced one of your goddamned comic books?"

A sneer gradually encroached upon his upper lip. Slowly, he shook his head back and forth.

"You think you can fool your old man? If you'd spend as much time doing what you're supposed to do as you do giving me the royal raspberry, you'd be way ahead of the game. Now get out of here."

I slithered out of the room, went upstairs, and turned on Murray the K on WINS. If anyone could treat shame with bombast, he could. But it didn't work. A pine needle in a forest, a pebble in a quarry, an ant in a jungle had more worth than me.

When I lost things, my parents called me names like "chowder head" and "cotton brain." They accused me of "sleep-walking through life" and of being "unconscious." It made me angry, but it became increasingly hard to deny what they said. Something was definitely wrong.

The day following the rocket launch, I casually asked my classmate Dennis E. if he noticed the broken window in Mrs.

Pitella's classroom. Tommy made it very clear he wanted to keep the rocket launch a secret, but I wasn't a top-secret kind of guy.

"You did that?" he asked.

"Not exactly," I said coyly.

I made him beg for the story and then related all the details. By the end of the day, the entire sixth grade knew what happened, and although I tried to put forth the impression that I had an integral part in this amazing feat, my associates greeted my braggadocio with skepticism.

My blabbering did establish that Tommy had considerable scientific skills and that he needed a sidekick about as much as he needed a PR man. After the rocket launch, he set the agenda, and his peers were all ears. When he said one afternoon he knew how to make an explosive gas called hydrogen, I wasn't the only one who wanted to watch.

Tommy waited until after 4:00 p.m., when most of the teachers had left the building, and then led several of our gang to the chemistry lab. There, with the confidence of TV's Mr. Wizard, he assembled the apparatus to produce the gas. Using copper wire, batteries, two pieces of copper pipe, and a metal tray filled with water, he made a machine that emitted hydrogen bubbles. Tommy placed a large beaker over the contraption, and when he judged enough gas had been manufactured, he quickly pulled off the beaker, slapped a top on it, and announced that we were ready for our first test.

A lit match held near the mouth of the beaker would cause an explosion, Tommy asserted. We were ready to take cover behind some overturned lab tables, but being a responsible scientist, he insisted our endeavors be transferred to the parking lot.

The air outside smelled of tree sap and bright yellow dandelions. In the tar-and-gravel lot, we clustered around the beaker, frequently looking over our shoulders for encroaching adults. Tommy produced a book of matches. When he asked who wanted to do the honors, he looked directly at me.

Instead of seeing the matchbook as an invitation to suicide, I grasped at this obvious chance for redemption. That afternoon on the Bronx River festered in my brain, and I wanted a chance to rehabilitate my reputation.

A considerable audience gathered. Dickie M., a swaggering athlete, had followed us down from the lab, as did Kelly J., the class ape with the musculature of a twenty-year-old. Van L., the student council president, strolled up and expressed thoughtful concern. A couple of girls, whispering feverishly behind their hands, squeezed into my growing audience.

With unparalleled nonchalance, I snatched the matchbook from Tommy's outstretched hand.

I lay down on the tar and gravel and stretched out so only my hand and the match were close to the beaker. This didn't work because of the wind. I then further demonstrated my dedication to self-destruction by kneeling, cupping the match with both hands, and gingerly advancing the flame to the lip of the beaker. Nothing. So I got a little closer and tried again. Nothing. Finally, convinced the beaker presented no threat, I leaned over it and lowered the match inside.

Orange haze, a whoosh, and a gasp of amazement from the crowd.

When my friends were sure nothing further was likely to happen, they approached me, their eyes wide.

Nancy N. walked up to me and ran her hand along my eyebrows and then to the top of my forehead.

"Golly, Bill, all your eyebrows and eyelashes are burned off! Are you okay?"

I was fine. My face felt a little hot, but that might have been because I had taken a terrible chance and made a fool of myself in the process.

I looked over at Tommy. He had a mocking smile on his face.

"Can I have my matches back?"

I tossed them to him, picked up my books, and headed toward home. On my way, I chewed on what had just happened. Tommy was a leader, all right, and I a born follower.

When I walked through the front door, Mom said, "What in the world happened to you?" I told her I had made some hydrogen in the lab and had blown myself up. I knew she'd gush over my initiative, and she didn't disappoint.

It represented one of the rare times I managed the alchemy of turning foolishness into good PR.

Yet any time I impressed my parents, my scheming ways would reverse whatever slight reasons for optimism I gave them. I didn't want to be a good son; I wanted to be a big shot. Although the hydrogen debacle represented a terrible setback in my efforts to be cool, I had plans to regenerate my image. My parents told me the following summer we would embark on a trip that would make our journey to Nova Scotia seem like a walk down the block. Their itinerary spelled opportunity for my ambitions.

CHAPTER 16: SENSE OF WONDER

Although my parents knew they had an asymmetrical warrior on their hands, they refused to let a knot-headed kid tie them down. They wanted to use their vacation time to travel, and luckily they had a destination resort: my maternal grandmother's Tucson hacienda. Time to head west!

Mom planned the trip with the help of the American Automobile Association, which sent us an impressive assortment of maps with a suggested route highlighted in yellow. They also sent a list of recommended places to stay. Her goal was to get there as soon as possible and to minimize potential for conflict.

When Dad inspected the packet prior to our July departure, he pronounced himself thoroughly dissatisfied. Although expediency persuaded him to use the turnpike system from New York to Chicago, additional travel needed to follow the Union Pacific Railroad's main line — and all motels west of the Windy City — needed to be as close to the railroad tracks as possible.

Dad constituted part of that strange phylum known as "railroad nut." Although a lover of baseball as well, he wasn't a baseball "nut" because his interest waned when the New York Giants weren't involved. The UP fascinated Dad because it was based in his boyhood home of Omaha and because he lawyered for the company. Yet *everything* concerning railroading captivated him: the semaphore, the switches, the massive train yards, and any kind of steam locomotives. Diesel engines also intrigued him, but they were far less dramatic than their predecessors. Also, they represented change, which he hated.

Had he the money, I'm sure he would have taken us to Tucson by rail, but reality dictated that the wheels that took us west would be rubber.

He outfitted the Pontiac station wagon with a luggage rack. Loaded with old-style rubberized cloth suitcases, Dad covered it with a piece of heavy-duty canvas and secured it with hemp rope. On a muggy summer morning, Dad summoned his family into the vehicle, carefully backed out of the stonewalled driveway, and headed for the George Washington Bridge.

As we descended into New Jersey, he let us listen to the radio. Perry Como sang, "Hot diggity dog diggity boom what you do to me..." He listened happily to Perry, but when the tempo picked up, he turned the music off. I resented his preemptory act, but the stink of the oil refineries soon distracted me. Then came the fresh air of rural New Jersey and the Delaware Water Gap. With only 2,100 miles to go, we were bored.

Mom had anticipated this problem. She employed something she rarely used at home: positive reinforcement. She had a basket full of snacks (raisins, animal crackers, gum) to be used as hourly inducements for reasonable behavior. These nibbles, capped by the promise of a cold soda pop at 4:00 p.m., proved robust incentives.

Yet temptation surrounded me during the ten-hour travel days. My parents assigned Mary Jo and I the middle seat and Anne to the rear. (The twins were left with the grandparents.) I amused myself by provoking Anne. I'd stick my fingers between the cracks of the seats to poke her, and I'd hear the clicking of her teeth as they just missed their target. This game generally didn't last more than a couple of minutes before Anne was screaming with rage, thus endangering my access to strawberry soda pop. I promised to be good and then within the hour resumed my provocations.

◆ ◆ ◆

My parents were very big on educational experiences for their children. They wanted to show us the vastness of the Midwest, and because it took us three days to cross it, we couldn't miss their point.

The farmland began in Ohio, but the limited-access, four-lane "super highway" held the reality of rural life at bay. After Chicago, the two-lane road crossed hundreds of miles of undulating wheat and swaying corn. Mirage after shimmering mirage radiated off the heat-packed pavement. Large black puddles lay by the road, rank with the perfume of ebony soil. We wrinkled our noses like downwind dogs. It was so un-Bronxville!

Every once in a while, fluting over the susurrus of rushing wind, came a sound so melodic we couldn't believe our ears.

"It's a meadowlark," Dad said. "It's the sound of the Midwest."

We caught the trilling several more times before hearing a loud thump coming from the overhead carrier.

"What was that?" we chorused.

"A meadowlark."

We whimpered our despair, causing Dad to eye his callow audience in the rear-view mirror. He took on a jocular tone, using his lisping, magnanimous millionaire voice.

"Woe, destruction, ruin, and decay;

The worst is death, and death will have his day."[29]

That chilled us for a while, but then the sound of rubber against asphalt took over, and once again ennui set in. Minute after minute, mile after mile, windows open, pollen-heavy air rushing through the vehicle and out again. Interminable rows of corn, then a barn, then more corn, then a grain elevator, then more corn.

Legions of white-on-green signs flicking by like frames of an unsynchronized movie. Many of them contained Native American names, and our father, with clarion-like elocution, enunciated the tribes associated with rivers. The Kankakee, the Maquoketa, the Wapsipinicon. He'd tell stories about the tribes that were as apocryphal as they were entertaining. For him, the names of the Great Plains natives had nothing to do with humanity or history; they recalled the warmth of his early years growing up there when everything had been simple and good. For us, the Midwest meant bugs, humidity, and monotony. For Dad, it resurrected the time before Bronxville, the time before the war.

The battles between settlers and Native Americans got Dad onto his favorite philippic — the resilient character of Midwesterners. Using the rear-view mirror to make sure he had our attention, he'd hold forth on the difficulties of farming and the hardships of the first settlers crossing the plains. He talked about soddies and their construction and about how the pioneers spent much of the winter underground, trying to survive blizzards that lasted for days.

"Then, just as the settler community thought they had things turned around, after fifty or sixty years of hard work, they had to face the Dust Bowl," Dad said. He spent ten minutes describing the ravages of that great drought on the country's midsection.

When he stopped, the pervasive hum of the tires took over.

That meant the task of providing entertainment passed to my mother. Who wanted to sing? Should we keep a list of license plates from various states? Who could be the first person to call out a state boundary?

And of course:

"Does your husband / Misbehave / Grunt and grumble / Rant and rave / Shoot the brute some / Burma-Shave."

One evening, as we were close to bedding down at a motel somewhere in rural Nebraska, I saw Dad looking at his watch. In those days he smoked cigarettes, and that night he burned through one after another. He checked his watch several times and then said, "Bill, come with me."

The gusty night threatened rain; thunder grumbled nearby. In the lee of the motel, lightning bugs sought a pocket of calm air. We walked up an embankment to the tracks, where the wind buffeted us as we waited.

I fidgeted. He told me to cool it.

"Your patience will be rewarded, William." Haut.

Within five minutes, we saw the locomotive light and then held our breath as the silvery train roared by. As it disappeared into the muted orange glow of the sunset, the illuminated sign on the back of the observation car glowed in the dark: *The California Zephyr*. Dad looked at me with a gratified smile. He threw an arm around my shoulder, and we walked back just ahead of the rain.

On the afternoon of the third day, the flat fields of corn and grain ended and the high desert of eastern Colorado began. The air rushing in the car window went from wringing wet to blast-furnace dry, and smelled of sand and herbs.

At a rest stop, I asked Dad what the odd smell was.

"Sage, but don't mistake it for what's used to season food."

That gave me a devilish idea I found impossible to resist.

I picked a sprig of the plant and, casually sitting on the front bumper, began munching on it. It had a biting and unpleasant taste, but it was a small sacrifice for the reward I had in mind.

Eventually, Anne asked me what I was doing.

"Chewing sage."

"What's that?"

"It's like Thanksgiving stuffing," I said. "Without the onions."

"Liar!"

Her brown eyes practically left their sockets as she expressed her disbelief.

"No, really! It's delicious! Smell it."

Cautiously, she lowered her nose to the twig of sage I held.

"It smells okay."

"Tastes even better."

I knew I had her. She was under the misapprehension I wouldn't discomfort myself just to trick her. I bit off a substantial sprig and masticated. As the bitter taste pervaded my mouth, I played my part.

"Emmm, delicious."

Still suspicious, she bit off a little piece, took it in her mouth, and slowly began to chew. At once her eyes narrowed. She spat out the nasty weed and emitted a shriek of outrage. She rushed at me, canines exposed and claws out. I took off and led her on a merry chase until Father boomed, "Knock it off!"

"But he made me eat something nasty!"

"Like what?"

"Sage!"

"He *made* you eat sage?"

"He tricked me!"

My little sister's anger turned to tears.

"Anne, come here," Mom said. "Wash your mouth out with water and have some crackers."

I looked at Dad and got the dirty eye. One word and I could forget my bottle of pop. I scuttled back into the Pontiac's middle seat.

For the next several hours, Anne poked her fingers between the seats and made taunting noises. I kept my eyes front and my hands in my lap. I had better things to think about than my pestiferous sister. Within the next few days I'd get an opportunity for creating bedlam that most of my Bronxville friends would die for. I had to ignore Anne and concentrate on executing my plan.

◆ ◆ ◆

Beginning midafternoon of that day, I paid close attention to the western horizon. I'd been told Colorado had tremendous mountains, and I started looking for something familiar, like the Presidential Range in New Hampshire. But all I saw were towering cumulous clouds, substantial but unremarkable. Eventually, I saw what I thought might be the outlines of a mountain peak but quickly dismissed what my eyes told me. I didn't ask anyone else to confirm what appeared to be blocking the path of US 24. Everyone knew mountains didn't come in that size.

My old man saw the same thing, but he didn't say a word. When the reality of what loomed out of the cloudbank could no longer be denied, I burst out, "Dad, look. Mountains! They're huge!"

"That they are, Bill. The one you see jutting out of the clouds is Pikes Peak, 14,114 feet above sea level."

He had never seen the Colorado Rockies either, yet Dad preserved the sense of wonder for me, knowing I would have an entirely different experience if I spotted it than if he pointed it out.

After four days of driving, we got close to our destination. We left the cool climate of Flagstaff, Arizona, crested the Mogollon Rim, and wound down the twisting road into the Sonoran Desert. We began the day crisp and enthusiastic, thinking the last few hundred miles would be a lark, but within a couple of hours the deeply thermal environment of greasewood and cholla invaded our un-air-conditioned car. Our expectations focused on our grandparents' swimming pool. We'd take our first dip that afternoon if we could just stay on schedule.

By early afternoon, we were just south of Phoenix and the temperature reached 110 degrees. Our fried family stopped at a grimy gas station, hoping for the relief of cold drinks, but they had only tepid orange pop, and we mewling children were ushered back into our hot metal cage. Dad claimed we really needed only two things to withstand the omnipotent heat: water and an ample measure of stoicism. Onward we drove, limping down the two-lane highway crammed with melon trucks, ramshackle buses, and migrant workers in cars that wheezed and stalled on the road's sandy shoulder. As we crawled along, my mother opened Anne's suitcase and found a pair of underpants. She saturated them with water from our thermos and let each of us take turns swathing our heads, necks, and arms with this poultice that provided a few minutes of relief but then made the heat seem even worse. When we cried for more, we were rebuffed in the name of conserving water in case we got stranded.

When we finally reached Casa Grande, we stopped again and this time found icy cold Coca-Cola, and nothing had ever been that good, so good we drained the seven-ounce, hourglass bottles in seconds and pleaded for more, but were told, nope, back into the car, this trip doesn't need a bunch of sick kids.

Another eviscerating hour passed, the desert grew dim, and our parents, possessing nothing but written instructions about how to get to our grandparents' house, began to discuss the issue of navigating the dusty back roads that led to our final destination, the adobe-walled compound and its luscious green swimming pool. When we turned off the main highway at Flowing Wells, darkness had descended on the desert. The heat still ruled, but there was a new threat. A strange noise came out of the desert night that seemed so unlikely, we discounted it at first, but soon the rumbling became real and we were inundated by wild thunderstorms sweeping in from the Sea of Cortez.

Saguaro cactus stood in relief against the purple desert night as lightning illuminated the Santa Rita Mountains south toward Mexico, and the smell of creosote infused the air like the redolence of a primitive civilization.

Slowly, uncertainly, we drove through the whiteness of the rain. As we crested a shallow ridgeline, Dad slammed on the brakes to avoid an arroyo roiled by a muddy flash flood. In the heavy rain, he turned the car around, and somehow, without aid of cell phone or map, found our grandparents' house. That night, he was our hero.

CHAPTER 17: NOGALES

A couple of days after we arrived in Tucson, we hopped in my grandpa's baby-blue Lincoln Continental — the kind with the suicide doors — and headed south.

The second we crossed the border, mobs of little kids descended on the vehicle with dirty rags, offering to clean our mirrors, our windshield, the entire car. They were smiling, friendly, and happy to dive to the ground for the pennies my granddad threw out the window.

"Hell, it's the only way to get through," he remarked mildly.

The main drag featured an assemblage of restaurants, curio shops, and pharmacies. The buildings were primarily one story of concrete construction. A few were made of granite blocks. None were wood — there wasn't a scrap of timber within five hundred miles of Nogales. Telephone and power poles heavily festooned both sides of the main street. We made slow headway because of men and women pushing carts laden with everything from melons to roasted meat. The odor of deep-fried corn suffused the air.

Finally, we parked and began a shiftless meander through the shops, looking for bargains. Of course, good deals abounded, but my grandmother delighted in hammering the humble merchants. She did so with the belligerent tenacity of a fighting cock, jabbing her forefinger at them until they begged for mercy.

For what seemed like hours, we inspected the goods:

lacquered orange maracas, velvet paintings of Jesus in his agony, cowhide chairs, brightly painted children's furniture, pots of every description, tooled leather purses and wallets, turquoise jewelry, a thousand earrings, corn husk flowers, heavy green highball glasses, punched tin chandeliers, mirrors and crosses, lacy white blouses, cowboy boots, and on and on it went.

Eventually, Dad and Grandpa said they preferred one of the cool, dark bars of which Nogales had such a fine selection. The women hadn't begun to think of surrender. I said I wanted to investigate the purchase of bongo drums and headed down a side street. No one thought of stopping me, because no one regarded Nogales as dangerous. They told me to report to a certain place at a certain time, and I happily agreed.

I planned to buy enough fireworks to keep Bronxville smelling like black powder for a year. I really did want bongos — it'd give me something to do when I was supposed to be doing homework — but the drums functioned as the cover I needed to complete my caper. My poor judgment served as a commentary on how badly I needed to be noticed by my peers. I'd recently completed a long stretch of penniless incarceration because of the Murballs episode, and if I got caught, another stint would begin.

Yet I convinced myself that this time I'd be wily enough to escape detection. I reasoned I didn't get caught that much; it's just when I did, I suffered draconian censure. I felt certain this particular scheme was worth the risk.

I had no trouble finding what I wanted and making it back to the meeting point in a timely manner. Our drive north went without incident. In those days, US Customs assumed a Lincoln filled with adults and kids belonged in the USA. They waved us through.

A couple of hours later, back in Tucson, we piled out of

Grandpa's car. I noticed Dad feeling his pants pockets.

"My wallet," he said. "I seem to have lost my wallet."

He began looking in the crevices of the car's leather upholstery, and I started feeling kind of sick. Granddad said he'd run inside and get a flashlight. At that point, I knew it would take something close to a miracle to save me.

Dad started fiddling with the power controls on the side of the seats. He saw this sort of thing as very decadent. In the fifties, only Lincoln and Cadillac offered power everything, and my father thought it quite silly. As he pushed the buttons, he clowned after the manner of a primitive grunting ape and showed mock surprise every time the modern marvel did something new that he thought absurd and wasteful.

Then he returned to his search. His hand reached under the front seat. His face changed from frustration to surprise. He pulled out a cherry bomb, examined it, and looked at me with the seasoned scorn of a prosecutor who knows he's got his man.

"You know anything about this, Bill?"

A thorough search produced about fifty cherry bombs, plus several ashcans and couple of packages of good old-fashioned firecrackers.

"Did it ever occur to you what might have happened to this family if we had gotten caught smuggling explosives into the country?"

No, I didn't think about it, because had the car been searched, it would have been obvious to whom the "explosives" belonged.

But I kept my thoughts to myself because the old man was really getting hot.

"Just because I didn't know they were there would have done me precisely no good. I am legally responsible for your actions, young man."

And so on and so forth — and for quite some time. Even though Grandpa found the wallet in the back seat, Dad remained on his soapbox.

He asked me what "uses" I had planned for this "ordinance." I spun him a tale about blowing up balsa wood airplanes — something that sounded much less sinister then than it would today. Still, he didn't believe me and badgered me for my real agenda. I dummied up.

The truth would have made things so much worse: the firecrackers were for demolishing mailboxes or to throw at dogs and Canadian geese. They were tools to terrorize my sisters and ideal for rolling down the sidewalk behind old ladies. The TV host Jack Paar lived in Bronxville, and making his life a living hell constituted a full-time hobby for some kids. Now I could join the fun. What use did I have for such ordinance, indeed!

Dad couldn't employ his belt in the home of my grandmother. I think he knew he would have lost his mother-in-law's adoration if she knew he beat his kids.

When we returned to Bronxville, my lockdown resumed. Dad revoked my newly restored allowance, grounded me, and assigned work details — just in time for the beginning of the school year. Although I deserved the punishment, it made me furious, and it certainly didn't give me the intended lesson. Like a failed entrepreneur who yearns for another chance, I examined my smuggling technique for flaws.

My next opportunity didn't come for nine years. My mother wrote me at my Illinois college, asking if I'd like to join the family in Arizona during spring break. I had a girlfriend I wanted to impress. I persuaded my parents to fly both of us in for seven days of poolside R&R.

At first it seemed as if fun might hold our family in its golden grasp. The sun reflected from glossy green leaves of lemon trees by the swimming pool. Everyone was splashing and laughing, and even the flashing water seemed to revel in our celebration of spring.

We were one family, lovingly assembled. That was the idea, and as we settled into that morning, the feeling seemed to hold. Perhaps it was the smell of the desert or the sumptuous ambience of my grandparents' hacienda, but whatever it was, an absence of acrimony prevailed, as did a sense that during this brief week, all the things that had happened in Bronxville were off the table.

My maternal grandmother loved being a hostess. She had lived in Bronxville in the 1930s, but after the war she divorced my grandfather so she could spend more time with her lover, a Puerto Rican mystery man that none of us ever met. Apparently her choices brought some degree of community castigation, so in the early 50sshe moved to Arizona. Eventually, she married Lloyd Ritter, a West Virginia coal and lumber trust fund beneficiary and ardent proponent of takin' it easy.

A few days after our arrival, we once again piled into granddaddy's Lincoln and headed to the border. And again, we did the ceremonial Mexican kitsch parade. As before, I had my own shopping list. I planned to buy a hundred *dexedrinos* at a side-street pharmacy.

Dad pulled me aside before I headed out.

"Bill," he said. "It's okay if you buy some firecrackers."

"Gosh, that'd be great, Dad. Thanks!"

I completed the drug purchase, gobbled a few before

crossing the border, and talked like a jabberwocky until we got back to Tucson. No one suspected a thing, except, perhaps, that I was even more full of myself than usual.

That was the trip's high point. The downside came quickly enough.

The next morning, Mom and my grandmother sat poolside, chittering like sparrows. My younger sisters and girlfriend were in the shallow end, mixing like fingerlings. Mary Jo, Dad, and I were in the middle of the pool, engaging in a playful splash fight.

Playful, until it got too aggressive.

Dad had sent a one-two double splash my way that sprinted up my nose. I choked, and my sinuses burned. I got mad and responded with a two-handed staccato burst that got faster as I closed in on Dad. He grabbed my crotch and squeezed. After I finished bellowing, I looked at him, wondering if perhaps there had been some mistake.

His eyes were bright, his nostrils flared, and his smile was gleefully sadistic. After holding my gaze long enough to make his point, he swam in a leisurely manner to the ladder at the deep end, hauled himself out, and set about making a Bloody Mary.

My mother and grandmother stopped their chatter and wanted to know what happened. My sisters and girlfriend flocked around and asked me what was wrong.

I waited for the pain to subside and then assured everyone I was fine; an accident happened while Dad and I were engaged in horseplay.

Later, I told my sisters and girlfriend what really occurred but didn't admit that my *dexedrinos* hangover might have caused me to get angry. I also didn't consider for a moment telling Mom or my grandmother. They thought Dad hung the moon. For them, his brilliance couldn't be challenged.

In the days following the incident, I puzzled endlessly about "the grab," because even if I'd asked for it, I thought squeezing my balls a rather unusual form of retaliation against one's son. I suspected Dad walked the jagged line between eccentric behavior and lunacy. He always pontificated about obeying the rules and moral behavior. Had he just snapped?

There were a few obvious answers — it was reprisal for my insolence. It was the ultimate rejection. It was the act of a man who wanted to reestablish the pecking order.

CHAPTER 18: THUMB MASTER

At twelve, I thought of my father as a mean son-of-a-bitch, and as I began to go through puberty, I devoted myself to rebellion and misbehavior.

Even though my firecracker punishment severely curtailed my opportunities for mischief, my anger had increased, and so had my desire to create havoc. I still had about forty-five minutes between the last bell and when I had to be home. I hoped Tommy C. would join me in substantially escalating our guerrilla warfare campaign.

The moment I saw his red hair bobbing in the crowd of students coming down the hallway, I took him aside. Even before I spoke, I could tell there was something different about him. A yellow mechanical pencil spoke loudly from the pocket of his neatly pressed plaid shirt. He'd combed his hair and shined his shoes. A different Tommy altogether.

Still, I didn't let appearances stop me. I put it to him straight away.

"You wanna start a few leaf fires after school?"

The prior year, this had been a regular feature of our extra-scholastic activity.

He hesitated a moment before he spoke. He had a small smile, as if about to tell his lunatic grandfather it would be better if he didn't drive.

"Bill, I'm not going to do that kind of stuff anymore," he said.

"What do you mean?"

"I just think it would be a better idea if I tried not to get in trouble."

"We never got in trouble. I mean, I got in trouble, but you never did."

"But I could have. I'll see you around."

And off he walked down the hall.

I felt like a tent had collapsed on me. My best buddy had blown me off. Now I had no one in the entire school I could call more than an acquaintance.

As I mulled over the stuff we'd done together, I could see I acted more as his fool than his friend.

During the weeks that followed, I surveyed my peers, searching for someone else with whom I could be friends. I had been rejected by the "in" crowd. Something was obviously wrong with me intellectually, I couldn't play any sport that involved a ball, and I was quite bristly about my inadequacies in the aforementioned endeavors.

I realized another rather unorganized cohort had escaped my attention. As a typical Bronxville classist snob, I ignored the blue-collar children, the children of the bank tellers and the barmen. I started paying more attention to them.

Kelly J., the ape boy who lived in half a house near the railroad tracks, inhabited those ranks. I always thought of him as a gonzo-fantastical sort. He had a Brylcreem hairdo, widely separated teeth, and laughed like a demented cartoon character.

We got to know each other as fellow Yankee fans. In those years, liking the Yanks became very unfashionable. They won too much! Most kids either rooted for one of the city's two other teams or for a club from some other city.

After a few weeks of small talk, Kelly invited me over to his house after school. I naturally expected his mother to be there, but Kelly said she'd be at work until 6:00 p.m.

Where Kelly lived made my head whiz. Not quite like Summit Avenue. His half of a large ramshackle clapboard house sat within fifty feet of the railroad tracks. The potholed gravel and mud parking lot in front prepared you for the smell of bacon grease as you entered the home through the kitchen. Floorboards showed through in places the linoleum had worn out. Dead flies lay legs-up on the windowsills. Brown spots splotched through the ceilings. My first visit to anything less than a superbly maintained residence made me very uncomfortable, but somehow I kept my mouth shut.

Kelly showed me into the living room. The windows seemed to have a gray tint, so I ran my finger down one of them and left a smudge. I furtively wiped my finger on my pant leg.

I looked around the room. In one corner sat an easy chair with an overflowing ashtray on one side and an immense, haphazardly stacked pile of *Look*s and *Life*s and *Glamour*s on the other. A yellow couch with plastic cushions covered one wall, a bookshelf cluttered with makeup, hair curlers, a kewpie doll with a broken hip, a crumpled package of cigarettes, and a collection of teaspoons next to it. An oversized tabby cat slept on the bluish shag carpet.

Kelly pointed to the couch and told me to have a seat. He departed but soon came back with two copies of *Playboy*. I had seen the magazine once or twice, yet it unsettled me that he possessed such scandalous material. What he proposed to do with it surprised me even more.

"You beat off much?"

"Uh, sure, lots."

"Okay, you take whichever mag you want. You do it out here, and I'll hit it in my room. Don't worry, I'll yell before I come back in."

My face hot, I grabbed one of the magazines.

"Don't you even want to check out the centerfold before you make up your mind?"

He grabbed a copy and let it unfold open to the Playmate of the Month.

"How about that, huh?"

"Ummmmm."

"You gonna take a look at the other one?"

I opened the other *Playboy* and looked at the woman displayed on the glossy paper. I made a show of comparing the two ladies, trying to bluff my way through chagrin, which quickly became sensory overload. I couldn't make a choice.

"Okay," Kelly said, "you take Miss July. She's got bigger tits, and that's what counts, right?"

"Uh, right."

"See you in a few."

I had a basic understanding of what Kelly asked me to do — at least in a theoretical sense. The facts of life biology class taken by all seventh graders covered masturbation. I had not actually tried it, however.

I focused my eyes on the woman's breasts and tried to feel sexy. I almost imagined getting somewhere when the tabby cat jumped on the couch and with a salacious purr began courting my affection.

I zipped up my pants and began to read the article on hip comedians. A short time later Kelly yelled, "You about done?"

"Yep. Come on in."

Kelly galloped back into the room.

"Pretty cool, huh?"

"Boy, I guess."

I walked home thinking Kelly was the most outlandish thing since Godzilla, but at least I had a friend, and as long as he didn't figure out the depth of my immaturity, things would probably go okay.

In the next few months, I picked up a couple more friends like Kelly. The son of the janitor at the Catholic Church, Jim G. The ward of a wealthy doctor, Karl K, should have been with the "in" crowd, but like me, he had an abrasive personality, and to make matters worse, everyone knew he was *adopted.*

One Wednesday afternoon that spring, Karl made it known he'd filched a bottle of vodka from his dad. He invited us — no, he *dared* us — to have a drinking party after school that day.

We went to a little park on a path leading from Garden Terrace to Sagamore Road. Although we would have been in the worst possible trouble had an adult happened by, we were well hidden by various flowering bushes, and the whoosh of nearby traffic muted our laughter.

Karl looked like he came from some border-state backwoods. He had washed-out blue eyes, thin, unhealthy blond hair, a small, pinched nose, and eyes too close together.

Today, however, a full fifth of vodka made him king, and he announced that to drink, we had to participate in an ancient ritual.

"In the old days," he asserted, "the pirates used to play a game called Thumb Master."

He explained that when he put his thumb down on the rock around which we all sat, the rest of us had to put our thumb on top of his. The last person to get his thumb on the pile had to drink.

My first swig of hard liquor will remain with me always. After the initial gasp and the burning sensation subsided, I felt like a withered plant infusing much-needed moisture. It enlivened my brain and filled every capillary with warmth and confidence. Earlier that year, during a long period of confinement to my room, I had vowed that if I ever got my freedom, I was going to have a good time all the time. In the park that day, I understood how my vow would be fulfilled.

Because of my slow reflexes, my thumb ended on the top of the pile most of the time, and I therefore drank a disproportionate amount of the vodka. But I had a great time. I never felt more self-assured or accepted. We all laughed and laughed. We polished off the bottle. I got really messed up.

I managed to stumble home, and when I arrived, I paused for a moment and did everything I could to appear lucid. I walked through the front door and hesitated on the landing on the way upstairs. To my left, about fifteen feet away, my mother stood in the kitchen. She got off the phone and lit an L&M.

"Mom, I don't feel too good. I'm going to bed. I don't want any dinner."

"Okay, dear. Goodnight."

She didn't approach me to hold her hand on my head to see if I had a fever. She didn't check for swollen lymph glands.

She may have been a little blasted herself. She drank Gallo dry sherry every afternoon and probably had several glasses under her belt when I arrived home.

That afternoon, she and I crossed a gradient, passing in opposite directions. For the first time, I used alcohol successfully to reduce the trauma of dealing with her, just as she had used it for years to deal with me, her husband, and the rest of our nutty family.

Today, I know exactly what she thought when I said I wanted to go to bed. "Great! One down, four to go!"

The night of my first drunk, I slept from 6:00 p.m. until 7:00 a.m. I recall feeling fairly good when I got up. I hadn't gotten sick to my stomach; in fact, I couldn't wait until I could do it again.

So it was with me and alcohol. I thought if I didn't drink Scotch, I wouldn't be like Dad, yet he and I did share one attribute: from the very start, I found I could consume considerable amounts without appearing intoxicated. I often got caught in situations that cried out for sobriety — like being stopped by the police or dictating a story to the city desk of my newspaper — and came out of the situation none the worse, even though I should have been thrown in jail or fired.

Although proud of this gift while still a young man, eventually it proved a bane, for it allowed me to drink well beyond the time I should have stopped. In my carousing years following college, I worried only occasionally about my drinking despite getting drunk frequently. Instead of focusing on the damage alcohol did to me, my family, and my career, I concentrated on ways I didn't act like my dad.

Almost all budding alcoholics search for reasons they shouldn't be classified as drunks. This is known as "denial." I denied being a drunk like my dad because I believed I had a fundamentally different way of looking at the world. Dad wanted to preserve all things patriarchal, white, male and Anglo-Saxon. I wanted to throw it all up in the air. Most important: I rejected racism while he embraced it.

CHAPTER 19: N***ER LIPS

My father knew few if any African-Americans before he joined the US Army. During the stateside portion of his service career, he drew the assignment of training African-Americans drafted into the Army from the rural South. As I grew up, he frequently recalled his months trying to instill military discipline into these men, recruits who had little or no education and a craw full of Jim Crow.

"Those people were animals," he said not once but at least a dozen times. "They had lice, they kept razor blades in their shoes, they couldn't even sign their own names!"

When he got to England, he found black soldiers with a newly inaugurated sense of self, and he clearly didn't like it.

I still believe the Negro race must be given greater equality of opportunity or else the whole country is going to be in an uproar, one letter said. *But I am definitely more prejudiced against them now than at any time before. In England, where they were given complete freedom socially, they did their best to push white men out of public places and in many cases succeeded. They had dates with white women and appeared publicly with them. To me, that was sickening. Of course, I realize this is an entirely subjective reaction, but it is there nevertheless. There is more than one half-caste baby in England now, to put it mildly. My experience with the Negro was that he becomes tremendously arrogant and overbearing when suddenly given a dose of freedom.*

I don't remember Dad ever mentioning ill-mannered Blacks in England, but his observations about African-Americans while I was growing up certainly were anything but positive.

Once, during the 1964 Harlem riots, Dad told me, "If you ever bring a n****r around this house, I'll throw him down the front steps."

He also said he wanted to drop an "A-bomb" on Harlem. I thought that since our house was about twelve miles from Harlem, his solution might involve a bit of blowback.

It made him uncomfortable that Black people lived less than three hundred yards from our house. Although red-lined out of Bronxville, thousands of African-Americans lived in the Village of Tuckahoe, just down the hill. For the most part, Blacks who didn't have business in Bronxville stayed away, but my father would frequently remind us we needed to be vigilant. Someday they would "rise up" from their squalor "down in the hollow" and come and get us.

Although I found it hard to believe the Blacks in Tuckahoe would "rise up," I became infected by his fear and therefore his anger. That made the thorny characters populating my life — bullies like J.P. — hard to finesse.

It wasn't long before I had another run-in with my tormentor, and what happened put me in the underclass of my WASP ghetto until I finally found my way out two years later.

We changed clothes for gym class in the boys' locker room. Painted bile green, it smelled of urine and chlorine. Pieces of stray clothing — a gym sock, a jock strap, or somebody's brown-striped underpants — littered the floor. Four large, opaque glass windows usually provided natural light, but as I arrived that gray January day, the only illumination came from a few bulbs hanging from the ceiling. Shadows masked the boys sitting on the benches, which was probably why I made the mistake of sitting down next to J.P.

His eyes blazed malevolence.

"Well, if it's not little Billy McBean."

"Knock it off, J.P."

"Or what?"

"Just don't."

"Okay, I won't do the stuff I usually do, how would that be?"

"Just great."

"Instead, I'm gonna tell you about your new nickname."

His atavistic buddies gurgled with mirth. One of them, the morbidly obese Johnny D., belched.

"We were just noticing how unusual your lips are for a white guy. They're big and fat — like a n****r's. So, from now on, you're N****r Lips. Isn't that cool?"

"You are just too funny."

"I know. But don't worry, I won't use your new name in school. While we're here, I'll just call you 'Lips.' Would that be okay?"

"You are such an idiot."

J.P. grabbed my wrist and began to bend my fingers back. I screamed like a poked pig, which delighted him. As a crowd of my amused peers gathered, J.P. kept the pressure on.

"What did you say?"

"I said you're wonderful ahahahah..."

"That's better. Do you like your new name?"

"No, I owowowow..."

"Say, 'My name is N****r Lips'."

I said it as quietly as I could, which prompted J.P. to increase the pressure. I yelled it out. The gathered crowd, about a dozen guys by now, shrieked with glee.

I thought J.P. would let me go if I cooperated with his effort to humiliate me, but he was just getting started.

"Johnny, do me a favor and fetch those underpants over there, will ya?"

"Oh, gross, man, why me?"

"Don't be a wimp. Just pick 'em up with your pen."

While Johnny carried out his task, J.P. said, "Mr. Lips, I don't want you to think I'm entirely mean. I noticed those underpants over there, and I was afraid they were yours. Didn't you tell me the other day that your parents fined you for each and every thing you lost?"

"Those are *not* mine."

"Well, just to make sure, I want you to smell them."

The idea of getting the underpants crammed in my face gave me a new burst of energy, and I managed to wiggle out of his grasp.

J.P. was about to pounce on me when Coach Farris walked into the locker room.

"What's goin' on here?" he rasped.

"Nothin', Coach," J.P. said.

"Well, hurry up, get dressed, and get outta here."

Although I was delighted to escape J.P.'s wrath, I knew

I'd hear from him soon.

I saw him the next day, standing with his cronies in front of Bellis. I cringed, but he made no move in my direction. He simply curled his upper lip and said, "How's it going, *N****r Lips*?" And he wasn't alone. The sobriquet achieved fad status almost immediately. I must have heard my new handle at least two dozen times.

By the second week, the insult mutated.

Lips.

Lippy Lou.

Lipper.

Lippy Lou the Leper.

At the time, I'd never met a Black person, but I could see most people in Bronxville shared my father's animosity toward them. Yet the taunting seemed, for the most part, benign. Many of the kids teased without knowing how much it stung. They had just caught on to my new moniker and wanted to be in the swing of things. They called me "Lips" in the same spirit they called the Spanish teacher "Chico."

A few, however, went out of their way to taunt me — Larry R. being the most unbearable.

The quarterback on the freshman football team, Larry also sat on the top of the pile in matters scholastic. He wasn't the type of guy who went out of his way to pick on people — but he made an exception for me.

Noting this, I wondered why. It occurred to me that I might be doing something that gave rise to my negative social experience at Bronxville High School. My sarcasm knew no bounds, and I probably led students using the middle finger to express dissatisfaction. I groused about teachers nonstop, and

I never missed an opportunity to make fun of someone even less socially fortunate than I.

So it was with small, pudgy, humble Bob J. Bedecked with red hair and freckles, he looked a lot like Howdy Doody, the puppet star of the popular TV show. Thus, every time I saw Bob in a setting where mockery would be tolerated, I'd sing the show's theme song: "It's Howdy Doody time, it's Howdy Doody time…" I don't recall once thinking that this probably hurt Bob as much as N****r Lips hurt me.

Gradually, my nickname became just plain "Lips," something I should have learned to live with but somehow couldn't. I never told Dad about it; I felt sure he'd have no sympathy. I also thought telling him I had trouble adjusting to life in Nirvana would cause him to say my problems were petty compared to those visited on him in the European Theater of Operations.

Although Dad frequently used his war experience to belittle my teenage problems, not all of his difficulties arose from the battlefield. Some of his animosity cropped up as he pursued his dream of becoming a great lawyer. On at least one occasion, he vented his bile and something quite good came from it.

CHAPTER 20: THE SPIRIT OF ST. LOUIS

One evening, my father got home in time to see his children choking down one of his favorite meals — liver and onions with bacon. The setting sun flooded our dining room with a rosy glow as it passed through the small beveled panes of the west window. He slapped a mutilated copy of the *Trib* on the hall table and placed his fedora on top of it. His tired eyes wandered over his brood of five. He lobbed a Haut in our direction.

"And how are my children tonight?" he asked with feigned magnanimity.

Our antennae went up. We knew one of several things might be in the offing — a quiz on state capitals, a lesson in phonics, or, perhaps, an impromptu lecture on *Brown vs. the Board of Education*, complete with a treatise on why Earl Warren should be disbarred. After all, he wanted to demonstrate his willingness to be involved with the upbringing of his children.

I knew saying nothing and keeping my eyes on my uneaten liver was clearly my best option. But I just couldn't.

"Dad," I burst out. "There's this really neat movie about this guy Lindbergh. You know, he was the first to fly over the Atlantic. Could I go Saturday?"

He sat down at the head of the table and gave me an appraising look. Mom, a lit L&M protruding from her lips, put a Scotch and water by his right hand.

"So," Dad said, using his mocking, cross-examination tone. "Who told you about Lindbergh?"

Thinking myself to be on very solid ground, I described the history lesson at school that day. I recalled the name of the plane, the airport from which Charles Lindbergh took off, and his triumphal greeting in Paris. This, I thought, was clearly a chance to impress my father.

As I finished, a sneer lifted the corner of his heavily whiskered lip. "Bill, you've been brainwashed."

"No, no, Dad, really, Mr. Porter told us all about it! And it's in our history book! Would you like me to show it to you?"

"I don't need to see it. I'm sure it's another example of academic certitude from some out-of-touch pinhead. I, unfortunately, don't need to read about Herr Lindbergh. Lately, I've gotten to see him every day."

"You see Lindbergh? Every day? Really? Gol, that's so cool! How come?"

"Because he's one of the firm's clients, and I've been given the task of dealing with his estate. It's a discredit to our democracy that the man isn't locked up!"

"Locked up? But he's a hero!"

"Balls! He's a Nazi sympathizer! He should be hung!"

Then, in a scoffing tone, he added, "He thought the German people were put under a terrible, terrible burden by the Treaty of Versailles and therefore shouldn't be held accountable for their actions during the war."

Dad paused, inspecting me like a bug he was about to squish.

"I assume you've covered Versailles in your studies?"

My parents in Vermont circa 1970 with his brother David's dog. Dad never went anywhere without a sports coat, while Mom favored a countrified look.

Bewildered, I stared at my plate. Many years later, looking at home movies of myself in similar situations, I got a pretty good idea of how I appeared to him. I couldn't meet his eye. My mouth hung open. I absent-mindedly reached down and scratched the mosquito bites on my legs.

"Christ!" he exploded. "Do they teach you little idiots anything!"

My mother, lighting another L&M from the butt of the last one, shot Father one of her terrible green-eyed looks.

"Peter!" she barked. She wasn't upset about Dad's tirade, but she didn't like it when he used the name of the Lord Our God in vain.

He paid no attention to her.

Instead, he launched into a screed on the First World

War, the Treaty of Versailles, the rise of German nationalism, how Lindbergh had tried to legitimize the Hitler government, and how Lindy had wanted us to join with the Germans to eradicate the USSR.

"Give the devil his due," Dad said. "Lindy had the right idea about wiping out Russia! Think where we'd be today if that damn Roosevelt had just listened to Churchill! We should have crushed the Reds while we were there and had the superior fighting force!"

Dad punctuated his point by thumping the dining room table with his fist, making cutlery jump. Mom brought him another highball.

"But I want *you* to know, Bill, that my dislike of Mr. Lindbergh isn't political. My loathing of him is entirely personal. I've had to sit with him in my office for much of the last several weeks, listening to him rant about the beauty of the German race. Bill, I've seen those people. I've dealt with them. I know what they're made of! They're arrogant and vile even in the face of total repudiation.

"I wish you could have seen your hero Lindy today. He acted like he was at Harvard, kicking off a highly endowed lecture series. He began talking about the superiority of German airplane design and then moved on to German philosophers, wines, literature, what have you. It was almost like he knew how I felt about the Reich and was amusing himself by rattling my chain. I fantasized killing him with my bare hands — but then I'd have no income, and you'd have no lovely liver and onions."

Cackle. Haut.

Dad sat back, but his hazel eyes never left mine. His face was an oval of red surrounded by coal black hair and an ominous five o'clock shadow. He was clearly warming to his subject. My sisters began to whimper. I could feel my neck and shoulders tensing up. My hands, in my lap, were clasped in a tight knot.

"I remember the day my outfit breached the German frontier..."

"Peter," my mother said from her smoky throne at the other end of the table. "I'll thank you not to get the children all riled up so close to their bedtime!"

Dad gave her a cold stare, and we worried he'd tell her to tend to the pots and pans. But he didn't. He reined in his fury. Taking his gaze away from her, he pulled out his pipe and fired it up. He then took a long pull from his icy beverage, got up, and without a word went up to his bedroom, leaving Mom with a cast-iron frying pan full of liver and onions.

The next morning, he was already eating his three-minute soft-boiled egg when I sat down at the breakfast table.

"Are you still enthralled with the idea of seeing *The Spirit of St. Louis*?"

Although I felt a surge of expectation, I carefully measured my answer. It sounded like he might be relenting, but you couldn't ever tell with Dad. He could be trying to find out if I still thought Lindbergh was okay despite what he told me. Maybe it was a loyalty test. Or he might let me go to the movie. I just couldn't tell.

"Sure, I guess," I said. "If you think it's okay."

"I was hoping we could go together, perhaps to the Saturday matinee?"

"Wow, that'd be cool!"

We were going to do something together! This almost never happened. Prior to this, we got haircuts together on Saturday mornings. Period.

Shortly after noon, Dad and I got into the wagon and drove to the movie theater. I felt like I had entered a parallel universe—the one I saw so often on TV in which dads and sons were buddies.

He dressed in his normal weekend regalia: a sports shirt, brown sports jacket, brown slacks, and his second-string wingtips. He needed the sports jacket to carry around his pipe paraphernalia. I dressed in an even more predictable outfit: oatmeal sweater over a button-down Oxford cloth shirt, chinos, and Bass Weejuns.

We arrived about twenty minutes early to make sure we got good seats. To my total astonishment, he bought me a Coke, popcorn, and a box of Milk Duds. It was my first contact with candy in weeks.

We settled into our seats. I could hear my friends who occupied the balcony. They emanated various farting and belching noises combined with catcalls and giggles. When I decided none of it was directed at me, I settled in, my mouth crammed full of candy and my heart content.

Dad began to talk about Lindbergh, but this time he didn't talk about the Nazi sympathizer—he talked about the hero.

"I was only seven years old when Lindy made his flight, but I still remember how excited everybody was. My dad told me it was among the greatest events in world history; he said it would change our civilization in ways no one could predict, and boy did he get that one right!

"For years afterward, he was the greatest of world celebrities. Then, five years after the flight across the Atlantic, someone snatched his kid. It was a leading story for most of the 1930s — it damn near eclipsed the Great Depression in terms of public interest."

I wanted to ask him about the child, but my mouth was so jammed up with Milk Duds, I couldn't make my tongue work. Yet Dad provided the information in his trademark savage, abrupt fashion.

"About two months after the kidnapping, they found the kid dead, right near the house. The investigation went on for three years before they caught the guy. He got fried in the electric chair."

Then Dad began to chuckle. "H.L. Mencken said it was 'the biggest story since the Resurrection.'"

I had no idea what he was talking about, and I didn't much care. The lights dimmed, and the cartoons came on: Donald Duck in all his furious glory followed by newsreels about Elvis being stormed by a mob of crazed teenage girls. I heard Dad rattling around with his pipe stuff, worried he was going to do something abrupt — but we were saved by the main feature. For almost three hours, all my troubles were softened by the story of Lucky Lindy, a guy with dreams that everyone — at first — dismissed. When the joyous crowd at Le Bourget Field hoisted him on their shoulders, the concept that anything was possible enthralled me.

As we drove home, I asked Dad if he had enjoyed the movie.

"Yes, I did. I think they took a few liberties with the facts, but overall, it was pretty good. It is, however, important that you remember one thing: Charles Lindbergh is no Jimmy Stewart."

He had already made this point many times over; I hadn't expected *The Spirit of St. Louis* to change my dad's opinion of Lindy. There was, however, something bugging me about our outing. Dad had never taken me to a movie before. In fact, Dad didn't go to movies, period. So why take me to a movie about a guy he hated?

So I asked, and he answered.

"Given the circumstances, how could I *not* go?"

Herr Lindbergh would want to know if Dad had seen the homage to his bravery.

Had I been a little older or of a more philosophical turn of mind, I might have reflected that I wasn't the only person making a rough going of life. It could have been an inspirational moment where I grasped my place in the universe and accepted my father as being stuck in the mud like me. But finding the road to popularity in Bronxville High School took up most of my time. My analytical ability was nonexistent, and Dad's lessons about the world were too complex. I wanted a bluebird on my shoulder, and when it wasn't there I blamed him.

The Lindy interlude soon crumbled around the edges, and within a couple of weeks the struggle between us was back on. Finally, the day came on which our conflict became intractable.

CHAPTER 21: THE DAY THE MUSIC DIED

On February 4, 1959, I was twelve. I looked through the mullioned window of our front door that grainy black-and-white night and saw Dad coming, trudging the final stairs up from the street. I waited. I wanted to be the first to say, "Hi."

At that moment, our rapport was wobbly but okay. Sure, he hated much of what I loved, but I felt oddly at peace with that. Dad was trudging through middle age with an out-of-skew mind, and even though I was just a dumb kid, I somehow understood that.

Or perhaps the emotions I felt weren't even that complicated. Maybe we hadn't fought for a while and I'd settled into the sentiment most boys have for their father: admiration bordering on hero-worship, a love for a guy who is all-powerful and could solve problems by casting a spell on them.

The moment he opened the door, I detected something different about him. As he removed his gray fedora, he seemed gleeful instead of his usual weary self. In fact, he seemed positively ecstatic — but at the same time sinister. His beard, like black iron filings, made him look like a gangster dressed up as a Wall Street lawyer. Locking his eyes on mine, he pulled the folded newspaper from under his arm. The headline said:

3 Rock-and-Roll Stars

Die in Iowa Plane Crash[30]

"Got three of 'em!" he said with enthusiastic belligerence. "Three of them in one blow! There is some hope!"

I grabbed the *Trib* out of his hands. The story was short, only nine paragraphs. It said Buddy Holly, Richie Valens, and the Big Bopper were all killed when their plane slammed into an Iowa cornfield during a snowstorm.

I don't remember what I said to him, but at that moment I knew for sure there was no hope for us. All the good feelings I had for him a few moments before, all the rationalizations for his iconoclastic behavior, evaporated.

My anger felt bottomless and as volatile as a mineshaft on the verge of explosion.

Yet I was also powerless.

Had I screamed at him, had I called him an insensitive pig, a ghoul and a sadist, it wouldn't have mattered a bit, for I know exactly what he would have said.

"William, the forces of nature have acted to cleanse our society of three punks who were making millions undermining the morals of kids too silly to know better. Their effort to bring this primitive jigaboo tripe into white society has got to stop. Now, to my delight, I find that God agrees with me."

Had I pursued the argument further, called him a racist and an idiot and a hatemonger, he would have acknowledged my point.

"Bill, you are right. I do hate rock and roll stars. But then again, I hate everybody."

All of this he would have said in a humorous tone — the same tone in which he related the tale of the unfortunate burgermeister. He loved the factious, which was why he had no problem saying he hated *everybody.*

At that moment I sincerely hated him.

That headline-in-my-face made me think of the time,

three years earlier, when he turned off Elvis right in the middle of "Hound Dog." Back then I thought of him as moody, but now I saw he didn't care whom he hurt.

Of course, Dad couldn't have seen into my psyche any more than I can understand why people like Insane Clown Posse. He couldn't have known that I sang Buddy Holly songs as I walked to school in the morning, or that "Oh Donna" was my first slow dance, or that "Chantilly Lace" represented the confidence I so yearned for.

Yet he had a deep-seated scorn for opinions other than his own. When I read the war letters, I stumbled across a passage that succinctly summed up his attitude. On February 18, 1945, he wrote Mom a letter trying to comfort her regarding difficulties she was having with her employer:

I'm afraid that life is a constant matter of adjusting to other people and working with them whether you like it or not. I find great solace in thinking privately, 'Aren't I smart and isn't he dumb?' It allows you to maintain your own self-respect and still get the job done.

He didn't apply the principle of silent egoism to his own family. He displayed his intellect and tried to bring us all up to his level.

Since I would not agree that rock 'n' roll was a communist-inspired plot, and because I continued to listen to it and play it in his household, he remained irritable toward me. The rock phenomenon showed American society "falling apart at the seams." He saw eerie parallels with ancient Rome just before the Visigoths poured over the battlements.

Rock seemed to have replaced Nazism on his hate list.

When Dad came through the door February 4, I hoped something familiar and warm would happen. I thought maybe he'd Haut, and then talk about politics or the Cold War or the inadequacies of the New York Central Railroad or someone he'd met at his office or something that happened on the subway. Dad often brought home a rich harvest of anecdotes, and even if he was too tired to be funny, he had the *Herald Tribune*, which, future newspaperman that I was, I'd snatch and read in my room in lieu of doing my homework.

Prior to that day, I viewed Dad as the successful, stern, all-knowing and highly competent, if overwhelmingly nasty, leader of the household. After that day I viewed myself as a prisoner and him as the screw. Now, there were no more rules — just like there are no rules in war. He set down regulations; I figured out ways to break them. I got caught, he meted out punishment, I inveigled ways around the punishment. A parent rules by moral authority, and he had lost his. We were done.

As I sat in my room that night, I didn't think about hurting Dad. I plotted to get away from him. I once again vowed to myself, "If I ever get out of here, I'm going to have a good time, every day, no matter what." I had no idea my adolescent vow meant that I was going to end up being as self-centered as my old man.

CHAPTER 22: THE ULTIMATE MEANNESS

To me, my father, the warm-hearted lad from Omaha, had clearly become an aficionado of inflicting pain. As I pored over the war letters, I wondered what turned him into a sadist.

The answer became clear as I read his correspondence following the Battle of the Bulge, when the Cannon Company and the rest of the 35th Division began to deal with Germans on their own ground.

March 10, 1945:

So far the German civilians we have encountered have been easy to handle. They are anxious to make friends and seem very bewildered when given the cold shoulder. Eisenhower's no-fraternization policy imposes heavy fines for being sociable with German civilians, but combat troops have no desire to be friendly with them.

In fact, most of us get a big kick out of booting them out of their homes and taking over for ourselves. I think it will do the German population a lot of good to experience being conquered for a change. Perhaps it will make them a little more cautious in supporting maniacs in their government. I certainly am doing all I can to disabuse them of the notion that they are the master race.

In fact, I am being just as mean as hell. My recon Sgt. and I accomplished the ultimate in meanness this morning. We took shelter in a basement from a German artillery barrage and found 12 German civilians there. On looking around we decided the basement would do very nicely as a company command post and fire direction. We promptly ran all 12 of them out including women and girls. I don't know whether any of them got hit, but it wouldn't bother me if they did. As far as I'm concerned they and some eight million like them started this and now it has come home to roost. You may have gathered by now that I don't like Germans.

The farther he got into Germany, the more he held the people as culpable as the soldiers. He became convinced of the merits of collective punishment.

April 19, 1945:

We have an example of German methods on the railroad tracks not far from here. A train carrying political prisoners of all nationalities was stalled and the Germans burned about 1,500 of them alive in locked cars and killed the rest with machine guns. The rest were hunted down and shot all over this section by kids and women. They are lying along the roads and in woods everywhere in their striped suits, most of them shot through the head.

Some 15 miles from here there is a pile of Poles numbering 350 who were all killed by machine gun fire at the approach of American troops. Many of these atrocities were not committed by the SS but by civilians. This business of making distinctions between these people and their leaders is so much rot. They are all made of the same stuff.

Other letters with similar language expressed hatred for German civilians. The more the Cannon Company suffered — and he had some incredibly close scrapes once inside Germany — the more indifferent he got to trying to preserve civilian lives.

The closer the army got to Berlin, the more appalling the carnage became. Finally, Dad's unit arrived at the ultimate German horror show, and perhaps the vilest American reaction to it.

April 22, 1945:

You have probably been reading a great many articles on the state of things in German concentration camps which have been overrun and you are probably wondering, as I used to wonder, just how true these reports are. My doubts are at an end. Yesterday I had the opportunity to view the remains of an as yet undetermined number of Polish and Russian political prisoners and prisoners of war. Now that I have seen the grim evidence of German brutality and bestiality with my own eyes I feel justified in saying that the newspaper reports understate the case if anything.

The place which I visited (Gardelegen) is not a concentration camp but a special slaughterhouse. It was a large stone barn with a corrugated roof and sliding doors. The Germans herded up to 400 prisoners at a time into this barn, closed the doors and burnt them alive with gasoline, phosphorous grenades and flares.

When I arrived, there were still some 350 charred corpses lying in the barn. A few in their agony had managed to squeeze out under the doors and the Germans had machine gunned these. I think that barn was the most horrible thing I've ever seen.

Behind the barn in a long trench were buried the remainder of the victims. Up to the time I arrived some 1,100 blackened corpses had been exhumed out of the one pit and as near as I could determine, there was still no bottom to the pit. All of the bodies, despite being badly charred, showed evidence of extreme starvation. The arms and legs were mere sticks. The smell of the place was beyond description — a combination of roasted flesh and decay.

The Army had every civilian in the nearby town at work digging out the corpses and reburying them in a separate place. Old men, young men and boys were all at work in that pit, digging out the burnt and rotting corpses with their hands and carrying them to their new place of burial. The officer in charge had Poles and Russians who had escaped from the same group as overseers, and were they doing a good job! Each one had a leather thong quirt and every time a Kraut stopped to rest he would get the quirt across the face or on the back. They also had a captured SS officer, one of those responsible for the massacre, working in the pit. We all derived tremendous satisfaction out of that.

CHAPTER 23: RAPE

On VE Day, May 8, 1945, spring was in the air, and so was rape.

The Russian Army ran Germany's streets virtually unchecked. The American Army operated under a nonfraternization policy, disallowing the troops to even talk to Germans, let alone bed German women. Yet rape happened, and many American authorities looked the other way.

The army transformed Dad's artillery company into an military police unit assigned to Hannover, Germany. They had the task of controlling the civilian population, which included native Germans, large numbers of men recently released from prison camps, and refugees of every stripe.

The city also served as headquarters for two brigades of Russian troops. The army ordered the MPs not to become embroiled with the Russians, my father said.

In Hannover, and all over Soviet-occupied Germany, women were being victimized by soldiers bent on revenge, conquest, and gratification. Russian journalist Natalya Gesse said the Soviet soldiers "raped every German female from eight to 80. It was an army of rapists."[31]

It has been estimated the Russians raped two million women during the invasion and in the months following the occupation of Germany.[32]

On May 14, 1945, my father wrote:

Occupation duty is proving to be something of a trial. These mad Russkies in our area are getting in our hair something awful.

In addition to robbing and looting German civilians, they have taken to fighting inter-camp wars among themselves. They raid each other in the dead of night looking for liquor and women and the vanquished lie dead along the streets and have to be picked up and carted away.

Last night I saw one of the better examples of their idea of sport. One Russian had dragged a girl up to his bedroom and when she refused to cooperate, he stripped all her clothes off and pitched her out of a third story window onto the pavement. I happened to be driving along the street about then inspecting guard posts and was on the spot when she came shrieking out into the street stark naked and dripping blood. She spotted me and my driver and made a bee line for us. I am not exaggerating a bit when I say the sight of her and the direction of her march scared me about as much as anything has since I have been over here. I didn't know whether to run or to stay and do my duty. My driver made up my mind for me. He slammed on the gas, dodged her and took out at top speed, thus saving me my reputation and earning my undying gratitude.

Something like that happens about every night in our area. We have ten camps (Lagers) in the area and about 5,000 wild Russians...Much of it (their misbehavior) is caused by liquor. They have looted vast stores of it and get wild drunk every night. They are causing us twice the trouble that the Germans are. The Germans sneak out every once in a while and cut our lines, but they don't cause any other trouble. It will be a happy day when we move out of this section. Our troubles may be in for some relief soon, however. This afternoon a Russian officer walked in...and announced that Uncle Joe had sent him to help us with them. We welcomed him with open arms...I hope his magic works... Nothing in my environment has prepared me for naked women who are streaming with blood.

Not all of the rapists in occupied Germany were Russian.

"There was a good deal of rape by (American) combat

troops and those immediately following them," wrote Australian journalist Osmar White, who served with American troops during the war. "The incidence varied between unit and unit according to the attitude of the commanding officer. In some cases offenders were identified, tried by court martial, and punished. The army legal branch was reticent, but admitted that for brutal or perverted sexual offenses against German women, some soldiers had been shot—particularly if they happened to be Negroes. Yet I know for a fact that many women were raped by white Americans. No action was taken against the culprits. In one sector a report went round that a certain very distinguished army commander made the wisecrack, 'Copulation without conversation does not constitute fraternization.'[33]

An examination of records at the National Archives in Collegeville, Maryland, makes it clear the 35th Division leadership, as well as the commanding officers of the 134th Infantry Division, worried about rape. When 35th Division troops began to occupy Germany in April of 1945, commanders summoned all company-level leaders to meetings that addressed fraternization and the subject of rape.

"There have been ten cases of rape reported in this area in the last 11/2 days," the April 4, 1945 minutes of the 134th Infantry Regiment Unit Journal reports. "Nine of them have been by colored soldiers but last night two white soldiers broke into an apartment and tried to molest the daughter of the woman of the house. She ran and hid in the attic... This type of thing must be stopped."

Leadership of the division appears to assume "colored soldiers" are more prone to such attacks than whites, because it was the last reference in the unit records to allege rapes by African American soldiers. In World War II, policy relegated most Black soldiers to rear echelon duties like kitchen work and trash collection.

The division issued frequent warnings forbidding talk to "Rhine Maidens." The leadership cited evidence that fraternization occurred even as the bullets flew.

"The VD percentage in the division is higher than it has been for a very long time," the minutes of a March 24th regimental meeting said. "It is strange to note that this increase came about while units were engaged in combat."

Obviously, soldiers had sex with women they found in towns they conquered. However, the brass said soldiers of the 35th were "cleared" of having raped anyone.

Although the army continued to enforce the policy as it pertained to Rhine Maidens, it gave the men permission to fraternize with "allied nationals" (the numerous women displaced by war who happened to be citizens of Poland, Yugoslavia, Russia, and many other countries) in early June.

In the early days of occupation, an accusing finger pointed at my father.

April 8, 1945:

Germany

Dear Mary Lou-

... Had an embarrassing experience yesterday. I had to line up the headquarters group for inspection by some Kraut gal who claimed she had been raped and wanted to make an identification. She passed down the ranks without making any identification and then stopped in front of me and looked me in the eye for a long moment. I thought sure she was going to accuse me, so I mustered all of my resources, stuck out my chin, put my hand on my pistol and

glared at her. She backed off.

When I turned around to dismiss the men there was a suspicious twitching on most faces. I'm afraid they would have liked nothing better than to have their platoon leader accused of rape. I glared at them, too, but I fear that had very little effect. I wish that I could speak German. Methinks I would have told that girl if I were to add rape to the list of my accomplishments I would sure as hell pick something better than her. I was denied that satisfaction, however, by my perennial linguistic ineptitude.

Nothing more for now, my darling. Take care of yourself and have the Martini makings ready, should I drop in to pay a call sometime this year. 'Night, baby.

Much Love,

Pete

P.S. I didn't rape her, honest.

This letter might be the most curious of any sent during his eighteen months in Europe. Was he so angry with Germans in general that he decided to take it out on a single German woman? In 1945, "denial by insult" still had a lot of efficacy, and almost anyone accused of rape might have used such a defense. But why would an accused soldier pass the allegation on to his wife?

While Dad was in Germany, everything good about him seemed to go out the window. When he got home, many of the good things returned. He was an excellent provider for his family. I gather his clients thought he offered quality service for the money they spent — at least until his drinking got too bad. My mother told me she believed he was always honest with her.

He came out of World War II with his ideals pulverized, and that made him angry — ferociously angry. He couldn't talk about it with anyone, because no one understood what he'd been through, even my mother.

Vets I've interviewed weren't in the least surprised. One said, "Anyone who hasn't been through the experience of war can't have the slightest understanding of what it does to a person. It turns you into an animal. Everything good goes out the window. That's just how it is."

Rapist or not, I'm certain the war involved him in things he didn't like thinking about — things of which I know nothing and never shall, decisions he made or didn't make. Shells that killed American troops, shells that could have saved somebody's son. Women and children he killed. People he left behind.

Sins. Sins I can't even imagine. Sins that weren't sins at all. Sins that could never be called anything else.

CHAPTER 24: THE LECHEROUS TOAD

I spent much of my adult life measuring my sins against my father's. Like: I quit drinking and he didn't. Or: I made a stand against the Vietnam War, but he bragged about his accomplishments as a warrior. Or: I chose the newspaper business to help society, where he chose to be a wills and estates lawyer to help the rich.

Now I think about how judgmental I was and I shudder, because I'm sure my actions would have mirrored his under similar circumstances.

One of the things I enjoyed feeling smug about was what he may have done to become a partner.

Most men with my father's education and background became a partner at his law firm in roughly seven years, which meant Dad should have gotten the nod in 1954. Yet as the years went by, the firm passed him over again and again. It caused him and my mother great anxiety.

One evening in 1959 or 1960, Dad got home in a sour mood. As usual, he plopped his newspaper and hat down on the hall table and sat down in his captain's chair at the head of the dining room table. He often opened our dialog with some odd pronouncement, but this evening's declaration was particularly curious.

"Children, your father works for a fat, vile, ugly, lecherous toad," he said in a loud, emphatic voice.

"Peter!" my mother said from her end of the dining room table. "That isn't appropriate dinner table conversation."

Dad Hauted at her and then began bantering using his comic voice, which involved opening up a hollow at the back of his throat and speaking through jowly lips with a slight lisp.

"Well, dear, it's the only time I ever see them, and I think they should know the sacrifices their father makes to ensure their welfare."

"Well, I don't, and I forbid you to discuss this matter any further!"

There was an edge to my mother's voice that she very seldom employed with Dad, at least in front of us. Most of the time, if she showed peevishness, he ignored her. The fact that he chose silence on this occasion whetted my curiosity. For one thing, I didn't know what lecherous meant. When I looked it up, I became even more inquisitive.

For years I tried to figure out what the problem was but couldn't ever determine exactly what my father had done to so aggravate his boss, who was an expert on estates and trusts and had established the Trust Department at the J.P. Morgan Co. He, my father, and other lawyers at Davis Polk worked with corporate executives to minimize the tax bite taken out of their estates when they died.

Dad worked with some extremely high net-worth individuals, not the least of whom was W. Averell Harriman, former governor of New York, chairman of the Union Pacific Railroad, and US ambassador to Russia. My father and many others who'd done business with Harriman called him "the crocodile" because of his penchant for taking a large bite out of the hide of people who annoyed him.[34] Harriman apparently liked my dad enough to assign him a considerable amount of the railroad's legal work, so it probably wasn't incompetence that held Dad back.

My suspicions always returned me to the word "lecherous." He seemed inordinately interested in improper sex. His war letters were full of claims that he didn't approve of sexual debauchery, and my personal experiences with him were scored by warnings against becoming sexually involved with women before marriage.

During research for this book, I questioned various relatives about the reasons for the long delay in Dad's elevation to partnership. My Aunt Althea, often present during those August summer vacations in Vermont, said Dad told her that his boss wanted my father to comply with his sexual demands. Dad had told her his boss said he had "a lovely mouth."

His boss had the power to blackball my father's applications for partnership. No explanation was ever required or offered.

Mom said he considered getting a job with another New York law firm but worried potential employers would think he "couldn't cut it" with Davis Polk. He and Mom also considered moving to Chicago but didn't because, according to them, success in Chicago wasn't anything like success in New York. Dad thought his father, who finished his career as associate general counsel at AT&T, would be disappointed with him if he didn't make it with a big-time NYC firm.

In the spring of 1961, he told us he was planning a fishing trip to Oregon with his boss. A few months later, he was made partner.

Whether Dad's partnership hinged on his capitulation is entirely speculative, though after his death Mom said she thought the stories about his boss were true.

Wall Street law firms traditionally test the mettle of associates, and it's possible Dad came up short for reasons relating to his wartime trauma. Obviously, almost all of the information about what happened at Davis Polk came from Dad.

Dad's promotion to partnership gave the entire family a tremendous sense of relief. It came with obvious economic benefits. My parents built a second home near my grandparents' house in Vermont, and my sisters were taken on trips to Scotland and on spring junkets to the Caribbean. Dad eventually got his new office, a monstrous room on the 44th floor of the Chase Manhattan Building with a view of lower New York Harbor. I visited once and remembered thinking he had become a "Master of the Universe," to use Tom Wolfe's phrase.

Yet he died a dozen years later at fifty-five. The multimillion-dollar financial legacy that everyone expected would accrue from his promotion never materialized. Dad maintained life insurance policies, so Mom wanted for little. Still, he didn't fully benefit from the immense satisfaction and influence one supposedly received from a Davis Polk partnership.

I believe status motivated Dad more than the millions he might have made. After all, Davis Polk and predecessor firms were home to President Grover Cleveland, John W. Davis, the Democratic candidate for president in 1924, and Lawrence Walsh, the independent counsel in the Iran-Contra scandal.

Although my father certainly never attained national notoriety, that didn't mean he lacked ambition for his only son. Dad finally attained a partnership in Davis Polk, and according to all that was holy, I would attain much greater heights—perhaps become the next Averell Harriman.

The improbability of this became apparent early on in my academic career. My second-grade teacher, Barbara Bowman, told my parents I was behind the curve in my early learning efforts. She said if they wanted to turn things around, they shouldn't put pressure on me. I'm sure Dad thought Ms.

Bowman's advice to be prattle, for the pressure continued. He sincerely believed one had to badger people to get results.

CHAPTER 25: BETRAYAL

As I absorbed my father's battlefield trauma, my behavior morphed from that of a childish miscreant to something more closely resembling that of the Hitlerjugend (Hitler Youth).

I entered my sophomore year at Bronxville High School high centered on futility. My internal dialogue felt like a phonograph needle skidding across a record. My fraternity of friends resembled the weed patch of our green little village, the crabgrass and thistle that grew along the river and down by the tracks.

Me and my buddies were guys who had nothing more in common than no one else wanted us. What little time I had after the final bell at school I spent with them, talking tough: what a punk that kid was, what a wimp was another, how our favorite upperclassman hero had beat up some out-of-town kid at a football game, how this girl "gave out" to anybody (except us, of course), and what plans we had for the additional persecution of poor Jack Paar.

A couple of the guys had a band, and they'd talk about getting the Bo Diddley beat right. One of the fellas had a daddy who bought him expensive toys, so we'd chat about that.

Much of the time, however, we'd moan about the injustice of life, and nobody had a more woeful lament than me.

"Dad's grounded me indefinitely," I said one day as we sat in the park off Garden Terrace, where we shared a box of Malt Balls. It was early October of 1961, and it had been a dry year. The leaves lacked any real color and blew off the trees in fragments, nicking our faces as they flew by under a gray, indifferent sky.

"Jesus, why?" someone asked.

The real reason: my chronic academic ineptitude.

But instead of telling them what happened, I said Dad grounded me because of bad grades from the previous year.

"Wow, that's a bitch," one of my buddies said.

"Yeah, it's like I get home, I go straight to my room. No TV. I get to come out for meals and when I'm working for Dad, that's it. On weekends, I do homework or work for my parents. I haven't been allowed to go to a single football game."

One of the guys, with a reedy, insinuating chuckle, said, "That Karen isn't gonna walk around forever looking at you. I saw big Allen A. giving her the once-over the other day when she was walking down the hall. Can't you see him and Karen in that convertible of his? There's enough room in the back of that sucker for a queen bed and end tables."

Guffaws, and my ears burning bright red. If Allen, the star halfback on the football team, decided to date Karen, I'd have no shot.

"We should do something about your dad, Lipper? We should teach him a lesson," one of them said.

I'd never told my friends anything about cheating on my report card, only about how happy Buddy Holly's death made Dad. I told them about all the hats and gloves and books and retainers I had to pay for, but never a word did I tell about how much money I stole from my parents.

Now, I had a choice to make: credibility with my friends or loyalty to my family.

When my friends suggested I do something to Dad, it sounded right, even if it felt wrong. I'd talked such a good game over so many months and so successfully withheld the other side, why wouldn't I want some kind of very open revenge? They all understood that I was too afraid of him to do anything myself, but if something could be arranged to bring him down, why wouldn't I sign off? What possible reservation could I have?

I thought of some of the viler tricks we played on people in recent years, trying to focus on the one perfect escapade to rob Dad of his dignity. I weighed the old saw of lighting a paper bag filled with feces at the front door so he could stomp it out, but I didn't want to live with the smell he'd grind into the carpet when he came back inside. I thought of putting sand in the gas tank of the car he wouldn't let me drive, but that wouldn't make him look foolish and would simply confirm his most paranoid conclusions about society at large.

Then I thought of the fun we had throwing eggs at cars on the Cross County Parkway the previous summer. We'd lob them underhand so they'd land on the windshield, causing the driver to turn on his windshield wipers and thus create a godawful mess. They were going much too fast to slow down and come after us on the limited-access highway, and it was fun to see their cars swerve and shudder in helpless rage. I'd like to see Dad that way.

"Why don't you guys egg him for me?" I said. "Just show up around seven thirty and ring the doorbell. The old man will come out. Don't worry. He's the curious kind. Then you can let him have it from the street and be gone before the cops get there."

"You're paying for the eggs, right? Four cartons?"

"No problem. When do you want to do it?"

"How about tomorrow night?"

I found myself agreeing with surprisingly few reservations. My anger with my father pounding in my temples and my need to be accepted by him always competed with getting the endorsement of my peers. Being pressured by the lowest rung of Bronxville society had little meaning at that point; they were the only friends I had, and my credibility was at stake.

If I faced accusations of having some connection with the miscreants, I'd just deny, deny, deny.

◆ ◆ ◆

I fixed my eyes on the red clock on the kitchen wall. Ten minutes to go. I made myself look away, but I could still hear the clock humming the overture of looming disaster.

I knew damn well I had concocted a plot likely to estrange me from my parents forever, but I didn't have the guts to call it off.

I hung around in the kitchen listening to my parents talk, something I never did. A voice inside told me to go upstairs and hide under my bed until it was all over, but an equally strong proctor urged me to stay there in the hope I might, at the last moment, spare Dad the coming indignity.

My father, too numbed by drink to notice anything amiss, seemed oblivious, but Mom cocked her head at me.

"Is there something we can do for you, young man?"

"Uh, no."

"Then shouldn't you be doing your homework?"

"Aren't we about to have dinner?"

"Not for another fifteen minutes, and until then, I'd like to talk to your father if you don't mind."

She looked at me through a pall of smoke, her eyes raisins among freckles.

Then the doorbell rang. Dad sat at the kitchen table, drinking Scotch, his shaved-and-powdered early morning face grown black with stubble, his hazel eyes recessed in their mournful sockets.

Although home a half hour, his business attire remained fully in place: dark striped tie knotted to a heavily starched white shirt and fixed to his collar by a silver pin, dark blue three-piece suit with a hint of pinstripe, black silk stockings held up by garters, and highly polished black wingtips.

"Humph!" he said, cocking a furry black eyebrow. "I wonder who that could be?"

He got up to answer the door, and I saw my chance, but I didn't take it. I could have said, "Dad, don't!" But I froze, caught between malice and fear.

He peered through the front door window, and seeing no one waiting in the twilight, he walked out on the front steps and got hit by a fusillade of eggs.

The four boys, standing in the street fifty feet below him, each had a carton of eggs — forty-eight eggs in all.

The assassins threw until the boxes were empty and then split up, running in different directions. They left the cartons on the street.

He raged back into the kitchen. His eyes radiated the feral gleam of an animal in mortal combat. Eggshell clung to his shining forehead, sticky albumen oozed through his wiry black hair, and yolk tattooed vile graffiti on his white shirt.

Mom stood by the stove, her hands clasped to her flowered cotton dress. Her green eyes, brilliant with shock, darted from Dad to me and back to Dad.

A shout jolted her into action.

"Mary Lou, call the goddamned cops!" he said.

As he wiped the egg off his face with a kitchen towel, he said nothing, but he glowered at me, a just-discovered traitor.

A few minutes later, the doorbell rang again. Dad went outside and briefly spoke with the cops. Then he came back and said, "William, come with me."

As we walked down the front steps to the street, his hand grasped my elbow tightly. Two cops waited, one with a nightstick. As I thought of what they might do to me, my insides shriveled. Dread welled up behind my eyes.

The sun had just set, but the spotlight from the police car shone brightly on an ivy-covered retaining wall in front of our house. The cop who did the questioning was a stocky, squat sergeant. He got within an inch or two of my face. His black eyes snarled at me.

"You better tell the truth, kid, or I'm gonna take youse to reform school right now."

When he spoke, I smelled a putrid combination of garlic and cigarettes. I jerked my head back in disgust, and he smiled.

The glib lies I imagined myself telling wouldn't come. I looked over at Dad, and I could see he didn't give a shit what happened. He was going to give me to these guys.

I think I protested my innocence for a few minutes, but it might not have been that long. In the end, I ratted out my friends.

When the cops left, Dad grabbed me by the neck and slammed me against the retaining wall. As his hands cut off my air, I thrashed with panic. I could smell the raw egg.

"You're either for me or you're against me," he said, spittle flying in my face, "and you, my little man, have just made your choice."

◆ ◆ ◆

The next morning, Dad left for work without a word. He wouldn't even look at me. As I waited for him to get home, I lay at the foot of my bed, gazing out the window toward Avon Road, looking through the wispy, dry leaves for Dad's bus. I knew it would be several hours before it arrived. I had plenty of time to think what might be in store for me, but given the heinous nature of the offense, I had no inkling.

Dad had clearly lost his dignity and with it his inhibitions. That worried me. In the past, his ambitions and his need to keep his law license restrained him. Now, those institutional barriers didn't seem so stout. I recalled the expression on his face when he told me about shooting men who'd refused to obey a direct order during combat. I also recalled the nonchalance with which he admitted to killing twenty people. For the first time I understood the chance one took putting too much pressure on a crazy person.

The atmosphere at school that day stood in obvious relief to the climate on the home front. Clearly, everyone knew something grave had happened, and all seemed on their best behavior. Sure, one of my co-conspirators hissed, "You fink!" A few girls pointed at me and stage-whispered, "He had his dad egged! Can you believe it?" But what I had expected — mass excoriation plus tar and feathers — didn't happen.

A gentle knock at my door interrupted my stupor. I hoped it was Mary Jo. We hadn't talked since the egging. I wanted to know that she, at least, still supported me.

Mom entered my room.

She wore a sleeveless yellow cotton dress that buttoned up the front. As with most of her wardrobe, the design attempted to cover bubbles of fat, her reward for having five children in seven years. Under her arm she carried a large brown legal envelope. Her eyes were cinched with worry, her mouth slightly pursed.

"Hello, darling, how are you? I didn't know you were home until I saw your books on the hall table."

She sat down beside me on my bed. She cringed, like I might explode.

"How did school go today?"

"Okay."

A silence followed, but I was too anxious to let it go on very long.

"What's Dad going to do?"

"Well, I don't know, dear. Obviously, he's very upset."

She looked at me as if peering at a pest, perhaps one of the little blond spiders that inhabited our house.

"We're wondering what would cause you to do such a thing?"

I didn't reply.

"Your father thinks you've fallen under bad influences.

We expect you provoked the incident, but we're quite distressed that those boys would commit such an act."

She spoke in a reserved, almost rueful tone. I wanted to gush forth a litany of complaints. I didn't, however, because I didn't trust her. I thought her meek behavior might be a ruse designed to pump me for more information about my friends.

So I didn't say anything, and in a few moments, the facade of concern fell and her anger came out full force.

"How could you?" she cried out. "How could you have anything to do with something like this?"

Now that she was showing her wrath, I felt okay about returning fire.

"Because I hate him! I hate him because he grounded me indefinitely. I hate him because he punishes me every time I make a mistake!"

For a moment, Mom said nothing. She looked out the west window. The pink of the setting sun lit up her face, exposing a hair growing out of a mole on her chin. My screamed statement seemed to have distilled the piss from her anger.

"I know you're mad at Dad, but I wish you'd try to understand him. He's been through a lot."

I had no idea what she meant.

She set the envelope on my bed, its fold-over top held in place by a tattered piece of string. Mom had labeled the envelope: "P.C. McBean's War Correspondence, 1944–45."

"I wish you'd read them. They're awfully good. I think they'd tell you quite a lot."

I picked up the envelope and opened the top. A plume of dust emerged that smelled like old newspaper. I peeked inside and saw hundreds of tattered, wrinkled pages.

I glanced at my mother's face, and it looked like someone had pulled a ligament in her soul.

"Please, Bill, just give it a try."

I could see the letters were a big deal to her, but I didn't want to have anything to do with them. It was just more homework, or worse yet, homework designed to make Dad look good.

But I didn't want her to cry either. She'd tell Dad, and I'd be grounded for *eternity.*

"Okay," I said. "I'll read them."

She looked at me, trying to determine my sincerity. I think she knew there'd be no deeper commitment. She sighed and got up off my bed, smoothing a wrinkle on my bedspread before looking at me again.

"Dinner will be in a half hour," she said before leaving my room.

I picked up the old brown envelope and weighed it in my hand. Briefly, I wondered about its contents. Then my fury swelled again, washing away all curiosity. I put the envelope in the bottom drawer of my desk.

CHAPTER 26: EULENSPIEGEL

The three weeks following the egging provided me with a preview of what life might be like if I decided to pursue the criminal arts.

Previously, when I committed an act that provoked the ire of my parents, retribution generally came within a few hours. By entering into a criminal conspiracy to have my father assaulted, I had taken a step up.

It was still just my room, but it seemed like the county jail. The familiar wallpaper depicted the cowboys cooking at their campfires, but it just wasn't the same. Even though I knew something would happen soon, it struck me as serving an indeterminate sentence, because I knew they'd never feel the same about me.

Like all guys under strict confinement, I chafed. I looked for any crack, no matter how small, that might allow me just a little wiggle room. That's why when I heard Bob J. bitching about his mother making him serve as an acolyte at Christ Church, I became very attentive. He didn't like the idea because it meant he had to get to the service forty-five minutes early and sometimes meant he had to do chores after church as well.

To me, this had a very promising sound. Like maybe if I were pitching it to Mom, I would need to get there an hour early and stay an hour after. Every time. The walk to the church went right past Karen's apartment building.

My parents would never have gone for the acolyte scam

had I not been hot on the Episcopal Church previously. At twelve, I had been confirmed as a member of Christ Church and attended every Sunday. My parents — who never went to church — liked it that I latched on to religion; had Dad known the church actively discussed the civil rights movement, I expect he wouldn't have thought my interest so benign. I loved being in the vanguard of this dialog. It was my one legitimate secret.

When I asked Mom if I could become part of the candle-bearing corps, she said, "Let me ask your father. We still weren't speaking. A short time later, I obtained permission and had just a tiny bit more independence.

My second Sunday as an acolyte, I focused more on getting a glimpse of Karen than on addressing my holy duties. I thought she might show up outside her apartment building. She didn't, and I almost committed the unpardonable sin of causing the 11:00 a.m. Holy Communion service to get off to a late start.

As I opened the church door, a billow of incense that engorged the eaves of the old stone edifice softened the rainbow of light filtering through the stained glass. I dashed down to the dressing room.

Mark P., my new friend and fellow acolyte, waited for me there. Tall and lean, with thick, elaborately styled dark brown hair that reminded me of *77 Sunset Strip* TV show star Edd "Kookie" Byrnes, he had a slight stutter and a sardonic sense of humor.

He dressed in our sacred uniform, the white surplice cascading off his arms and chest like new snow off an evergreen. A Marlboro smoldered in his hand. His hazel eyes viewed my frantic efforts to change with amused tolerance.

"Your d-dad still got you chained up?"

"Yep, bolted and shackled."

I told Mark that Dad permanently grounded me because of bad grades. He attended Riverdale, a private school in the Bronx, and didn't know anyone at Bronxville High School. I had no intention of telling him about the egging. He represented my new start.

"Too bad. I got this fabulous blonde I could hook you up with. Built. *Friendly*."

"That's wonderful."

"Well, what sense d-does it make to ground someone for months over a few bad grades?"

"More than a few."

"Still, all he's d-doin' is givin' you a bad attitude."

"Tell me."

"This girl, her name is Lynn. She really wants to meet you. I told her you were solid. We could d-double. My mom will give me the Bonneville any time I want it."

"You're killing me."

"Tell me this: what time d-do your parents go to bed?"

"About nine."

"So we pick you up around nine thirty. We have a little rumpus, I have you back by midnight. Who's gonna know?"

"Maybe nobody, but if my Dad figured it out, there would be blood!"

"No!"

"Oh yeah!"

Father Barrett stuck his head in. "Would it be too much to ask?"

◆ ◆ ◆

As I came out of church, I saw Karen walking down the sidewalk, heading into the shopping district. She wore seersucker shorts, very short seersucker shorts that seemed to make her long, sinuous legs even longer. Yet I knew if I pursued her I'd be quite late. My parents knew exactly when church let out. They had checked up and weren't going for my story of having to stay late.

Dad waited for me as I walked in the front door. "We'd like to talk to you for a moment, William."

He looked his most mournful, prune-like dark pockets under his eyes, cheekbones ruddy and populated by a day's worth of dense black bristle.

He motioned me into the kitchen. The hammer hadn't come down yet from the egging, and I knew the moment had finally arrived. It wouldn't have surprised me at all if there'd been a casket waiting for me. I could envision my mother in her best black skirt, white silk blouse, and white gloves, gesturing for me to climb on in.

But when I turned the corner from the dining room into the kitchen, Mom stood there, dressed in her customary weekend outfit, a blue-and-pink-striped cotton blouse and denim pedal pushers. As ever, a wreath of smoke wrapped her head.

I looked at the countertop and saw the Scotch bottle had been uncorked.

Dad sat at the kitchen table. I propped my butt against the kitchen counter and folded my arms tightly across my chest.

"We have decided," my father said, "that you have fallen under bad influences."

Hearing those words had an immediate and almost miraculous effect on my body and brain. All the arched tension, the Armageddon fight-or-flight, dissolved. I was off the hook! Till Eulenspiegel (the merry prankster of Strauss' tone poem sentenced to death) would live!

"We also think your academic difficulties need to be dealt with by specialists," Dad continued.

He used his strong legal tone, as if giving a closing statement to a jury. He didn't invite feedback.

"Your Uncle David ran into similar difficulties when he was your age."

My ebullience shattered. *Holy shit!* I thought. *Gow!*

"Your grandfather Alan found this great little school for him near Buffalo that gave your Uncle David the tools he needed to really turn things around. I've made contact with the head master of the Gow School in South Wales, New York, and he's agreed to do some testing on you next weekend. We'll be going up there together."

Dad looked at me for a reaction, but I had nothing to say to him. Uncle Dave had told me about Gow. He said in retrospect he was grateful to his father for sending him to the school, but when he first arrived there, he hated it. "I'd never seen so much snow in my life!" he told me.

"Do you have any questions for us?" Dad asked.

"When do I start there? Like do I have to pass these tests to get in?"

Dad erupted in laughter. "Oh, no, no, these are in*telli*gence tests, son, in*telli*gence tests," he said, like I was stupid for not picking that up in the first place. "And as to when you'll be given admission, that's the unfortunate part. I wanted them to admit you the first of the year, but they said they needed to wait until September. So we'll just have to try to put up with each other until then."

Dad and I made the four-hundred-mile drive to the academic outpost called the Gow. It much more resembled a sequestered mental health facility than a prep school. I linked academia to the classical architecture of the Bronxville School. The Gow School had retrofitted a collection of farmhouses for academic purposes. The school built two structures, an unimpressive administration building, and a two-story clapboard dorm. It had soccer fields in abundance and a ski hill with a rope tow. Gow offered baseball and tennis in the spring. That constituted the sum and total of the athletic program. A small convenience store several hundred yards from campus offered a source of sugar. Otherwise it was me, a hundred other guys, and the remote hills of western New York.

As I looked around, I began to understand the freedom of exile.

CHAPTER 27: UNKNOWN BUT TO GOD

To everyone's surprise, I did quite well on the IQ tests. That delighted Dad. I think he suspected he had sired a hopeless cretin who needed to be assigned a cottage industry. He proposed to reward my "effort" with a trip to Washington, DC. He said nothing about forgiveness, but I inferred he wanted things to go better between us, a sea change that made me ebullient.

The night before we left, my excitement made sleep impossible. We'd travel to DC by train, a thrilling prospect. Despite my animosity toward him, Dad's adoration of the rails had rubbed off on me. We got to Penn Station early so we could give the Pennsylvania Railroad's Capitol Limited a thorough inspection.

Most of our attention went to the behemoth electric engine that would pull the long string of maroon and gold cars. Painted dark green, the locomotive looked like a prehistoric bug. The engine had two pantographs on its roof, connecting it to the electrical wires above. The locomotive's flanks rippled with vents that served as gills for the mighty motor within. A fishy ozone smell made it seem more beast than machine. One massive golden eye cast light far down the dark tunnel under the Hudson River.

When it came time to get on board, I thought crossing that yellow stripe separating the platform from the bottom step of the railroad car meant we'd stepped into a new epoch. We were going to Washington together, and we were going to have a ball.

The Capitol Limited had only been under way for an hour before the atmosphere began to change. The train halted to hitch on a diesel engine. The electrical lines didn't go all the way to Washington, but for some reason I felt disappointed. It illustrated the fragility of my newfound optimism.

Then, a short time later, raindrops began skidding off the windows, and by the time we got to DC, a steady drizzle enveloped everything.

All the pictures I'd seen of Washington featured a bright blue sky. When we stepped out of the station and onto the street, I saw the precipitation turned light gray granite dark, blending the city's pillars and domes with the mist. On the sidewalks, innumerable black puddles hampered our progress. Even the pigeons seemed to be sulking.

Yet the Lincoln Memorial benefited from the rain. Old Abe, sheltered under a portico held up by Doric columns, seemed to brood more heavily in foul weather. His great throne was covered so he could do his thinking in comfort.

I read the Gettysburg Address on the wall:

Four score and seven years ago our fathers brought forth on this continent a new nation, conceived in liberty, and dedicated to the proposition that all men are created equal. Now we are engaged in a great civil war, testing whether that nation, or any nation, so conceived and so dedicated, can long endure. We are met on a great battle-field of that war. We have come to dedicate a portion of that field, as a final resting place for those who here gave their lives that that nation might live. It is altogether fitting and proper that we should do this.

Tears welled in my eyes. A rich white brat with nothing but opportunity in front of me, I wondered how deeply horrible it must have been to be Black and a slave.

"He was a great man, huh, Dad?"

I looked up at my father. Dressed in his accustomed attire — a gray fedora with a black silk band and a formal gray wool overcoat —he gazed down at me, his big black eyebrows bunched.

"Who told you that, one of your liberal teachers?"

"Well, them and everybody else."

"Everybody, huh?"

"Well, I don't know. Maybe not everybody."

"Did you know that the central issue of the Civil War wasn't slavery?"

"Uh, no."

"The Civil War was fought over a clause in the constitution that says *all rights not specifically* delegated by the constitution to the *federal government are reserved for the states.* Before the Civil War, the Constitution didn't forbid slavery. Lincoln used military power to do away with the principle of states' rights."

"Dad, do you really think that states' rights is more important than slavery?"

"I do, Bill, especially when you look at the practical result. When the slaves were freed, hundreds of thousands of them came north without the education or the experience to deal with an industrialized society. Now you can't walk the streets at night."

"You can in Bronxville," I said.

"Which is why we live there. But they're all around us! Tuckahoe, right down the hill, is nothing but Negroes!"

"But Dad, Lincoln was a Republican. I thought you liked Republicans. All Republicans."

"I am very fond of today's Republicans, but only because they were modeled after a new icon."

"Who's that?"

"Calvin Coolidge."

Haut.

◆ ◆ ◆

After the Lincoln Memorial, we went to the Capitol, and after that to lunch. Without pause, Dad explained the inner workings of the US government as seen through the eyes of a conservative Wall Street lawyer. He emphasized what he viewed as excessive government spending enacted by congressmen who had been elected by an ignorant populace. I started reading the *New York Times* two years before and had engaged Dad in dinner-table political discussion — so his views came as no shock. I had not, however, realized he planned to use our trip to Washington to expound upon those views.

Dad didn't want to go anywhere near the Kennedy White House, but he did have one last destination on his sightseeing list: the Tomb of the Unknown Soldier. The rain had evolved from a spattering annoyance to a downpour, so it took us a long time to find a taxi to Arlington. I tried to stay under his umbrella, but by the time we reached our destination, I was drenched and shivering. My complaint drew a cackle and the commonplace "Compared to France, this is nothing."

A formidable marble sarcophagus guarded by four soldiers, one side of the crypt bore the phrase *Known but to*

God. Neo-classic columns marked the sides of the tomb. In between the columns were Greek figures representing Peace, Victory, and Valor.

The tomb included an amphitheater so the public could witness the changing of the guard. On a dry day we could have been seated, but the wetness forced us to stand. As we waited for the ceremony to begin, the wind began to gust, and I tried to crowd closer to Dad, but he had the umbrella cocked to one side so it covered his head but not mine.

"Dad, I'm getting wet!"

He didn't respond. I looked up at his face, but the man I knew was gone. The assertive, rounded, and naturally well-formed facial features had given way. His eyes were black holes, and his face had crumpled like a leaf that survived a long winter. His mouth was a knot.

The ceremony began. The sergeant in command ordered off the soldiers on duty. The replacement soldiers marched in, and one by one, the sergeant inspected their uniforms and did the white glove test on their weapons.

As the ceremony concluded, Dad began to speak. His throat clogged and his words were hard to make out over the beating of rain on his umbrella. I strained to hear but could only pick up a couple of phrases:

Thought it was safe... I made it back... Why didn't you?

I got even colder and wanted him to put his arm around me, but he wasn't there. I looked around for something familiar, something that might ground me, that might quell my rising angst, but I saw only people milling about and my father staring at the sarcophagus, transfixed. The rain stripped the air of almost all human references — perfume, cigarette smoke, the hotdog cart — all driven to the ground. I could only smell the dirt on the drenched paving stones. Finally, without a word, he turned and left, and I struggled to keep up.

CHAPTER 28: PUPPY LOVE

Following my acquiescence to the Gow idea, the tension between Dad and I lessened considerably. He lifted my grounding and restored my skimpy allowance. I tried my best to behave (if you didn't count my unabated larceny). I had an excellent reason for obeying the rules: my sixteenth birthday approached in June. I hoped if I could show some modest improvement in the classroom, a driver's license might be in my future.

Until then, I could depend on my buddy and fellow acolyte Mark. When I told him I could fly again, he said, "Great. I'll tell Lynn we're on next weekend. We'll d-double at the d-drive-in."

Mark looked at me, expecting an affirmative gesture, and when he saw apprehension, he said, "Well, we don't need to start with the d-drive-in if you d-don't want. We could d-do a regular movie or go bowling or..."

"I don't know if I can do any of that."

"Why not? It's all we've been talking about for months!"

"I just meant I could leave the house on Saturday afternoons."

"You gotta be shittin' me!"

I mumbled something about the necessity of spending more time studying.

"Why don't you d-do that Saturday afternoon and go out on Saturday night like a normal person?"

I said I'd think about it.

My problem with girls went beyond common shyness. I could talk only to Mary Jo and my other sisters. The egging may have hurt my father's feelings, but it hurt mine a lot more. My ego had become friable. I thought Dad deserved every single egg that yellowed his bright white shirt, but there weren't many boys who could hatch plots against their father and not feel traitorous. Add to that snitching on my co-conspirators, and I had precious little evidence upon which to base a positive self-image.

My cowardice felt like a centipede that had crawled in my ear. No one had any respect for why it happened, nor did they understand how I could have been such a creep. I wanted to explain how afraid I'd been, but none of that mattered now. The centipede had made its nest, and every time it got up and resettled itself, I felt a little sicker.

My lack of eagerness to date Lynn astounded Mark. As we bombed around, he decided he was going to talk to me about it.

"You still thinking about spending Saturday night studying?"

"I really need to keep up."

"You know, you don't need to be afraid of Lynn."

"Who says I'm afraid of her?"

"Bill..."

"Just because I take school seriously."

"Bill..."

"You private school guys think you have it so tough..."

"Okay, forget Lynn. Just forget it. It'll take you home right now so you can get even *more* studying done!"

"Oh, for Christ sake!"

"For Christ sake what? You're so full of shit, you should be a guidance counselor!"

"When did you get so slash-happy?"

"When my best friend started rejecting my efforts on his behalf."

"That's really the way you see this?"

"Of course I do. You spend months pissing and moaning about your nonexistent social life, so I persuade my top recruit to go out with you, and now you're acting like a socially retarded nimrod."

"You really think she'd like me?"

"For the love of God, if I didn't, would I be putting my reputation on the line? I got considerably more to lose here than you, Billy boy."

"Well, maybe if I get really a lot of stuff done this weekend..."

I had never been on a date. I'd danced one slow dance with Nancy N., with whom I had had an "Oh Donna" slow leak, quasi-sexual experience at Teen Center. Of course, I danced with dozens and dozens of girls at Miss Covington's Dancing School every Wednesday night since fourth grade, but I hated them and they hated me, and we didn't talk. We just did the foxtrot.

This girl Lynn, better-looking than any Bronxville girl, this girl who had consented to a date with "really solid" me, now had to be impressed. I had to dream up some way to astound this chick.

Six days elapsed before the Saturday night in question. During that time, I thought about opening parries.

I knew I had to start with a joke, so I consulted *Mad* magazine. I had to stay away from Alfred E. Neuman, I knew that, but I thought about avant-garde cartoonist Don Martin. Then it occurred to me that a fifteen-year-old boy shouldn't be reading *Mad* at all. When my mom told me that, I blew her off, but when Mary Jo confirmed it...

That killed my source of jokes. I read the *New York Times* and the *Herald Tribune* every day, which meant I knew a lot about politics and world affairs. The previous Sunday, a bunch of people had escaped from East Berlin through a sewer under the notorious wall separating the two sides of the city. I asked Mary Jo if she thought that might be a good opening topic, and she just rolled her eyes, which pissed me off, so I said to her, "Okay, what do *you* think I should do?" and Mary Jo said, "She's a *Hastings* girl, how should I know?"

For the rest of the week, my brain ran on emergency overload. My ears strained for all things flip or glib. I considered dirty jokes, what-if jokes, mind-game jokes, religious jokes, knock-knock jokes. For a while I considered blonde jokes, but even I understood the insane risk of that. By Saturday, the simple act of saying "Hi" to her became more twisted than a Gordian Knot.

I expected Mark at 5:00 p.m. and had just gotten out of the shower at 4:45 p.m. when he showed up. Dripping wet and still tucking in my shirt, I ran down to his car.

I opened the rear door and saw Lynn, a blue-eyed blonde

with mischievous eyes who would have made Jesus tumescent.

I nearly blubbered with panic. Earlier that day, I had been practicing my moves on my pillow, confident I could squeeze just about anything. Now, I felt terror growing in my shoulder blades and neck. I closed the rear door, wandered around to the driver's window, and said to Mark, "Hey, bud."

"Hey, bud yourself. Get in."

"Well, um, what are we gonna do?"

"What are you talking about? We're gonna go to the movies."

I tried to mime to Mark that Lynn was too much of a good thing, and I was freaking out. I don't know what I expected him to do except what he did, which was say, very loudly and very impatiently, "*Bill*, get-in-the-car!"

That brought clangors of laughter from Mark's date Judy, as well as Lynn, and it made my ears fire-engine red. The occasion might be an even bigger disaster than I thought possible.

I couldn't imagine what I was going to say when I got in the back seat. My brain shrieked for me to run, but instead I got in the back seat and managed to say, "Hi."

Lynn took it from there. When I awkwardly attempted to shake her hand, she took my hand in both of hers and held it there. Her hands were wonderfully warm, so warm that my body chemistry began to shift from cold scared to hot, willing and agonizingly stiff. She started to ask me about myself. Did I have brothers or sisters, what kind of music did I like, had I seen *Lolita* yet?

As Lynn talked, Mark caught my eye in the rear-view

mirror and mouthed his prediction about what I might accomplish with Lynn, and I nearly died, sure she would to catch him and ruin everything.

As Mark drove, I tried to lead a conversation comparing The Duke's performance in *The Alamo*, which also came out that year, to *North to Alaska*, which we were supposed to see that night. No one seemed very interested, and the second we got to the drive-in, I figured out why.

Mark pulled the Bonneville into our space and turned the car off. Then, instead of lowering the window and grabbing the sound box, he put his arm around Judy, pulled her in, and began kissing her. Their smooching echoed throughout the car. I cringed. I felt betrayed and angry. What was I supposed to do now? I didn't even dare look at Lynn.

With my hands clenched in my lap, I stared straight ahead at the screen, watching the Road Runner do his thing. I think I watched that desert demon harder than I ever watched anything in my life. Then I felt Lynn's hand on my neck, and I jolted away from her.

"Hey," she whispered. "Come back here. I'm not so bad."

"No, no, I'm sure you're not."

She got extremely close to me and whispered in my ear. "Mark didn't tell me you were going to be so nervous. My Coke's got a little rum in it. Want a taste?"

"God, yes."

I took an inappropriately large swallow.

"There," Lynn said. "Now we'll taste the same."

She giggled, and when it became apparent I didn't get the joke, she whispered, "Do you know how to French kiss?"

I almost ruined everything by saying yes, but by that time so much warmth had been created, I just had to trust her.

"No."

"Well, it starts when a boy and a girl touch each other with the tips of their tongues."

CHAPTER 29: DESPERATE

Frantic to see Lynn again, I did the unimaginable: I asked my parents for help.

I approached Mom first. “Mom, you know that girl Lynn I told you about?”

“You mean the one that has made my little boy totally lose his composure?”

“I haven’t totally lost...”

“It’s all right, dear. Your mother is acquainted with puppy love.”

“It’s not, it’s, well, never mind. It’s just that she wants me to take her to a movie and Mark can’t get his car... It’s kind of an emergency.”

“It’s nothing of the sort.”

“Well, okay, it’s not an *emergency*, it’s just that I don’t want to disappoint her.”

“What are you proposing?”

“That you drive me to Hastings, drop me off at the movie theater, and then pick me up when it’s over?”

“Certainly not! As far as I’m concerned, if you want to date, you have perfectly good girls right here in the village. But feel free to ask your father.”

So I went up to my room, stared out the west window, and watched for his bus, this time not in fear of corporal punishment, but in anticipation of being told no. I think I would have been glad to take twelve whacks from his belt if he'd just give me break this once. But I felt hopeless. If I found Mom's sarcasm hard to take, Dad's would be a killer.

Despite what Mom said, I kind of thought she might put in a good word for me, so I waited a few minutes after he got home before making my case.

When I walked into the kitchen, he sat at the kitchen table nursing a Scotch and water. He looked tired. His eyes were bloodshot and his face, heavy with late afternoon beard, seemed to sag. I didn't like my chances.

He addressed me before I could say anything. "Your mother tells me you're in a transportation pickle."

"Yeah, pretty much."

"I will be your chauffeur."

"You mean you'll drive all the way to Hastings, take us to the movie, and then pick us up after?"

"That's exactly what I mean."

"Oh, my gosh, thank you!"

The evening would certainly be a step down from the one we had spent together at the drive-in, but Lynn said she wanted to go to *The Manchurian Candidate,* and I was desperate to be with her, so I thought Dad's offer was a lot better than nothing.

Dad's magnanimity puzzled me, for a while, but I eventually theorized the psychodynamics of the egging had taken an unexpected turn.

The first part of the evening went well. I feared Dad might lay a Haut on Lynn, but he restrained himself. I worried Lynn would mock me for bringing my dad on our date, but she treated him like the King of Siam.

The unforgettable part of the date occurred after the movie. The film, a tale of brainwashing and assassination, had thrown a scare into both of us, but we reacted in totally different ways.

It struck me mute, but Lynn apparently needed reassurance — so as Dad drove us back to her house, she made her move. She started by inching up on my hand. When I felt her fingers, my eyes went right to the rear-view mirror, and sure enough, Dad was watching.

She inched closer, put her hand on my face and launched into lip lock. I didn't know what to do. My tongue hid from her tongue. My eyes looked into Dad's eyes. Lynn, sensing my hesitance, turned it up a notch and seemed close to climbing into my lap when Dad pulled up in front of her house.

I walked her to her front door. We said an awkward goodnight. I could tell she noticed I wanted to stay out of trouble with Dad more than I wanted to be passionate with her, so I tried to choke out a few words of explanation.

"Oh, don't worry about it," she said and disappeared into her house.

On the way home, I expected acerbic comments, but Dad had something else in mind.

As I got into the car, he fired up his pipe. After filling the car with smoke, he pulled away from the curb and said, "I'm wondering if you've given any thought to how Kennedy won the election."

Dad thought "being part of our lives" mean inculcating us with his political opinions. Although my date had been disastrous, I knew listening to him would be a good way of expressing my gratitude. He knew I hadn't given Kennedy's win any thought whatsoever.

"He bought it. In Chicago. Cash on the barrel head."

"Really?"

"Really. I'm sure you remember election night. By 1:00 a.m., it was still too close to call, and then suddenly precincts in Chicago started reporting huge pluralities for Kennedy."

"Yeah, so?"

"That crook Joe Kennedy bought those votes from the mayor of Chicago, the *honorable* Richard Daley."

"Now how do you know that?"

"You're just going to have to take my word for it. I know."

I said nothing, so Dad resumed his disquisition.

"You know about Joe Kennedy, I assume?"

"Are you talking about JFK's dad?"

"You're damn right I am. Biggest crook in the United States of America."

Dad's pipe went out, so he started steering with his knees so he could refill the bowl. We drove southbound into glaring headlights on the Saw Mill River Parkway, a road in those days without a center rail.

"All during prohibition, he ran booze into the US and paid off every politician and police officer on the East Coast. But the heart of his scam was a triangle-trade involving selling opium to the Chinese, using that money to buy liquor in Scotland and Canada, which he sold in the US and then poured into even greater sums into opium purchases."

"Really?"

"Bill, the man was born Boston shanty Irish. Do you think he got rich on his good looks?"

"Actually, I heard he got rich in real estate."

"For Christ sake, son, where do you think he got the money for the real estate investments?"

"I dunno. From investors?"

"You, laddy boy, are hopelessly naive."

CHAPTER 30: "UNCLE"

When school let out in June of 1962, report cards were issued, and mine marked a true watershed: no Ds, and there was a single, wonderful, outstanding B. My mother examined it like a hen eying corn, but she couldn't deny it. I had gotten a B in social studies.

Capitalizing on my feat, I asked her the same question I had asked her at least a dozen times since the beginning of the year: "Does this mean I can get my learner's permit?"

She responded just as she always had. "Ask your father." This time, it was me who stomped my foot.

"*How* can I ask him? What's the best *way*?"

"Make an appointment with him at his office. Put on a jacket and tie. Go down there and make your case."

I knew most boys didn't have to take a train and two subways to ask for a learner's permit, but by this time I also knew that to get anything accomplished, I had to get him before he began drinking. Scotch whiskey made him mean; it was an undeniable fact. If I wanted him to be reasonable, I had to catch him in the eight-hour non-medicated window he reserved for his clients and his colleagues.

It had been eleven months since his elevation to partner. I expected the trappings of office to be grander, but he remained fixed in his moderate associate-sized quarters — enough room for a large desk, a few chairs, but little more. He did have a splendid view of the Chrysler Building, its intricate art deco silver spire reflecting the morning sun.

Dad saw me gawping and said, "The powers that be have said a corner office with a view of lower New York Harbor is in my future. The current occupant is meandering toward retirement, so they've asked me to be patient."

His office impressed me. Human society for thousands of years had concentrated on new ways of elevating its most successful members: kings on their thrones, judges on their high benches, but not too many people had been raised up to the extent my father had — but good God, at what cost? When he got that coveted corner office on the forty-fourth floor, would he be happy?

"My secretary said there was something of an urgent nature you wished to speak to me about."

I launched into my pitch. I began with improved grades. I pointed out my cheerful completion of household chores. I talked about my career as an acolyte, which by now had been going on for many months. I even said I no longer tortured my sisters — as much. I asserted I felt a new, more responsible self burgeoning from within. I laid it on so thickly that by the end Dad was chortling.

"From Bolshevik conspirator to ideal son in nine short months."

I knew I had overdone it. I should have just come out and asked him. I prepared myself for a long ride home, but Dad said, "Bill, I will allow you to get a learner's permit, but I do so with grave trepidation. I would love to be proved wrong, but I think in your heart of hearts you are a hot-rodder."

"No, sir, I am not. I promise."

"Well, I hope that's the case, and I'm prepared to give you a chance, but the second I see any evidence of anything other than grandmotherly use of my vehicle, I'll yank your driving privileges just like that!"

He snapped his fingers to emphasize the point.

I said, "Okay, sure," and I stepped out of his office building, at last ready to ride on the broad highway to freedom. Within the next few weeks, I learned to drive and soon drove all alone in my family's two-toned green Bonneville with its 356 horsepower V-8 engine. For a month, I reveled in adulthood's opening chapter.

One day I entered the Cross-County Parkway from a very short on-ramp — one which I believed required pedal-to-the-medal acceleration. I pushed my foot to the floor, and the engine gave out a gratifying roar. The car lurched forward, but then I heard a loud clunk, and the Bonneville lost power. I smelled burning rubber and hydrocarbons. Smoke came from under the hood. The car rolled to a halt, never to move again. I learned later the lynchpin holding the transmission to the drive shaft had snapped.

The destruction of his car made Dad angry, but not apoplectic. He simply demanded I hand over my driver's license. In those days, New York licenses were paper, making it easy for him to tear it into long, skinny pieces.

"As I anticipated, William, you have a heavy foot, and because of that I am now forced to spend thousands of dollars to buy a new car. We'll talk about a new license in a year, but in the meantime, you're grounded."

I, of course, put up a very strenuous effort to convince Dad that the car's mechanical failure had nothing to do with me. People floored Bonnevilles every day, and nothing happened. I even got our family mechanic to so attest, but it made no difference.

"Bill, do you remember me telling you to drive like a

grandmother?"

For weeks I hung around the house, grounded, fielding telephone calls from Mark and others in my new group of friends. They were going to Jones Beach. Come hear Monk at the Blue Note. These really weird Tarrytown chicks who played guitars and smoked Camels were having a party. I missed all these things because I was grounded, and at that point in my life, being grounded made no sense, especially being grounded indefinitely. I had about six weeks until I had to migrate to the gulag called Gow. All my new friends, this wonderful new life I had created, would be left behind.

Thinking these thoughts, I found myself once again at the foot of my bed, looking out my west window. Gray skies oozed out heavy humidity. The buzz of cicadas pervaded the neighborhood, blanketing everything with their monotonous drone. Blue jays soared from one tree to another, crying "bored, bored!"

I knew Dad sat downstairs having lunch. He had a Saturday afternoon ritual: he'd fry up four pieces of Canadian bacon and then crumble them into a saucepan of bean and bacon soup. While his meal warmed, he'd open a beer and read the *New York Times*.

I began wondering why I let him keep me in the house. At one time he seemed very tough, but in recent years, his belly had become more formidable than his brawn. In fact, his deterioration evidenced itself in all sorts of ways. He became short of breath walking up the stairs from the street. He coughed relentlessly. His facial skin, once so vital and ruddy, had developed a thousand fissures.

I, by contrast, felt like a sixteen-year-old boy. I had the energy and strength of a two-year-old Great Dane pup. I'd developed more than a little fighting experience. I'd lost my share, but I'd also learned how to size up my adversary.

Dad still had the requisite anger to fight, but he'd allowed his brawn to atrophy. I felt motivated, a fundamental factor in any physical contest, plus I had the element of surprise on my side. I wanted to leave, and I knew he couldn't stop me.

I went downstairs and walked into the kitchen. He looked up at me, his eyes venous and sad.

"I'm going down to the school field and hack around," I said.

"No, you're not. You're grounded. If you're bored, I can certainly think of work that needs to be done."

"No, Dad. I need to get out of here. I'm going."

"*No, you're not.*"

"Yes, I am. Bye."

I headed into the dining room toward the front door. I felt him grab me from behind. He put me in a headlock and tried to pull me to the floor. I resisted, and he redoubled his effort. He wheezed, and I could hear liquid percolating in his lungs. He smelled like pipe tobacco and beer. I managed to get my arms around his midsection and heaved. We crashed to the floor, and I landed on top. I pinned his wrists and put my face an inch from his.

"Uncle?" I screamed. He struggled a little, but I clearly had him beaten. He sounded like a broken accordion.

"Uncle?" I screamed again, louder this time.

"Okay," he gasped. "Okay."

I got off and headed toward the door.

He called after me, "So you can take your old man, but

don't forget, I have the power of the purse, Bill. I have the power of the purse!"

I chuckled when he said that. He'd told me repeatedly to anticipate, and for once I'd taken his advice.

During the weeks of my imprisonment, my resentment built like steam in a pressure cooker. I'd remembered how his face creased with malice as he tore up my license, and I'd wanted to hurt him.

Theft presented a way to wrench emotional satisfaction from the situation. I suppose I could have gotten a job, but this angry, entitled Bronxville teenager vetoed that option quickly. For several years, I'd been financing myself by dipping into my mother's purse. Yet she'd taken to counting her money, making me chary of this avenue to riches.

One weekday morning, acting on whim, I waited until my dad went downstairs to read the *Times* and then wandered into his bedroom to inspect his wallet. I really didn't think I'd have much of an opportunity to steal from him, but curiosity got the best of me.

His fat, rectangular bifold wallet lay on a huge pile of change and subway tokens. Worried the change would make noise or spill onto the floor, I lifted his wallet very gingerly. My ears fairly twitched in an effort to hear him begin to mount the staircase. When I opened the billfold, I gasped at its contents. I fanned out the top half-dozen notes: hundreds, fifties, and twenties beyond number! Quickly, I slid the bills back in and placed the wallet squarely on top of the change pile before scampering back to my room.

In the succeeding days, I thought about the implications of stealing from him. I decided he had no idea how much money he had. Alcoholism had claimed him. He'd quit talking to his family, with the exception of Mom, and from what I could glean through the closed kitchen door, he spoke to her only in monosyllables or in short sentences. He didn't stagger or slur his words, but his face had turned the color of beef left out too long. His physique, once so starched and ready for action, had turned to pulp.

I decided he could no longer protect himself. I tiptoed into the bedroom nearly every morning for months, taking one or two twenties each time. By the time I won our physical struggle, I'd stashed a bundle. He could hang himself with his purse strings, for all I cared.

As I walked toward the school, I thought about how he couldn't control me anymore, that I had my freedom and he didn't have jack shit to say about it.

About twenty minutes after leaving home, I faced a strike zone outlined in chalk on the brick wall of the school. I picked up a tennis ball on my way there and began throwing it at the chalk rectangle. I imagined myself as Yankee pitcher Whitey Ford, like me a lefty. Ball in hand, I came to the set position, looked over my shoulder to check the runner at third, and then threw the ball at the rectangle as hard as I could. My percentage of strikes to balls: about one to ten.

As I pitched, I thought. I physically overpowered Dad, but what had I achieved? I still had zero prospects for the future. Despite my solitary B, I still couldn't handle school. I knew he wouldn't kick me out or disown me. He had too much interest in my success to do that, but at some point I had to take a hand in my own future.

As I threw the ball against the wall, I didn't think at all about how Dad must have felt that day. Later, I realized that I had Dad egged and then a few months later manhandled him. I'd turned into the artillery shell, and his large Bronxville house had become his foxhole. His despondency that summer day in 1962 must have been deep indeed.

◆ ◆ ◆

We never discussed our physical struggle. We just went on living in the same house, barely being civil to each other until the day came for me to leave. As Dad and I launched into the nine-hour drive to Gow, he resumed his discourse on the Kennedy administration, this time focusing on JFK's connection to the Vatican. But the noise from passing trucks and cars blessedly made his words indistinct.

When we finally pulled up in front of my new school, I felt renewed shock. The word school couldn't really be applied to Gow. Outpost, maybe? Yet I resolved not to let my sarcastic, contrarian attitude get me in trouble.

Before I left Bronxville, a school guidance counselor suggested to me that I authored many of my own problems. He acknowledged that my parents contributed to my problems, but he told me I had let my tribulations master me. With my fellow students at Bronxville, I acted negative, caustic, reactionary, and occasionally downright rude. He didn't use such bald terms. He employed social work code words, but I got the point.

I decided treating Gow like a punishment would be a big mistake. I vowed to be open, positive, and friendly. To my amazement, it worked. From the first day at there, I got along with everyone.

During the initial weeks, this optimistic mindset held. During the warm weather, my emotions stayed fairly positive, and as fall ripened, the maples and oak on the steep hills surrounding Gow provided the kind of solace given by color. I thought even if this place seemed lonely, it had beauty. Red, yellow, and orange leaves floated down into deep ravines, making them like down bedding.

When I'd been at Gow for a little over a month, the Cuban Missile Crisis hit the airwaves. The school didn't have TV, but we all had radios — and though callow, to a boy we knew what nuclear war would be like. We had studied World War II. Many had seen Gregory Peck in *On the Beach*, the film version of Nevil Shute's post-apocalyptic novel. It seemed likely that South Wales would escape the devastation, but Bronxville, just sixteen miles from Times Square, would not.

I called Mom from a payphone near campus. As I listened to the telephone ring, wind buffeted the booth and clouds skidded across the moonlit night. When she answered, I had difficulty hearing her. The connection crackled and faded, making her voice sound remote. I remembered her saying, "Well, I suppose we can only hope for the best." That seemed inadequate to me. I found myself longing to talk to Dad, desperate to get his take on the news.

The missile crisis passed, but the loneliness didn't.

In November, the hillsides became gray and purple, and then one astonishing morning, they turned white. From then on, the whiteness built on itself until it ruled everything. Paths burrowed through it, but merely making way wouldn't overcome the emotional effect of that much snow. I couldn't escape this crevasse.

Finally, Christmas came. I took the train from Buffalo to New York. I thought about nothing other than Lynn, but when I got home, she wouldn't return my calls. Mark gave me the bad news: a mutual friend, Bill Y., had taken over, and Lynn had fallen headlong in love. Intense pain came with this news, because during almost every hour at Gow, I dreamed of resuming our succulent osculation.

Mark lessened my funk. He suggested if I hated Gow so much, why didn't I apply to Riverdale? I wouldn't need to live with my parents; I could live in the dorm. Big-time fun! Every

Friday and Saturday night, kids signed a log stating their alleged destination, hopped on the subway, and spent the evening in Manhattan. Curfew? One a.m.!

I thought it sounded considerably better than South Wales, but even if my dad agreed to the transfer, my grades wouldn't allow admission to a school with Riverdale's scholastic reputation.

Mark suggested talking to admission director Russell Ames.

"He's a hell of a guy," Mark said. "Why don't you just give him a call?"

CHAPTER 31: DAD RETREATS

Riverdale had a wonderful reputation, and after I managed to talk my way in, I never earned a grade lower than B.

Following my first year at my new school, Dad told me he didn't want me hanging around Bronxville all summer because I'd surely get in trouble. Instead, he got me a job at the Union Pacific's Zion Canyon Lodge in southern Utah. I reveled in the adventure and overcame the culture shock. The following summer, I worked on the north rim of the Grand Canyon. All of this came thanks to Dad's connections with the UP. Growing up with him had been torture, but in just a few years I'd transformed from bullied to bulletproof. My confidence soared to entirely unjustified levels.

After four years at Lake Forest College in Lake Forest, Illinois, I had vague career goals, but I really wanted the riotous living of Chicago in the early seventies. I crawled the bars and sampled the women I met there. I went to all the protest rallies and thought myself a jolly cavalier of the new epoch.

Although tremendously entertained for a while, eventually I lost my way — primarily because I'd developed a penchant for amphetamines while living on Chicago's north side. My home at 72 Summit Avenue, a prison for so long, became my safe haven.

The fact that I'd resorted to a "geographic cure" by fleeing Chicago didn't seem odd to me. I thought myself rather smart and prudent. Any independent observer would at this point have diagnosed me as an alcoholic. Yet I thought I had things well in hand. I drank only beer and thus thought myself safe. Much later on in my drinking career, someone pointed out that one beer equaled one shot of whiskey, so if I drank eight or nine beers, I qualified as a sot. Still, I managed to avoid any major repercussions in my early years of alcoholism and therefore engaged in the favorite pastime of all drunks: denial.

Observing my parents' condition, I being twenty-three and they being fifty, gave me all the moral high ground I needed. A lot had happened during my six-year absence, very little of it good. Alcohol is a ruthless creditor, and when it came time for my parents to pay up, it wasn't pretty.

Mom, who always appeared to be the more moderate drinker, became the first to get diabetes. Suddenly she found herself in hospital, near death.

Faced with the possibility of losing his wife, all the armor Dad had accumulated in the army and on Wall Street fell away like so many plastic parts. During the two nights she spent in the hospital, he acted like a man who had just seen his child drown. His famous composure walked away from him like a casual acquaintance. He wept. He held his hands over his eyes and bleated with pain. No longer could he hide behind his hard-shelled and churlish front.

"What if she doesn't make it?" he cried to no one in particular. "I can't do this without her. I just can't. I can't..."

His grief astonished us. We thought him totally immune to emotional pain. The gradient had shifted, and we were dumbstruck. For the first time in the two decades we'd lived with him, he showed palpable fear. When he said that he couldn't "do this," we assumed he meant our family, or perhaps life itself. My sisters and I couldn't quite understand what he was talking about. His outright panic scared us, but most of all, we didn't know what we could do for him. Since we had seen so little of comfort given, we didn't know how to give it.

I had no idea how to cope with my own emotions. The old world I knew and hated seemed to be morphing into a diminished cosmos I knew I would like a great deal less.

Although Dad led our family, Mom lived at its center, and if the center wouldn't hold, I didn't understand how anything would work. Of course, it never occurred to me that Mom's drinking might have any relevance to me.

I wished I could have been more upset about my mother's condition, but the normal love a boy felt for his mother had evaporated many years before during harsh recriminations about bed-wetting and lost hats. We each viewed each other as a management problem: me dependent on her economic largesse and thus had to be diplomatic; she duty-bound to encourage her son, who'd just landed his first journalism job at the *Tarrytown Daily News*. Still, I'd told her so many lies, she probably wondered if I in fact had a newspaper job, or if it was just something I'd made up to look good.

My effort to comfort my father exposed my own lack of empathy.

"How do you feel, Dad?"

"How do you think I feel?"

"Not very good, I expect."

"They said she could die!"

"But she also could live."

"But if she doesn't?"

"I don't know, Dad. Let's try not to think about that,

okay?"

He looked at me with the eye of a man who had seen too much death but whose eyes asked for comfort. I knew nothing about comforting anyone — not Dad, and not my sisters. I focused on my new life in Tarrytown, period. I had the emotional depth of a shellfish.

I patted him a couple of times on the shoulder. I wondered how I'd gotten this far down the road without having genuine family ties, the sort of bond that would allow me to naturally and unaffectedly hug my pa. Yet at that moment, giving him a bear hug felt as impossible as reversing the long, terrible history between us.

I therefore numbed my pain with alcohol, and plenty of it. Susan and Joan managed to get a meal on the table, which we ate in silence. No one spoke a sarcastic word, no one tried to devil anyone else. No one knew how to extend the hand of love to a man who had been through so much.

Dad seemed to be doing fine mixing his own drinks, so we just watched two days of his anguish until finally the doctors declared Mom stable and allowed her to come home.

She acclimated to her insulin shots fairly quickly and had no problem moderating her diet so her blood sugar remained stable. In a few weeks, the old sherry glass reappeared, just above eye level, inside a kitchen cabinet. It mystified us how she could resume her old drinking habits without ending up in the hospital again, but she claimed she had greatly moderated them, and so our commonplace existence at 72 Summit Avenue resumed.

Yet something had changed with Dad. He became much more moody, like he couldn't forgive her for scaring him. Arriving home in the evening, he'd sit at the marred, porcelain kitchen table, Scotch and water in a sixteen-ounce glass sitting in front of him, and he watched her as if she might slip away at any moment. He watched her as he glumly completed that day's ossification, and his face, suffused with violet, looked like a landslide.

Mom, however, seemed to have made a new arrangement with life. She became even more involved with Christ Church. She got to know all the ministers, frequently invited them to the house on Saturday evening, and fed them Rock Cornish game hens or her famous ham soup. Eventually, Dad fell in line with this new order of things, and they became über-Episcopalians together. He even allowed himself to be drafted into the church's vestry.

But if Dad tried to get closer to God, or if he learned any real practical lessons from his spouse getting diabetes, he didn't let on. He continued to drink like a college sophomore.

As 1971 slipped into 1972, Westchester-Rockland Newspapers promoted me to the county bureau in White Plains, the chain's central news organization that supplied the member papers with news of relevance to the entire circulation area. I rewarded their confidence by attempting to establish a chapter of the Newspaper Guild, AFL-CIO. The organizing effort took eighteen months and ended when the employees voted against authorizing the Guild as their collective bargaining agent. The vote expedited my move to Colorado.

During this period, I occasionally spent a weekend in Bronxville. Sanity, in my experience, is a relative thing, and the lunacy of my family sometimes felt more stable than the madness of the organizing drive.

One day, talking to Mom, she let it slip that one of the law firm's senior partners had asked her to persuade my father to drink more moderately. The partner said Dad carried a fifth of Scotch in his briefcase. It startled me when she said this, but she had no confidantes. Lonely and worried, she had to tell someone.

Although Mom informed Dad of the partner's call, nothing changed. Whatever paralyzed his heart also abolished his antic behavior. He no longer Hauted. He didn't rave about communists or Black people. Dining room table quizzes ceased entirely. He no longer had dinner with the family. He ate separately in the kitchen and then went to bed.

During Thanksgiving of that year, my sister Anne brought her African-American boyfriend to the house. She marched Levon — from Tuckahoe! — into the kitchen and introduced him. Dad looked up at him like an old dog. Slowly, he offered Levon his hand. Having dispensed with the formalities, he returned his eyes to the kitchen table. Anne made an effort to prod Dad into expressing his anti-miscegenation views, but she might as well have goaded a stone.

I, according to the fashion of the day, had long hair and wore a torn blue jean jacket and bellbottom pants. He said nothing. I raved ceaselessly about Vietnam. He said nothing. I smoked ounce after ounce of reefer in my room, and although the odor of it suffused the premises, he said nothing.

He did, however, retain one remnant of passion: his love of steam engines. For years, he had indulged in Iron Horse Rambles, and sometimes I went with him.

In the spring of 1971, he invited me to accompany him on an excursion from Albany to Montreal. I didn't particularly want to — these expeditions tended to run ten to twelve hours, and whether you stuck your head out the window or huddled in the bar car, the coal dust found its way into your hair and clothing. The excursions offered rank food, and the company tended to be decidedly odd. But I said I'd go, because he had been decent about my extended period of unemployment following college and because even though the trip annoyed me, I thought he might be dying.

I didn't anticipate that Dad would finance one of the strangest sexual experiences I've had before or since.

The weekend began sedately. Dad and I caught The Empire Builder at Grand Central Station and sat in the bar car, chatting amiably. We both had entirely too much to drink by normal standards, but in this respect we McBeans had pioneered a new paradigm.

We arrived in Albany late that night, and early the next morning we caught a cab and crossed the Hudson River on our way to the train station. The previous evening's drizzle had been blown away by warm gusts from the south, and the river glistened green under the day's new light. We arrived early at the dowdy depot in Rensselaer so we'd have plenty of time to inspect the engine. I felt sure Dad would be enthused by whatever form of smoke-belching monster the tour organizers provided us, but at the same time I knew he would judge the engine inferior to the colossal locomotives that hauled him to Hanover during his college years.

"I wish you could have heard it, Bill. It was magnificent to lie in your Pullman bed while the whistle screamed and the engine took on that hill leading up to White River Junction. Man, I'll tell you, it was really something."

As he told me about the steam engine's effort to climb the grade to White River Junction, he got his arm moving like a driving rod linked to a steam engine's power wheel and replicated the noise of those old locomotives. It was a queer spectacle, but given the crowd around the train that morning, he fit in nicely. He dressed in casual clothing, but on his head he wore a black-and-white-striped engineer's hat. Around his neck hung a red bandana.

After we took our seats and began our northward journey, I decided to explore the train for a place to smoke a joint. I knew I could get stoned in the toilet if need be, but the facilities on these ancient trains tended to be smelly, and anyway, I thought there might be someone aboard who'd share my enthusiasm for the pernicious weed.

As I stumbled forward through the lurching fifteen-car train, I saw rail enthusiasts poring over timetables, talking eagerly about the Union Pacific's 4-8-8-4 Big Boy locomotive versus the 2-6-6-6 "Allegheny"-type engines. Many teetered out of the windows with a ludicrous disregard for safety.

Finally, I reached the baggage car. It had two wide-open doors guarded by flimsy gates. A tall, slim girl in blue jeans and a brown ski sweater stood there. She held a joint to her lips. I gaped at her, and she smiled.

"Want to get high?"

"Far out," I said.

Soon we were zonked and giggling about the otherworldly train fanatics. Before long, we went in search of beer and munchies.

Donna had fashion model cheekbones, a luscious mouth, and a very easy manner. It didn't take us long to outline our motives. Mine were those of a typical male dog. She wanted to piss off her boyfriend, who had coerced her into going on the trip and had thereby marked himself for extinction. After we smoked a second joint, we began a gentle dance toward intimacy.

Steam excursions, however, aren't designed for lovers. We snatched kisses between cars. When the train unloaded its passengers so fans could get photographs, we found a copse of bushes that allowed us to escalate our desire. Then we briefly experimented with lust in the toilet, but thought a Montreal hotel room a better option.

Satiating our passion presented us with strategic difficulties. Donna's boyfriend happily let her roam the train — it allowed him to fully indulge his passion for steam. But when we reached the end of the line, he'd be looking for her. She decided to simply disappear when the train stopped in Montreal and meet us at our hotel.

I, however, couldn't imagine what I would tell Dad. He already knew Donna and I were together and didn't seem to mind. Donna asked to be introduced, and Dad politely pulled his head inside the window, shook her hand, and made respectful inquiries about where she went to school and what she envisioned as a career.

I was grateful that he didn't embarrass me, but the fact that he knew we were together made accomplishing our ultimate goal a tactical challenge.

As we entered the hotel in Montreal, I asked Dad what the sleeping arrangement would be. He told me I had my own room.

"I will want to retire at a considerably earlier hour than you," he said and then flauted — for the first time since I'd been home. I asked him if he minded if Donna joined us for dinner, and he readily assented to the idea. Following a cordial meal, we told Dad the Montreal nightlife needed sampling. Soon we were together in my room, drinking beer and smoking a last joint.

As she deposited the smoldering roach in the ashtray, she grabbed me by the corduroy collar of my blue jean jacket and led me into the bathroom. Immense, tiled in white porcelain, with green trim and a fleur-de-lis pattern repeated on the decorative scrolling at the ceiling and again on the shower curtains, it featured a heated floor. Two fluffy bathrobes hung on the door. Best of all, the smell: iris and lavender. We, by contrast, stank of coal and needed to undergo an olfactory makeover before we could proceed.

As we stood together in the shower, we watched with amazement as the water, coming off our bodies and heading toward the drain, turned black.

When I crawled into the warm silkiness of the bed, we had what must have been, for her, a very mediocre sexual encounter. For me, the tryst was terribly exciting — until I felt the soles of her feet flat on my back. Her big toes began to massage the muscles under my scapula. My body, headed pell-mell for ejaculation a moment earlier, came to an abrupt halt. I rolled off her.

"What the matter?"

"How did you do that?"

"We all have our talents. Mine is being especially limber."

"Oh..."

"Most boys like it, but if you'd rather I be a little more conventional, I'm happy to oblige."

She went on to show me several things that had never crossed my mind before then. As she moved from one erotic technique to another, she'd say sweetly, softly, "I'd like to try something else, but I don't want to make you uncomfortable."

She made me very comfortable. Before that day, I was relatively inexperienced despite my two years of marriage that ended in 1970. That night, I felt like I was transformed into a man by a woman I'd never see again.

I had agreed to meet Dad at 7:00 a.m., and I suffered more than a little grogginess as I entered the hotel dining room.

"Well, William, did you sleep well?" he asked, using his most magnanimous tone.

"Actually, I had sort of a hard time getting to sleep," I responded.

"I'll bet you did." He leered, leaving no doubt that he knew exactly what had happened. "I'll bet you did!"

◆ ◆ ◆

Paris

Nov. 5, 1944

Dear Mary Lou:

...Paris is indeed a remarkable place. It is Times Square on New Year's Eve and a four-alarm fire all rolled into one. The inhabitants are celebrating release from curfew and other restrictions. The streets are jammed from dawn to dawn. When Parisians sleep and when they work are two things that I am unable to figure out. They seem to spend all of their time in cafés and walking the streets. A package of American cigarettes is the key to the city.

My first afternoon I decided to devote to sightseeing and accordingly set forth. My first action was to get terribly and completely lost in the Metro...The Metro is worse than the Lexington Avenue line any five o'clock of the week. I was jammed against a comely mademoiselle so tightly that it reminded me of the hydraulic presses I studied in physics. Unfortunately the mademoiselle took advantage of the situation to make improper suggestions. I have never claimed to be a man of the world and I turned very red, much to the amusement of spectators who were eavesdropping. Having always had somewhat of an aversion to being in the public eye, I suffered the agonies of mortification before I could escape...

Love,

Peter

CHAPTER 32: A "NEWS" OBIT

In 1973, I decided to join Mary Jo and her hippie boyfriend in southern Colorado, where they lived in a little adobe house. I needed another geographic cure after my failed attempt at organizing the labor union in New York. The effort had helped plunge me into even more drinking, and I thought leaving New York might be just the answer.

For about five months, I did hard manual labor in southern Colorado. One fall day, a couple of weeks after frost made its first appearance where we lived, thirty-five miles west of Trinidad, I got a note from Mary Jane, a woman I'd fallen in love with during my high school job at Zion Canyon. She said she'd gotten a divorce and invited me to visit her in Salt Lake. About a year later, we married.

At around that time, I took my second professional job at the *Colorado Springs Sun*.

One afternoon in 1974, I answered my newsroom phone and heard the voice of an old family friend telling me of the death of my father. That my mother didn't call herself didn't surprise me in the least. When the word came in that Dad had suffered a fatal heart attack during a board meeting of the Morgan Guaranty Trust Co., she called the church. They volunteered to take care of everything, including calling the children, so she could get some serious pain relief under way.

It did surprise me that Dad died at fifty-five. Although I knew he had heart disease, he had stopped drinking nine months prior to his death. I hoped he might become a brilliant old man.

The circumstances surrounding his swing to sobriety humbled him. His doctor, noting substantial swelling in his legs, suspected congestive heart failure and ordered him hospitalized.

The doctor had previously warned Dad about drinking, to no avail, so when he entered the intensive care unit, they sedated him and put him in four-point restraints. The doc ordered he be kept in that posture until the delirium tremens passed.

My sister Joanie told me when the DTs struck, Dad broke out of the restraints, shed his hospital gown, and ran buck-naked down the corridors of Lawrence Hospital in search of a Scotch bottle before being captured by the nursing staff.

A few days after the DTs shook out, the hospital released Dad, shattered but sober. His medical problems, however, weren't confined to his cardiovascular system. He had diabetes as well. Dad's squeamishness about needles caused his doctor to prescribe oral insulin, a drug known even then to cause heart attacks among patients with cardiac illness.

Of the five of us, probably the only child who truly grieved the loss of her father was his youngest, Susan. She picked me and my wife up at the airport for the memorial service. As we walked away from the arrival gates at JFK, we faced a vast sea of terra cotta terminal floor, populated by relatively few people, for the hour was late. My eyes surveyed the outer edges of this pinkish-gray expanse and finally picked up my sister, still a hundred yards distant. She wore an oatmeal sweater, copper-tinted blonde hair, and outsized glasses. Even from afar, I could tell her walk didn't have its usual sparrow-like confidence.

As she got closer, I could see that grief hung on her like a sodden fishing net. Her entire demeanor sagged. It seemed forever before we narrowed the gap between us, but when we finally did, I saw tears cascading down her face. She put her arms around my neck and clung to me, heaving with grief.

I had been away from home much of the time, but she had watched him drink and drank with him. She gave him a ride to the train in the morning and almost always picked him up from the station in the evening. He shouldn't be burdened with the final leg of his commute, a half-mile bus ride followed by a long walk up the hill to our house. Although in her early twenties then, Susie eventually would achieve no more longevity than he, and for the same reasons: alcohol and tobacco.

In Bronxville, Mary Jane, my sisters and I spent our time in the basement smoking weed and drinking beer while my mother commiserated with friends and relatives in the kitchen upstairs.

As we talked about his demise, I can't remember one kind word being said, a remarkable thing considering the man raised us in an exclusive New York City suburb, made sure we never went without, took us on cross-country vacations, and paid college tuition for all five of us.

During the memorial service at Christ Church, I wondered what made him turn to God. Obvious answers, when dealing with a man like Peter McBean, seldom sufficed. I had a bundle of "young man" answers but little insight. I speculated that he got old, sick, and afraid of death. I thought Mom wanted him to go to church with her, and he thought getting with the program easier than resisting.

I'm sure Dad would have been pleased by the military element to his funeral. His law firm required all the firm's associates, well over a hundred in number, to attend the memorial service. Men stood at the head of each aisle, checking off names.

At one point during the service, I found myself thinking about how much his personality changed in the year before his death. He became truly meek. Several months before his demise he said to Mom, “If I die, please put a cookie in my hand before you bury me.” The thought made me sob.

As I sat in the front row of Christ Church, I tried my best to think of things I liked about him. He had many virtues: original humor, his splendid sense of satire, and his willingness to supply us with the tools we needed to be successful. Of course, at the time, I had no conception of the bravery it took to live a quiet, orderly suburban existence after experiencing such a harrowing wartime career.

The memory that comforted me most, as I sat in Christ Church listening to the drone of Gospel readings, floated in from the deep past. Sometime during a Vermont vacation, Mom had struggled to get her five kids ready for a visit to family friends. She wanted her brood to be as presentable as possible and ran short on time.

I had needed to have my fingernails cleaned before we could leave. This wasn’t something I could be expected to do in an acceptable matter — I’d been rooting around in the dirt for days, and cleaning me up would take a fingernail brush and an adult armed with a pointed instrument.

My mother usually cleaned my nails, and it wasn’t a pleasant process. She used brute force and speed, and I usually broke away and fled outside, knowing once I passed the screen door, she’d never catch me.

I viewed Dad the fingernail cleaner with trepidation. Mom used barbaric methods; could I imagine what Dad’s would be like?

And yet that moment with him turned out to be an island of calm in an otherwise chaotic relationship. As he cleaned each nail, he kept his eyes trained on mine to make sure he didn't inflict any pain. In those eyes, and in the relaxed expression on his face, I saw the father I'd always wanted.

I also thought about my tenth birthday party — but not about receiving the radio, which I should have been grateful for but wasn't. I thought about the following Saturday, when I'd invited most of the boys in my fourth-grade class to festivities at the Scout Cabin down by the odoriferous Bronx River. There would be ice cream and cake, and that always played well. Dad, however, had another idea — he would organize a softball game.

I couldn't get my head wrapped around the idea of Dad as master of ceremonies. Would he Haut? Would he quiz my friends about vowels versus consonants? Would he yell "AT-TENT-HUT" at the top of his lungs? The prospect of Dad being the pied piper of the diamond had me worried.

Yet when he got out there, he'd transformed himself from stern disciplinarian to the magnetic man. He had more charisma than Roy Rogers. My friends loved him, and as he pitched for both sides, he provided a hilarious commentary. To top it all, I got two hits! This was a minor miracle, since everyone knew I couldn't hit a ball off a tee.

It was by far the best birthday ever. I wanted it to go on and on. Somehow, Dad had done the basic adolescent PR work I couldn't manage. For one afternoon, I felt wildly popular and entirely happy.

When I returned to reality, I sat in Christ Church, still immersed in grief, bitterness, and regret. Obviously, Dad had his moments, but given the time we spent together, a few good things didn't add up to a eulogy. I decided I was glad he was gone, because now I could close the books on him permanently and forever. Whenever vestiges remained in my brain I'd simply block out.

The morning following the memorial service, the *New York Times* arrived on the front door mat. Mom usually waited until later in the day to read it, but on this morning, she opened its pages with a snap. Five days had elapsed since Dad's death without an obit. Often over the years, I heard my parents discuss whether this person or that person deserved a news obit in the *Times* (as opposed to a paid funeral notice). Once becoming a partner in my father's firm, mother assumed Dad's demise was worth at least some mention. That morning, the *Times* printed a hundred-word news obit.

"Thank God!" she whispered.

CHAPTER 33: MOM'S TRAUMA

Mom circa 1972

From then on, Mom had no one with whom to share her trauma. She'd met the challenge of fighting psychoneurosis and raising five children. Nothing prepared her for the isolation of being a widow. She didn't have that firm bedrock of a good childhood to fall back on.

She spent her early years in relative opulence, since her father inherited a family-owned wholesale grocery business that operated out of Manhattan. In the Depression, however, the business shriveled, as did her father's finances. He had to borrow from a Princeton classmate to send her to Swarhmore.

Her dad, Ken Sills ("Princeton, class of '16," he'd never fail to say), did manage to keep the family in Bronxville and send his daughter to summer camp in Maine. There she achieved notoriety when, at about fourteen, she saved a toddler from drowning. I found out about this in an old newspaper clip. Mom never mentioned her heroism as I grew up, though we heard plenty about Lake Webb and even went there once.

During the war, Mom worked at Macy's in Manhattan. She had a demanding boss named Gertie. Macy's hired Mom as a buyer out of college and by the end of the war promoted her to human resources. Her notes indicated that the store involved her in many of its operations, including a stint as a secret buyer who tested sales clerks' skills.

While Dad lived, Mom functioned as caretaker for the misunderstood genius. She kept her head down and did the work. She cooked and read us stories. Mom the automaton made sure a multiple vitamin rested in the hollow of our spoons at the breakfast table seven mornings a week.

It rarely occurred to me that my mother had more than one dimension until the day of her 1993 funeral. She died of cancer of the oesophagus, a disease I'm reliably told one gets from smoking and drinking.

On several occasions before her death, I heard her bitterly proclaim, "It's my own damn fault." Most of us had already quit cigarettes and wondered at our mother's inability to understand her peril. Yet we considered it part and parcel of dealing with a high-functioning drunk. With the exception of Susie, we all held a grudge against our mother because over the years her accounts of our behavior unleashed the wrath of our father.

The morning prior to her funeral service, we five siblings drank coffee, told jokes, and looked out the living room picture window at the foggy Connecticut River Valley. We heard a car crunching the driveway gravel. Heather, my daughter from my college marriage, arrived. We said hi and then continued with our levity.

Heather didn't laugh — she made no effort to hide her dismay. "What is *wrong* with you people?"

Mom had "adopted" Heather and had shown her a generous, loving side unfamiliar to us. She looked each of us in the eye and stopped at me. "This is your mother's funeral, not a party!"

"Heather, you have to understand we had an entirely different experience with her than you did," I said, but I knew we were being boorish.

I should have shut up and apologized, but I couldn't stop talking. I launched into a detailed and painfully inappropriate explanation about Mom's failings. One or two of my sisters joined in, but it didn't last long. Heather's stern eye reduced us all to silence.

The funeral took place on a high knoll in the Dummerston Center graveyard. Vermont wore its brightest green that May day. In addition to family and friends, a coterie of gay Episcopal priests attended. Mom loved to party with those guys. A bagpiper played "Amazing Grace," and although to some of us her life seemed neither amazing nor graceful, none of us had yet become wretched enough to sense the grace of God in all things.

She spent most of her life trying to cope with the childhood damage inflicted by her mother. When Mom started shopping for a husband at Swarthmore, she looked for a straight arrow because her mother's indiscretions had so disrupted her childhood home. When she met my dad, she found his single-minded devotion to her very compelling. He wanted only one thing from her: a traditional marriage with clear boundaries. Both of them held the concept of "moral relativism" in low regard.

During those years, Mom became riven by her lonely responsibilities. Her sister Josie, who had been very close to her, felt her best friend had floated away on a wave of booze.

"She began drinking an awful lot...I couldn't count on what her mood was going to be, or how she was going to be, or anything, from time to time."

During casual conversations with me — ones not included in my two recorded interviews with her — Josie made it clear that Mom drank during all four pregnancies. When she was pregnant with the twins in 1953, Josie recalled that Mom drank "heavily."

At the time, my seven year-old mind didn't focus on her drunkenness. I concentrated on my incompetence as a second-grader. It had me in a swivvet. Parent-teacher reports from that era accorded me kudos because I wasn't stepping on other children's paintings *as much*. My fogginess irritated Mom. I'm sure she wanted to be the warm bosom of motherhood, yet when I spilled a glass of milk, her wrath boiled over: "Oh, for criminy sakes, Bill how *could* you!"

I grew up with an irascible, tight, twisted, tense, white-knuckled, vexed human being. But despite her emotional problems, she took motherhood seriously. She read to her children every day at lunch, something I looked forward to greatly. She cooked many good meals and despite the drink performed her duties as a housewife in a manner that, I gather, met 1950s standards.

My sister Joan said Mom "busted her hiney" being a Girl Scout leader for the troop in which she and Susan participated. For years, Mom showed her civic pride by dressing up in her Girl Scout uniform and marching in the Memorial Day Parade.

She did more than that, though. A maid to former US

Senator Jake Javits, a Bronxville resident, had a child named Isabella Gonzalez. Latina daughters of embassy families living in Bronxville gained acceptance, but being a poor Latina must have presented a daunting situation.

Mom made it her business to assure Isabella had an active role in the Girl Scout troop — but she went further than that. She intervened in party plans to make sure the girls invited Isabella, and because of Mom's sponsorship, the other girls gradually accepted Isabella, Joanie said.

Mom wanted very badly to be seen as exemplary, but while she tended five children and a psychoneurotic husband, it proved impossible for her to show the outside world her goodness. Maybe that's why in the years after Dad's death, Mom became a church lady.

This didn't happen immediately after Dad's death in 1974. She and Dad had been companions of the first rank. The death of her only ally made her feel like a scrap in the wind. Married thirty-two years, they survived the war and its aftermath, raised five children — all of whom managed to stay out of prison — and together they steered their way into an opulent law firm partnership.

And now she got to enjoy the fruits of this work alone! Life didn't interest her without her husband. She suffered from serious diabetes at the time of Dad's death. On as many as a dozen different occasions, friends, family, and members of the general public found her in a coma and near death because she'd "forgotten" to take her insulin. One time, this happened at de Gaulle Airport and she spent the night in the American Hospital in Paris — but then caught up with her Swarthmore tour group and continued to party as if nothing had happened.

Yet she found purpose and lived another twenty years, primarily because of one of the gay priests who attended her funeral, Father Charles Scott of Christ Church. Scott talked her into doing a newsletter for part of the Diocese of New York. This project lasted about five years and brought her in touch with an entirely new cast of characters, mostly men and women from the church's left-leaning activist wing. It gave Mom a new identity and hope.

Some found her new persona attractive. To Mom's dismay there were widowers in the village who thought her quite tempting and tried to court her. Shortly before she made the decision to move to Vermont, she told me, "I'm so sick of Dick G. chasing me around the couch, I finally just had to tell him."

"Tell him what, Mom?"

"That I'm not a sexual person!"

Those words made me cringe. Her primary social life since my dad's death was with the aforementioned gay priests, and in my naiveté I assumed this choice centered on her interest in the church and her love for the priests, some of whom the family had known for years. I hadn't realized how alone she was and how alone she wanted to be.

She moved into a maple-trimmed house Dad built before he died, located right across the road from the old wooden house our family used for vacations in the 1950s. Susan and Joan also settled nearby, Susan so close she could drop in just about any time.

One morning, she walked into Mom's house and found her with a half-gallon of Scotch over her shoulder, giving herself a hillbilly-style eye-opener.

"God, Mom, at least use a glass!" Susan said with disgust

as she stomped out.

Mom tried as best she could to be productive following her move to the country. She started a local newsletter called *Voices of Dummerston* that operated for years after her death. She also became deeply engaged in helping the Church of England's faltering efforts in Uganda.

But her continuous attempts to improve herself and the lives of those around her weren't enough to save her from the grinding self-hatred she'd picked up being the daughter of a "playgirl."

While Mom lived in Vermont, she kept a journal that eventually fell into Anne's hands. An extended datebook for the most part, she recorded dinners, cocktail parties, and her activities around her new house in Vermont. On a few occasions, however, the account became intensely personal and provided a reflection of her pitiful self-regard.

One of her biggest grievances about Vermont life focused on Joan's refusal to let her babysit her daughter's new child, Duncan. Instead, Jan Scherer, Joan's mother-in-law, got the nod. When Jan got too busy, she'd occasionally call Mom and ask her to help.

This arrangement made Mom seethe.

This morning I was finally summoned to Duncan sit, she wrote in her journal July 15, 1985. *Duncan is really an extremely alert, responsive and attractive two-year-old. The trouble is that two-year-olds bore me. However, I kept him very happy for an hour and one-half while Jan did errands. After all, I have been begging for this as a matter of principle, and in the same spirit wish I had been allowed to do more.*

Trusting Mom with children wasn't something that happened often, and even when children weren't involved, she had a hard time dealing with her progeny. Her journal reflects a fight with Susan over lunch in which Mom said or did "something awful."

"I won't say what it was because it will live with me always."

I don't know what that beef was about, but at roughly the same time she got into a large hoodoo with Anne over not being invited to a late summer barbecue Anne organized for her own friends. No amount of explaining would convince her that sometimes twenty-somethings don't want sixty-somethings around.

Living in Colorado, I missed much of this. When I came back to visit with my family, the palpable friction seemed to be centered on alcohol. I drank even more than usual — being on vacation — and Mom drank just as she always did, often leaving no one competent to drive a car other than my wife, who hesitated to ask her mother-in-law for the keys. She knew Mom *wanted* to drive so she could be included in the fun.

She wrote perhaps the saddest part of the journal a few years before she was diagnosed with cancer. She obviously had no idea how much trouble she was in.

Her October 26, 1986 entry said, *Things started going downhill on Thurs. eve. I was watching TV, got up for something, not realizing my left foot was asleep and fell. I hurt my foot quite badly and it still hurts, but I'm walking on it.*

Then on Friday morning when I was practicing (piano), I became aware there was blood on my nose. It looks as if I'd run into something, but I couldn't have unless I blacked out. I don't think I did but the thought scares me, living alone...I will probably have to go to the doctor on Monday...

She did go to the doctor. He ran a battery of tests and told her to return in a couple of weeks. When they reconvened, he said her liver wasn't functioning properly and that she should stop drinking.

Mom said she gave the matter a second's thought and then told her physician she would probably "cut back after Christmas." She said her doc understood this kind of thing was an "adult choice." She didn't cut back, and the following year, after her annual physical, she waited for the doctor's scolding telephone call. When it didn't come, she assumed the problem had vanished.

When I learned in January of 1992 that Mom had cancer and that it had been misdiagnosed for nine months as a respiratory infection, I felt subsumed by depression. The last thirty years of her life boiled with resentment — against the death of her husband, against her children, and against herself for not being able to quit tobacco and drink.

For days, I summoned up scenes from the past where I had slathered her with mockery and scorn, sometimes behind her back but often enough to her face. As month after month of cancer treatment tales came to me through my sisters, my heart filled with pity and shame.

I thought primarily of how insolently I acted toward her, especially after 1962, when I escaped Bronxville. I thought myself justified because she always told Dad of my misdeeds and therefore it was she (not I) who brought about his draconian discipline. In the last years of her life, she let her children know she asked Dad to dole out the punishment because she didn't want to be viewed as the sole bad guy.

In May 1993, doctors told Mom the cancer had metastasized to her lungs. She could expect to live only a few more weeks. Unlike many, who fought cancer to the end, Mom conceded meekly. The night before she died, she requested Mary Jo to read Thomas Gray's *Elegy Written in a Country Churchyard* at her bedside.

In the poem, the writer ponders whether the low-born people buried in the churchyard might have had significant, unrecognized talent. The poem praises the dead for the simple, honest lives they lived.

Mom memorized large passages of the poem and often quoted it when she wanted us to value simple goodness. She quoted Gray often enough I knew her favorite lines:

Large was his bounty, and his soul sincere,

Heav'n did a recompense as largely send:

He gave to Mis'ry all he had, a tear,

He gain'd from Heav'n ('twas all he wish'd) a friend.

CHAPTER 34: MY DODGER PENNANT

I can think of no more convenient personal quality than blaming others for your problems. If you're convinced in your soul that you are the most unworthy of individuals, refusing to take responsibility is your only option.

I didn't stop blaming my parents during a spiritual epiphany. It took deconstructing the whole mess, looking at the individual parts, and then putting them back together again. Only after doing that — and writing about it for a decade — could I adjust my perspective.

My new point of view didn't include letting my parents off the hook. Their alcoholism convinced me to use booze to relax. They criticized me so much that I became a thin-skinned and defensive adult. They embedded in my psyche a pustule of fear that caused me to have panic attacks.

Psychologists believe children exposed to trauma — like my dad's beatings and sadism — are susceptible to a host of emotional ailments:

- Depression and anxiety
- Intense emotional upset
- Substance abuse
- Anxiety disorders
- Academic difficulties
- Nightmares

- Behavioral problems[35]

I suffered from all of the symptoms cited above, and they blended into a perfect storm the day Dad decided to take me to a baseball game.

A fanatical Giants fan, Dad hated the Yankees with everything he had. Of course, that meant I had to be a very vocal Yankees fan.

Between 1950 and 1960, the American League Yanks won the World Series six times, including once over the Giants. In 1955, the Dodgers won a World Series victory over the Yanks, which delighted my father.

While Dad's eloquence and rationality extended to many things, baseball summoned up his partisan self. He thought me jejune and ripe for conversion. At every opportunity he'd try to turn me into a National League fan (and therefore a potential recruit to the Giants).

"Bill, the National League is obviously superior to the American League. The statistics are undeniable. The Yankees get to the World Series every year because of light competition. Who wins the All-Star game? Every year? The National League."

He was nearly right about that. Between 1950 and 1956, the National League won five of six All-Star games.

"Okay, Dad, so why do the Yankees win the World Series so much?"

"Luck," my father said emphatically.

Our baseball banter, which began when I was roughly seven and continued until the Giants broke his heart and moved to San Francisco in 1957, often became a little too tart. Slightly sour turned rancid when my dispirited old man decided, on the last year of Brooklyn's tenure, to take me to the first major-league game either of us had ever attended in person.

Dad never went to the Polo Grounds. It would have entailed another trip to Manhattan when he had to travel there five days a week. He watched the Giants on our little black and white TV. During Sunday double-headers, he'd sit in front of the box from 1:00 to 9:00 p.m., drinking beer and eating double-mayo tomato and onion sandwiches.

I turned into a Yankees fan largely because of the Giants' stellar 1954 season, which ended with a 4-0 sweep of the Cleveland Indians in the World Series. I had to listen to Dad's irritating talk about his boys from April until October. He viewed the Giants' foes with the same vitriol he generally reserved for communists and Blacks. Because my mother didn't give a hoot, he'd talk to me about his heroes' struggles. To him, I'm sure my disinterest mirrored all my other problems. I didn't get math, I couldn't read very well, my attention span was zip, my mouth hung open most of the time. My disinterest in the Giants must have seemed like a direct rejection of him.

When it became obvious that two National League shrines, Ebbets Field and the Polo Grounds, would soon be demolished, Dad's sense of history overwhelmed him. Since he knew I wouldn't attend a Giants game, and because he couldn't set foot in Yankee Stadium, he saw Ebbets Field as a compromise.

One Saturday in midsummer when I was ten, we jumped in the Pontiac wagon and pointed the orange hood ornament toward the heart of Brooklyn. I pouted as we crested the Whitestone Bridge and then made our way, slowly, toward the park. We weren't going to see the Yanks, so who cared? After the bridge, the world went from neatly trimmed suburban green to blowing newspapers and city gray. The grimness of it confirmed my worst expectations. Certainly the Bronx wasn't this ugly! I crossed my arms and hugged them tightly to my chest. Dad soldiered on, fought horrendous traffic, and got us there in time for the national anthem.

My peevish attitude let up a little as we came out of the tunnel leading into the stadium. I'd never seen grass so green. City buildings crowded around the outfield fences and made Ebbets seem like a quaint little theater.

Since the game didn't involve the Giants, Dad modulated his rhetoric. He made a concerted effort to explain some of the game's more arcane aspects. He'd read up on Ebbets Field's "ground rules," or regulations exclusive to the venue in which we were sitting. His commentary piqued my interest, and the occasion might have ended up being positive for us had it not been for his generous offer to buy me a souvenir. My eyes sorted through the blue-and-white Dodgers regalia and spotted a Yankees pennant.

"Please, Dad."

"No. Choose something else."

"Oh, Dad, come on! Please!"

"I didn't bring you out here today to encourage your slavish devotion to that team."

Dad held his hand up, signaling he was ready to buy. "One Dodgers pennant, please."

He handed me the pennant, and I threw it back at him. It fell on the grimy pavement. I stomped it and then disintegrated into a bawling fit that lasted until we got back to Bronxville. At the game, we established our common bond: we each held to our unreasonable positions, irrespective to how much it hurt the other.

Both Dad and I were traumatized. We'd psychologically destroyed each other.

Resetting our relationship at that point may have been beyond the skills of even the best twenty-first century practitioners. I'm sure counseling could have benefited me and perhaps helped me make the most of the many blessings I had, and if Dad had managed to stop drinking, he might have been happier and lived a longer life, but our bond had as much hope as a stone dropped in the deepest part of the ocean.

I'm sure he thought he'd done everything he could, but I thought he'd done nothing at all; worse, I believed he'd done his best to break me.

CHAPTER 35: DANGERS OF SECONDARY TRAUMA

Anticipate, the mantra Dad urged upon me several times a week for years. Yet I'm sure he didn't foresee PTSD, and I'm certain he couldn't imagine what it would do to his family.

Although many were aware that warfare turned some people into lunatics, serious research on PTSD didn't begin until after the Vietnam War. The investigation of secondary traumatic stress didn't start until twenty years after that, and it's still in its infancy.

Although much work still needs to be done, experts have concluded the best thing a family can do to prepare themselves for the impact of a veteran's return is learn the facts about PTSD and secondary trauma in advance of the homecoming.

The most difficult fact to master may be that soldiers who have experienced intense combat often form new families: their brothers in arms. The feelings of loyalty and love forged by life-and-death stakes are often more intense than those with a marital partner.[36] Obviously, this is an incredibly hard fact for the soldier to admit and for a spouse to accept.

PTSD isn't inevitable, and not every combat soldier is afflicted. Nonetheless, a prepared spouse should look for the basic signs of trauma in their returning soldier. Here are some basic PTSD symptoms:

- Nightmares

- Flashbacks
- Becoming upset following a trigger event, like a car backfire
- Avoiding events because of fear it will bring back memories
- Avoiding contact with friends or family
- Feeling dead or hollow inside
- Emotional numbness
- Disinterest in formerly enjoyable acts
- Hypervigilance
- Insomnia
- Unnecessary worries about safety
- Irritability[37]
- Sexual Disinterest[38]
- Domestic Violence[39]

There are many useful books out about PTSD and secondary trauma, but I think by far the most accessible information is available from the US Department of Veterans Affairs (www.ptsd.va.gov). The VA has gotten a reputation for failing veterans and their families in many ways, but this online resource is voluminous and easy to use.

Usually, there's a honeymoon period when a soldier returns, but experts say it seldom lasts very long.

Sometimes, households are reduced to war zones within days of a soldier's return. Two studies indicated women afflicted with PTSD initiated more violence than men, though some psychologists said not enough research had been done to draw conclusions.[40] About half the partners of veterans with PTSD indicated they felt "on the verge of a nervous breakdown."[41]

Many experts agree the first step toward healing the family is to get the soldier on the path to a solution. This can sometimes be initiated by a spouse who knows the symptoms of PTSD. After a soldier begins the road to recovery, the family can enter therapy.

The goal is to stop secondary trauma before it begins, but sometimes it's too late. Most children won't have the slightest idea of what's happening to them, but an educated partner can often recognize that certain children are playing predictable roles in the family dynamic. For instance:

- The "over-identified" child experiences many of the symptoms of the parent with PTSD.
- The "rescuer" or "hero" child takes on adult roles to compensate for the parent's problems.
- The emotionally uninvolved child receives little psychic support, resulting in school difficulties, depression, and/or anxiety and relationship problems later in life.[42]

In the twenty-first century, dealing with trauma is much different than it was after World War II. Perhaps the primary reason is multiple deployments. It's not uncommon for soldiers to be deployed five times for a year or more. This gives PTSD a far greater chance to take hold, and it makes the pressure on the primary caregiver — often the spouse of the soldier — even greater.

The necessity of service members getting therapy first brings up a daunting problem: career military members sometimes fear that getting therapy will hurt their careers, and many others, perhaps 50 percent, refuse to get treatment after they're diagnosed.[43]

Another fact that families need to understand is that compared to a battle zone, civilian life can seem boring and superficial to a vet. After dealing with the day-to-day problems in Iraq's Al Anbar Province, listening attentively to a parent-teacher conference might seem a little trivial. Many a vet's solution to this problem is to round up some buddies and go to a bar.

This oft-employed dodge leaves the partner at home trying to attend to his or her own worries, which often include children who believe their military parent's indifference means a lack of love.

Experts offer a host of palliatives for such situations. Psychological therapy by a *qualified* expert is the most often recommended line of treatment, but there are many reasons such treatment might not be possible. Many families can't afford psychologists. VA treatment is free if the vet is qualified to receive it, yet anecdotal evidence I've gathered indicates that getting qualified is difficult and frustrating. Also, many live in rural areas and must drive for hours to get to a VA center.

Here are a few self-help suggestions for caregivers and children to follow:[44]

- Stress is contagious, but so is relaxation. Let children see that you, the caregiver, know how to relax and take care of yourself.

- Be patient and talk fears through to a positive outcome.

- Sometimes a child's fears seem silly, but let him know you have a plan to address his concerns.

- The power of positive affirmations is often overlooked. Teach your children to say, "I am calm. I am relaxed. I am safe."

- Practice controlled breathing to curb anger and anxiety. Breathe in 2-3-4 and breathe out 2-3-4.

- To help your children fall asleep, use muscle relaxation. Start with their legs. "Now you are going to completely relax your legs," and then proceed up the body.

- Take a warm bath or shower an hour before sleep.

- Plan healthy social activities with friends. Isolation can be a big enemy — avoid it.

- Use alcohol in a very moderate way. Don't take drugs unless they're prescribed.

- Exercise and eat right. This is often easier said than done, but to steal a line from a famous sporting goods manufacturer, "Just do it." Getting aerobicized is a better solution to problems than drugs, alcohol, or venting anger.

The PTSD problem is slippery and amorphous, especially because no one seems to be able to get a handle on the numbers. Soldiers reporting PTSD directly after the war varied from 15 percent to 30 percent. Yet 25 years later, the number went up to about 80 percent.[45] Some estimate that 20 percent of soldiers returning from Iraq and Afghanistan have PTSD, but estimates vary from 4 percent to 31 percent and higher.[46]

The statistical picture is further blurred when traumatic brain injury (TBI) is considered. TBI is generally caused by a blow to the head. Although entirely different from PTSD, some of the symptoms, like mood swings, depression, and anxiety, are the same. That adds about 260,000 Afghanistan and Iraq veterans to the force with the potential to cause secondary trauma.[47]

When my father came home from the European war, I don't believe anyone was equipped to anticipate his needs. Of course, his family did its best. My mother fondly anticipated having that red-headed baby boy. Everyone told him how much they admired his bravery and how glad they were he'd gotten home safely. He didn't have significant financial worries.

For his part, Dad denied the war had done anything other than made him a little "jumpy" at times. He wished he had a little more than two weeks to decompress before starting law school, but he heeded his father's warnings about a job market already glutted by returning GIs.

Yet Dad had a relatively placid reentry. His wife adored him and, I believe, suspected he might be shell-shocked. She had read a great deal of popular press, and plenty of articles warned wives their spouses might be scarred. Yet she fell into a trap that awaits so many nonmilitary spouses: in order to commiserate properly, she felt she needed to drink with him. I have no idea how many details of the battlefield he shared with her, but judging from the detail Dad gave us, I'm sure her immersion in gore was considerable. She had, after all, received his explicit letters and surely asked follow-up questions. Dad, for his part, was a talker, especially when oiled by alcohol. Knowing him, I'd be willing to bet his sadism evidenced itself as he supplied his wife with bounteous detail. He enjoyed seeing people shudder. It amused him. Gradually, her companionable drinking gave way to medicinal consumption — to the point where her sister later said she was getting shellacked while pregnant with my twin sisters, eight years after my father's return.

To be fair to her, even if she had followed today's recommended protocol for wives of returning military men, her fight would have been daunting. Of course, she might have restrained her drinking, but if she'd taken other recommended steps, how far would she have gotten? Dad would never have gone to a psychologist. That would have meant admitting he had a problem, and, in his mind, would have risked leaking word of his condition. They had no way of knowing their children suffered from secondary traumatic stress — research on the disorder began in the 1960s and didn't become public until substantially after that.

She obviously had prepared herself for problems, because she tried to calm his nightmares and was there to offer daily commiseration. She understood the deeper meaning behind his letters from the war zone and tried to pass that understanding to me. While she might have had more resources if their situation were happening today, many of the same issues still occur. It's difficult to get warriors to seek psychiatric help or take meds, and if a soldier suffers PTSD while still in the military, it's entered on his or her military record. Many things haven't changed.

In 1946, deep war wounds didn't surprise Americans who had coped with World War I survivors' "battle fatigue."

Most ignored the effect of shell-shock on families. The study of transgenerational transmission of trauma began in the mid-1960s with the children of German concentration camp survivors.[48] After that, research into the basic problems besetting soldiers and their families gained momentum.

Today, as America tries to cope with PTSD-afflicted service men and woman from Iraq and Afghanistan, there's a lot of advice available but no sure-fire cure for secondary trauma.

I expect my experience with secondary trauma isn't unusual. I spent years having no idea I was afflicted. In my thirties, I suspected I had a drinking problem, but I thought it the product of an intentionally hedonistic lifestyle. Then, when I was forty, my hangovers featured major panic attacks — events that drove me into treatment and ended my drinking career. I thought abstaining from alcohol would stop the panic attacks, but I was wrong. They occurred periodically, embarrassed me to death, and left me profoundly puzzled. It wasn't until I was well into the research for this book that I began to understand the roots of my anxiety.

Perhaps my encounter is like that of others suffering from secondary trauma. Their lives are off course, their behavior borders on the bizarre, alcohol and chemical abuse causes them trouble, and they have no idea how this state of affairs got started or what to do about it.

People already afflicted with secondary trauma need to get help from a qualified therapist — which means a therapist with experience in treating trauma. If drugs and alcohol have become a problem, twelve-step programs are available. In my experience, these programs work only if the participant really *wants* to get sober. Panic attacks, depression, and other symptoms of secondary trauma only get worse if drinking and drug abuse continues. In my case, thirty years of sobriety plus medication have removed most of the symptoms of secondary trauma. I can cope with the remaining symptoms because finally I understand the psychodynamics of the problem.

My experience hardly qualifies me to give advice. I'm not a psychologist, and being married to one for over forty years doesn't count. Yet my very brief 1962 experience with Mr. Harris, the Bronxville Public Schools counselor, helped me immensely. We spent very little time together, perhaps two hours total, yet his message helped me turn around my approach to the world — at least for a while. Simply stated, he said although I had reason to act in a negative fashion, it was getting me nowhere. He suggested I be positive with people, express an interest in them, and quit complaining about my problems. As I said previously, his advice worked wonders.

In college, I suffered a few emotional setbacks that allowed me once again to wallow in self-pity. At the time, of course, it seemed like genuine pain, and I used nature's great pain reliever: alcohol. I didn't think at all about what alcohol had done to my parents. I didn't drink Scotch, after all; I drank beer. When a nurse told me one beer equaled the alcohol content of an ounce of whiskey, I scoffed. What did she know?

When I got into alcohol in a serious way the late 1960s, I had no idea I was using it to substitute for endorphins depleted by secondary trauma. Alcohol substituted for endorphins, and when the effects of booze subsided, my body cried out for more. I swirled in that cycle for roughly twenty-five years.

During my recovery, I learned an incredibly useful fact about myself: my primary problem wasn't that I craved alcohol; it was that I was selfish. And not just a little bit self-obsessed — egomaniacal would be closer to the truth. Getting rid of this major character defect proved to be quite a bit tougher at forty than when Mr. Harris suggested basically the same thing when I was fifteen. It took going to thousands of twelve-step meetings and creating an inventory of my grudges, wrongs to others, and fears. It was a major pain in the butt — and absolutely necessary if I wanted to go on living. Not everyone needs such an extreme solution, but I had a very strong intuitive feeling that if I'd tried a less rigorous fix, I would continue drinking.

Coincidental to my efforts to stay alive were my attempts to keep together a family that was truly worn out by my antics. Although I thought when I returned from the treatment center, they should lay palm leaves in my path, they didn't see me as heroic. On the contrary, they thought I was a "sober asshole." Some family members offered extended commentary on my misdeeds. As I listened to their screeds, I thought about my counselor Jeru, who said, "Their side of the street is their business. You keep your side of the street clean."

I washed dishes, cooked meals, and read bedtime stories. I resisted fighting with family members who held grudges. I kept on going to twelve-step meetings and somehow remained sober.

The question is, how much damage did I inflict on my family during thirteen years as an untreated drunk, and in more recent times, with our divorce? How much of that damage was counterbalanced by twenty-five years of effort to serve that family?

It's too early to judge. Although much of my family seems to be living a relatively placid existence at present, there are and will continue to be speed bumps. Time will be the judge of that. And even if I live to be a hundred, issuing the final scorecard is not my job.

CHAPTER 36: BRONZE STAR

For decades I stumbled in my effort to put my relationship with my father in context. Was he a warped human being who corrupted me? Or was he a victim who made a superhuman effort to deal with circumstances that vanquished lesser men?

I remember a friend who spoke of being repeatedly raped by his father as a child. He wanted to break away, to tell someone, but his father said if he didn't submit, his little sisters would be next. My friend escaped by joining the Marines. They sent him to Vietnam. He graduated from college and had a successful career, but alcoholism and bad choices plagued him. He made a serious effort at recovery but failed. Today, he's a wet-brain in a nursing home.

Now that's trauma, the kind of hardship that's almost impossible to overcome, even though my friend tried repeatedly. Relative to that, I went through very little. Still, I wallowed in self-pity for years.

I stopped drinking in 1987. I didn't take that step because my alcoholism hurt my family, or because of trouble with the law. I didn't stop because my work suffered or because I held up a mirror and became nauseated by what I saw. I stopped because I wanted to live, and one day it abruptly became clear to me that the privilege of life would be taken from me unless I changed my ways.

Excessive drinkers would rather do anything than face the facts about themselves, and I definitely fit that description.

While I drank, my policy was to lie rather than tell the truth, especially when the truth involved telling my wife my whereabouts or the company I kept. I figured if I told her the truth, then lied, then resumed trying to tell the truth, my chances of escaping detection (for secret drinking, misuse of money, etc.) were not good. But if I told her stories made of whole cloth each and every time, there was no truth to keep straight!

Predictably, she knew me for a liar and suspected I might be flat-out crazy. Nevertheless, she really didn't know vital facts that would have blown the marriage apart.

I would have drunk myself into an early retirement from life, just like my father, had it not been for the extreme anxiety I created by being such a nefarious liar. I had created a web of mendacity so thick, I lost track of what reality was — and then the panic attacks began.

For some, a panic attack can be little more than a state of high agitation from which they can recover by blowing into a paper bag. There are those who suffer from symptoms resembling a heart attack. For others, it's a paralyzing assault of psychosis where contact with reality can be fleeting.

From the onset, I counted myself among the psychotic group. True, the warning signs of total emotional collapse had been present for many years, but my denial attributed my problems to mixing pot with wine, or psychedelic mushrooms with whiskey. Then there came a day when the wall holding back all the mental mud collapsed and I was surrounded by darkness, unable to breathe.

On a mid-February morning in 1987, I went to work at my job at the *Denver Post* after administering my normal morning medicine: four Tylenol and a pot of coffee. I had just left my wife and thought myself on my way to divorce. The night before, I had stocked my new apartment with a full bar:

wine, whiskey, and beer. To my surprise, I reduced my inventory by 90 percent in one evening.

As I stood at my desk, I started reading a piece of legislation — the foundation of a story for the following day's paper. My mind would not coalesce around the words. My ability to focus wasn't there.

A normal drunk would have slipped across the street for an eye-opener, but I, standing in the early morning quiet of the newsroom, became convinced that the countdown clock to chaos had started ticking.

As the wild stampede in my mind grew, I called my wife and asked for her help. I begged her to come rescue me. I told her I worried about making a horrible scene if I stayed at the newspaper, so I asked her to pick me up as I walked south on Broadway. She reluctantly agreed. I put on my winter coat and left.

Juggling an eel is easier than managing an oncoming panic attack. Authenticity and fantasy merged. My judgment, which had been a staggering companion during my tenure as a drunk, wandered off. In its place came virulent fear. My mind was fragmenting, and there wasn't a thing I could do about it.

Walking toward Broadway, I felt sure I'd get hit crossing the street. I had a fight-or-flight episode with nobody to battle and nowhere to flee. Each person on the crowded sidewalk seemed threatening. An armed security guard gave me a look, and I became convinced he'd shoot me. I wanted to fall to the sidewalk and cover my head with my coat, but adrenaline made that impossible.

I darted this way and that like a bug and then, trying to collect myself, stood stock-still in the middle of the sidewalk. Buffeted by crowds, I once again became frenzied. I floated on an ocean in a rubber raft rapidly losing air. I couldn't remember how to swim. The waves were towering over my head and curling.

As I began walking south on Broadway, past Denver's Civic Center Park, I warily eyed the homeless folk there, only to discover they were eying me! I knew they could sense my helplessness and would come after me.

Then I saw my wife driving past in her red Sentra. She looked straight ahead, her forefinger characteristically pressed to her front teeth. She hadn't seen me.

I was on my own. My psychoneurosis had finally come full bloom.

I continued walking south on Broadway, toward I-25 and the looming Gates Rubber factory. I knew the farther south I walked, the fewer witnesses there would be to my inevitable slaughter. I convinced myself death waited on the next block.

At Ohio Avenue, I found a public phone. I didn't want to use it because my call would be an admission of my insanity. But I was beat. I absolutely had to ask for help.

I told the police dispatcher I was having a seizure.

"Mac, you're not having a seizure. If you were, you wouldn't be talking to me."

"Well, I'm having something!"

"Okay, stay right there. Help's on the way."

"How long?"

"Soon as they can get there."

Click.

When the Denver paramedics showed up, they knew

exactly what the problem was. One of the guys took the forefinger and pinky of my left hand and waggled them rhythmically.

"Don't worry, bud. We're going to take care of you. Everything's gonna be fine."

The hospital matched me up with a psychiatric social worker. Roughly twenty years my senior, she wore a mud-hen-brown suit and aqua-rimmed glasses. Generous amounts of rouge covered her dispirited face.

I earnestly explained my symptoms. I didn't ask for medication but certainly wanted it. The social worker knew me. She'd seen me hundreds of times. In a beleaguered tone forged by decades of telling miscreants the truth, she said, "Mr. McBean, you may want to consider that you have a problem with alcohol."

I had never admitted it, even to myself, yet this lady spoke the right words at the right time. I realized I needed to get help. From then on, I dedicated myself to recovery.

A couple of days later, I launched into twenty-eight days in an alcohol treatment center in Lakewood, Colorado. My primary counselor's name was Jeru, twenty years my senior and a recovered alcoholic himself. He looked pallid and whiskery under the fluorescent light, but his eyes were black and sharp.

He asked me if I resented anybody.

"Well, myself."

"We'll get to that. Who else?"

"Mainly my father, I guess."

"What'd he do?"

"About everything you could imagine!"

"I doubt that. Give me some examples."

I told him about the sarcasm, fines, and work details, the things I lost, the belt beatings — everything I could remember. I also told him about the egging. It was like acid belching from a boarded-up mine.

"Have you ever considered writing any of this stuff down?"

"What for? He's dead. The quicker I get him out of my head, the better."

"How long ago did he pass?"

"I dunno, it was '74, so about thirteen years, I guess."

"But he's alive, you know that, right?"

"In my head?"

"Bingo, and if you let him live there, he'll get you drunk."

"So what am I supposed to do?"

"Write him a letter. Hold him accountable."

"And then what? Burn it in some airy-fairy campfire ceremony?"

"Oh, no. You're way too smart for that."

I wrapped my arms in front of my chest and looked at the floor.

"What I was hoping," Jeru continued, "was if you wrote the letter, you might get a more focused idea of what actually happened. You suffered a lot of pain, I get that. But was that the entire picture? Did you handle your side of it as well as you could have?"

"I was just a kid!"

Jeru bunched his gray eyebrows and cocked his head. "Well, give it some thought, okay?"

I thought about the letter, even started it once or twice, but I feared attempting this high-wire act might cause me to lose my balance, and if I lost my balance again, I'd fall and keep falling.

◆ ◆ ◆

Even after I committed to sobriety, I hadn't finished screwing up people's lives. I wanted to feel better, but I didn't understand my problems weren't rooted in my family difficulties, or PTSD, or my hornet-of-a-wife. It was self-centeredness.

The night before going into treatment, I still felt very shaky — on the verge of reentering orbit. My stoic spouse tried to restore my equanimity by getting me to sit in a tub of hot water. As I sat there, and she hovered by my side, I decided the key to serenity was telling her my greatest secret — that I had a girlfriend. I was very sorry, knew it was wrong, and would break it off.

My admission shattered her, yet remarkably the marriage didn't end. It went on for another twenty-nine years before finally petering out. But it put a keen chill on family life for quite some time and made the "pink cloud" of recovery like jogging with nitroglycerin.

The details of my attempts to be a father are best left for another time, but certainly while I drank, my children came second and often had to contend with my surly hangovers. That they're all talking to me today, and doing well, is an undeserved gift.

Yet, to varying degrees, they suffered from my secondary trauma.

When I was twenty-three, I had left my wife and first child. My ex, out of necessity, quickly remarried — to my best friend at the time. The man was a drunk, so he served as my proxy. She survived the ordeal primarily because of her mother's dedication.

I had remarried at twenty-nine to Mary Jane, my former girlfriend from Zion National Park. She had two children by a previous marriage, and we had a son together. Our union was difficult from its inception, and although it takes two people to screw up a marriage, I did more than my share. My newspaper career was in full swing by then. I worked nights at the *Colorado Springs Sun,* and when I got off work, I drank with my fellow scribes.

After landing a job with the *Denver Post* in 1978, difficulties with my wife became unmanageable. We separated several times, once for fourteen months. The effect on my two oldest step-children was immense, but they still managed to flourish in a material sense — they graduated from college, got married, and had children. Their psychological damage is literally untold. Although there have been a few brief, harsh exchanges about my bizarre behavior, they understandably don't want to discuss their psychological distress. The son born from my second marriage seems to have suffered the least, although he was and is unhappy that we divorced.

It's too early to tell whether the traumatic wave set off by World War II will affect my children's children. They all seem to be doing relatively well, but in my experience, psychological problems tend to ripen with age. They have great parents who are moderate in their drinking habits, so they have a good head start.

Yes, the fact that my family hasn't imploded is a gift. Christianity calls this gift "grace." I'm not a practicing Christian, yet my moral framework, such as it is, is made up of Christian principles. I know I should forgive my parents, and I do. Things I learned as a lad at Christ Church — on my acolyte caper — reemerged as I aged, things like "Judge not least ye be judged" or "Let he who is without sin cast the first stone."

It's preposterous that I harbored hatred of my parents for so many years. And yet in the hidden back-bayous of my memory, I maintained secret shrines dedicated to things Dad did when I was seven. Maybe even younger. When I wanted to revel in self-pity or to justify some unpardonable act, I'd let my mind into those back rooms. I'd say to myself, "I can't be expected to act like a normal human being because of these things that happened."

That had to stop. Yet even though I forgave my parents, I really don't think it's my place to absolve them. Whatever my invidious memory believes happened back then, it's now between my folks and God.

◆ ◆ ◆

Dad bought me my freedom in more ways than might be obvious here.

First and foremost, without knowing it, he taught me never to base career decisions solely on money and prestige.

In the early 1960s, Dad may have compromised himself to obtain his coveted partnership at his law firm. He became significantly more depressed after learning he'd won his prize. His experience made it very clear to me that if I wedded myself to a finite goal, I lined myself up for a devastating result.

Although his career lessons were inadvertent, he supported me in some very important choices I had to make as a young man.

By allowing me to attend Riverdale, he set me on the road to pacifism and to a code of beliefs that allowed me to successfully apply for Conscientious Objector status after I was reclassified 1-A during the Vietnam War.

Dad knew every step of what went on between my draft board and me. He knew I'd been reclassified, that I planned to fight it, and that I was considering all options, up to and including going to Canada. He never said a word. In fact, he eventually agreed to be one of the signers of a full-page ad against the war in the *New York Times*. But he never told me that. Mom did.

Although anything I say about Dad's unspoken support for my CO status is speculative, I have a few guesses. My skirmish with the Selective Service system occurred during the two years before he sobered up. I think he was too immersed in his own problems to worry about mine. His open opposition to the Vietnam War occurred after he quit drinking. Yet I think it's possible he thought about Bronxville boys who'd been killed in action. He may have rethought what World War II did to him. Since he didn't talk about it, it's really impossible to know.

Irrespective of my dad's support, my parents provided a substantial "protective factor." Academics who study PTSD like to talk about the development of the ailment in terms of risk and protective factors.[49] In my case, the risk factors included being exposed to Dad's PTSD while I was growing up and my use of alcohol to tame the ensuing anxiety. However, my protective factors were weighty indeed.

In addition to family backing for my CO status, I had the education to craft a technically perfect application and connections willing to write letters tailored to fit the Selective

Service regulations.

Over the years, the gifts Dad gave me have emerged like rocks in a receding stream. His greatest legacy was his sobriety. It lasted but nine months, and because he refused to go into any kind of therapy, it was pretty rough around the edges. Yet he proved it possible.

He also proved himself to be a monument to stoicism.

Instead of sounding off about how unhappy he was or how badly his psychoneurosis afflicted him, he buckled down and did what had to be done. Because he didn't go off the rails, I got the best education my limited wit was capable of handling. During the years I struggled to bring up my family, either he or the money he earned back-stopped me, so when things came up, I had somewhere to turn. When he died, I inherited enough money to buy the house I'd always wanted.

Perhaps most important, he helped me deal with my difficulties, even though I didn't appreciate it at the time. Years later, when someone told me I had nothing but "high-class problems," I thought about "This is nothing compared to France." My problems, compared to his, were fluff in the wind.

Although he hated newspapers, he read them assiduously and thus confirmed their importance. I loved them and turned them into my professional career. As I wrote thousands of stories over twenty-three years, and as I interviewed bank robbers, judges, politicians, and everyone in between, I often thought about his most consistent admonition: "Anticipate, William, anticipate."

Trauma's poison is greatly diluted if the sufferer can be persuaded to tell his story. Just telling the story, however, isn't enough. Odysseus told his story, but when he returned from his journey he slaughtered Penelope's suitors.

During my trek with my father, I did everything I could to hurt him, and my efforts, combined with his excesses, left him totally defeated and me coping with a lifetime of regret.

As far as I'm concerned, Dad was as brave as Odysseus. Brave not only because of his World War II role, but also because he faced the relatively mundane work of law and raising a family without succumbing to the urge to give in to his psychoneurosis and do something more interesting. I could tell there were times when he wanted to act every bit as harshly as his Greek counterpart, but somehow he held back.

Yet the war imprinted him with a kind of permanent fear he just couldn't shed. After reading through all his letters, I concluded that the day he got his Bronze Star was particularly emblematic of the peril that nailed him with a lifelong stamp of anxiety. Out of this anxiety came a rage that extended to practically everything, especially things beyond his control: changing mores, his children, his boss, to name but a few. I often got the impression that he wanted to freeze that frame of his life just after the French lass threw him the egg and just before he muffed the catch.

The day he won the medal, the Cannon Company and the rest of the 134th Infantry had just crossed the Rhine into Germany, and the fighting had taken on that extremely ferocious quality it assumes when a despairing prey feels cornered. The 134th was having an extraordinarily difficult time making its objectives, and foot soldiers, immobilized by enemy fire, couldn't move another inch unless the artillery team did its job.

When he sent the Bronze Star citation home, he enclosed the following note:

May 15, 1944

The main purpose of this letter is to enclose an award of the Bronze Star Medal. This is an order: This is family property and I don't want anyone else nosing around it. A recommendation went in for me for the Bronze Star last fall and was turned down. That one was a good deal more deserved than this one is. That's the way the Army works. This one is 90% balderdash. Please don't show it around. I am easily embarrassed, as you well know. I also have the Purple Heart for minor abrasions from a stray piece of shrapnel the night they knocked the CP (Command Post) down over our heads.

Unfortunately, the fact that I have no children keeps these medals from doing me much good. Points (who got sent home depended on a complicated points system) *are what count, and I just don't have enough to get out on. All I hope is I get some leave and have some time at home before the next phase of this miserable mess* (the war with Japan) *catches up with me.*

CITATION FOR THE BRONZE STAR MEDAL

To FIRST LIEUTENANT PETER C. MCBEAN, 01308988, 134th Infantry for heroic service in connection with military operations against an enemy of the United States in the vicinity of Westerholt, Germany on 30 March 1945. When Cannon Company, 134th Infantry was ordered to cover the combat team artillery, Lieutenant McBean, Company Executive Officer, together with an enlisted man voluntarily went forward to survey the area for this operation plotting gun positions and placing orienting markers. Despite the fact that the area was subjected to three enemy barrages, his tenacity of purpose and disregard for personal safety made possible the successful accomplishment of the mission.

I checked his war correspondence for March 30, 1944, and no mention was made of this incident. I checked for several days after. No mention. I suspect he didn't mention the Westerholt incident because it comprised a routine task. Also, the "heroism" described in the citation didn't make a very good story. This is the second thing I had in common with my old man — a love of storytelling. He had a much better story for that day than the ordinary infantry mishmash:

I crossed the pontoon bridge (over the Rhine) around midnight and found the experience somewhat harrowing. There was some long-range shell fire falling near the site, but the chief thing that made me perturbed was the presence of aircraft. Several times while I awaited my chance to cross, strafing planes dove the length of the bridge sending me diving into various declivities.

The planes weren't the worst menace, though, as they were tremendously inaccurate in their strafing and bombing. The wall of ack ack that greeted each arrival was the chief menace. What goes up must come down and I didn't want any of it on top of me. All the time I was waiting to cross I kept sweating out the possibility I would get caught on the damned floating bridge way out in the middle of the Rhine just about the time a plane made a pass. Sure enough, right in the middle of the river, the column stopped. A jeep had slipped off the tracks ahead of us and stalled us all. Of course, while we sat there and sweated it out, a plane gave the bridge a good going over. I repented all my sins out there in the middle of the Rhine. He missed clean and I got the vicious satisfaction out of seeing him shot down on the shore.

And therein lays the most rueful aspect of this account: that I didn't get to hear his best yarns, just the accounts he wrote to Mom. He died too soon to tell his greatest stories, and I was too young to have any of my own.

As I stacked up Dad's war letters and began putting them back into the old brown envelope, I found myself daydreaming about the times we might have had if he hadn't died so young. I saw us sitting alone at the dining room table in Bronxville. We would have talked warmly about the problems we had in making our way through life. We would have discussed our history without fear and without blame, with reconciliation hard fought for and finally won.

I dreamed I would have told him about the progress our family had made since his death in 1974. I would have said that with the exception of Susie, his five children all had lived full lives, had beautiful children, and couldn't wait to see him Haut again.

I would have had trouble telling him about my domestic difficulties. I would have struggled to tell him that I couldn't face adversity during my career as a father and husband. I would need to tell him that time and again, when the going got tough, I got out, leaving the fate of my children in the very capable hands of my wives. The trauma I put them through was awful.

He, by contrast, was the unsung guardian, the unacknowledged hero. Despite his psychoneurosis, his nightmares, his alcoholism, thirty years of three-hour commutes, and the daily pressure of his legal work, he never retreated. Peter McBean never ran. It's the kind of personal bravery for which I'm still searching.

Acknowledgements

To begin, homage must go to my three sisters, who put up with my need to replay the past. Without their consent and patience, this book would not have been written. I made them all read the raw manuscript at least once, which caused some of them substantial unhappiness. In the end, they agreed to go forward with publication, and I'm grateful.

Marna Reed, my partner, gave me encouragement every step of the way. The decision to self-publish wouldn't have been taken without her endless advocacy. Most writers need love in their corner and I'm so grateful she's in mine.

Many writers belong to a critique group, an I'm no exception. Members of the Taxi-writers Critique Group of Denver combed through multiple versions of my manuscript. They made many good suggestions, most of which I adopted. Their best counsel was to stop whining. It's always good advice. I'm also beholden to Frank Gay and Barbara Wright, who read early versions of my manuscript. Mike Henry at the Lighthouse Writers Workshop in Denver also was kind enough to read an early draft.

I couldn't find many veterans who wanted to help me with this book, but Michael Lindsey spent untold hours talking to me about PTSD. More than anyone else, he helped me with my perspective on the phenomenon. Also, Mike McPhee was generous with his time and advice.

Among the more odious duties of published authors is to help aspiring writers become successful. For the time they spent reading my book and writing blurbs, I'm indebted to Gwen Florio, Jim Carrier, Heather Lyn Mann, Mark Stevens and Lou Kilzer.

Carol Green did yeoman's work editing my manuscript. She came up with a lot of good ideas, including ways I could avoid making a fool out of myself. Whether she was successful remains to be seen.

Then, there's the woman who got me started down this path, Shari Caudron, memoir teacher at the Lighthouse. Thank you, Shari, for starting me on this long road towards self-knowledge.

Thanks to Asya Blue for her splendid cover, and to Allister Thompson for copy editing, Noo Saro-Wiwa for proof reading and Kiersten Armstrong for her work on my author website.

Finally, there are many, many others who helped in some way, or perhaps were just kind enough to listen while I raved on about my family. There are many; I couldn't come close to remembering all their names. May they be blessed.

Bill McBean
Minneapolis
Oct. 13, 2020

INDEX

Endnotes

[1] Thomas Childers, *Soldier From the War Returning*, Houghton Mifflin Harcourt, 2009, p. 232.

[2]https://www.ptsd.va.gov/understand/related/problem_alcohol_use.asp (8-8-19)

[3] *The Shock of Peace: Military and Economic Demobilization After World War II*, James Stokes Ballard. Washington, D.C.; University Press of America, 1983.

[4] https://en.wikipedia.org/wiki/M101_howitzer

[5]https://www.wearethemighty.com/articles/this-is-how-hedgerows-made-the-invasion-of-normandy-a-living-hell

[6] http://www.unk.com/blog/no-need-to-relive-the-trauma/

[7]https://www.ptsd.va.gov/professional/treat/specific/vet_partners_research.asp (8-8-19)

[8] http://www.jhartfound.org/ar2011/

[9]http://articles.chicagotribune.com/2013-02-27/news/ct-x-0227-divorce-after-50-20130227_1_divorce-rate-marital-estate-health-insurance

[10]https://www.publichealth.va.gov/epidemiology/studies/new-generation/ptsd.asp (8-8-19)

[11] *The Common Sense Book of Baby and Child Care* by Dr. Benjamin Spock, Duell, Sloan and Pearce, New York 1946.

[12]https://www.sidran.org/wp-content/uploads/2018/11/PTSD-and-Children-of-Survivors.pdf

[13] *FIRE MISSION! The Siege of Mortain, Normandy, August 1944*, by Robert Weiss, Burd Street Press, 1998, p. 51.

[14] http://www.coulthart.com/134/chapter_5.htm

[15] Ibid.

[16] https://en.wikipedia.org/wiki/Liberation_of_Paris

[17] Dr. Robert Scaer, *The Trauma Spectrum, Hidden Wounds and Human*

Resiliency, W.W. Norton & Co., 2005, p. 80.
[18] https://adultchildren.org/literature/laundry-list/
[19] Michael C.C. Adams, *The Best War Ever: America and World War II*, p. 70.
[20] Scaer, Ibid., p. 44.
[21] Ibid, p. 54.
[22] Ibid, p.75.
[23] http://www.coulthart.com/134/chapter_6.htm
[24] http://www.coulthart.com/134/chapter_8.htm
[25] http://www.coulthart.com/134/chapter_8.htm
[26] http://www.coulthart.com/134/ardennes.htm
[27] https://www.britannica.com/event/Battle-of-the-Bulge
[28] http://www.coulthart.com/134/chapter_9.htm
[29] Shakespeare, *William, Richard II*, Act III, scene 2, line 102.
[30] *New York Herald Tribune*, Feb. 4, 1959
[31] http://www.theguardian.com/books/2002/may/01/news.features11
[32] https://en.wikipedia.org/wiki/Rape_during_the_occupation_of_Germany
[33] White, Osmar (1996). *Conquerors' Road: An Eyewitness Report of Germany 1945*. Cambridge and New York: Cambridge University Press, pp. 97–98. ISBN 0-521-83051-6.
[34] https://www.washingtonpost.com/archive/politics/1986/07/27/w-averell-harriman-dead-at-94/53b333ce-5a6a-4b15-900f-3c12342794bd/
[35] https://www.nctsn.org/what-is-child-trauma/about-child-trauma (8-9-19)
[36] *After the War Zone: A Practical Guide for Returning Troops and Their Families* by **Matthew J. Friedman** and Laurie B. Slone, DaCapo Press, 2008, p. 117.
[37] *After the War Zone*, p. 152–153.
[38] Ibid, p. 161.
[39] Ibid, p. 66.
[40] https://www.frontiersin.org/articles/10.3389/fpsyg.2017.01394/full (8-9-19)
[41] http://www.nccp.org/publications/pub_938.html (8-9-19)
[42] http://www.aaets.org/article188.htm
[43] https://www.psychologytoday.com/blog/curious/201409/11-

reasons-combat-veterans-ptsd-are-being-harmed

[44]http://www.familyofavet.com/secondary_ptsd_children_coping.html

[45] "Veterans statistics: PTSD, Depression, TBI, Suicide." Veterans and PTSD. Sept. 20, 2015, web accessed June 29, 2016. https://www.hillandponton.com/veterans-statistics/ptsd/

[46] Ibid

[47] Ibid

[48] https://en.wikipedia.org/wiki/Transgenerational_trauma

[49] http://www.nap.edu/read/11674/chapter/8

Made in the USA
Monee, IL
20 March 2021

62429224R00187